IN RETROSPECT

4/6/17
To Brianna Jo T. Fejeran!
With Best Wishes
[signature]

IN RETROSPECT

JUAN NEKAI BABAUTA

Copyright © 2016 by Juan Nekai Babauta
All rights reserved. No part of this book may be reproduced in any form or by any electronic or mechanical means including information storage and retrieval systems without permission in writing from the publisher.

Cover Design: Ron J. Castro

ISBN: 978-0-692-81898-5

Library of Congress Catalog Number: 2016921534

First printing: January 2017

Printed by Clavano Printers Cebu City, Philippines

This book is dedicated to my parents, Santiago M. Babauta and Carmen Nekai Babauta.

Table of Contents

Acknowledgments xi
Introduction xiii
Chapter 1: My Youth 1
    My Childhood 1
    High School in Vermont 3
    Eastern New Mexico University 7
    University of Cincinnati 8
Chapter 2: Public Service During the Trust Territory Period 10
    Commonwealth Health Planning and Development Agency 10
    The Board of Education and the Board of Regents 13
Chapter 3: Senator in the CNMI Legislature 17
    Self-government? 19
    A Full Agenda 20
Chapter 4: Resident Representative to the United States 23
    Office in Washington, D.C. 23
    Property Tax-exempt Status 24
    The Close Up Foundation 26
    Environmental Health Issues (PCB Contamination) 27
    Kennedy Center for the Performing Arts 34
    Navajo Code Talkers 36
    American Memorial Park Court of Honor 37
    U.S. Armed Services Academy Appointments 38
    Interagency Group on Insular Areas 39
    The Garment Industry, Immigration, Minimum Wage and Labor 42
    Punishment from Congressman Tom DeLay and Jack Abramoff for Not Conforming 48
    Recognition for the Marianas Marine Scouts 51
    Astronaut Chiaki Mukai Visits Saipan 54
    Veterans Cemetery on Saipan 55
    Telecommunications and Rate Integration 56
    Voice of America Relay Station on Tinian 57
    The Gates Millennium Scholarship 58
    Marianas Included in National World War II Memorial 59
    Other Accomplishments 59
    Lessons Learned 60
Chapter 5: Governor 63
    Public Security, Public Safety, and Emergencies 64
    Relations with Other Countries 66
    My Medical Examination 67

    Tort Reform to Save the Insurance Industry 67
    Adult Correctional Facility 68
    CNMI Integrated Fiscal Plan 69
    Iraq Defector 71
    President Bush on the Iraq War: "It's a matter of time." 72
    My Education Initiatives 73
    First Western Micronesian Chief Executives' Summit 74
    My Assistant for Carolinian Affairs 76
    Keeping SARS at Bay 78
    Rota East Harbor Redesigned 78
    Tinian's Harbor 79
    Council on Physical Fitness 80
    Japanese Royalty Visit Saipan 81
    The NMC Pacific Gateway Project at La Fiesta Mall 83
    Secretary of the Interior Visits Saipan 85
    Rota Judicial Complex 86
    Covenant Section 702 Funding Agreement 86
    Stateless Persons 87
    Approved Destination Status – China 88
    Tinian High School 89
    Paseo de Marianas Pedestrian Mall 90
    Japan Airlines Ceases Flights to Saipan 90
    American Memorial Park Visitor Center 92
    Tournament of Roses Parade 94
    Tanapag Cemetery 95
    Puerto Rico Dump and DEQ Award 95
    Hemodialysis Unit at CHC 98
    Land Compensation 99
    A Marianas Volcano Observatory 100

Chapter 6: Activities After Serving as Governor 102
    CEO, Commonwealth Healthcare Corporation 102
    Publisher *Homeland Magazine* 106
    My Participation in the 2009 Saipan Marathon 106

Chapter 7: Reflections 108
    Lieutenant Governor Diego Tenorio Benavente 108
    Governor Lorenzo I. Deleon Guerrero and the UN on Termination of the Trusteeship 110
    The Chipping Away of the Covenant 112
    Consultations under Section 902 of the Covenant 115
    Labor, Immigration, and the Minimum Wage 118
    Extension of the Federal Minimum Wage 121
    Compact Impact Funding 122

Submerged Lands and the EEZ 125
The Controversy over Tax Issues 127
The Controversy over the Territorial Clause... 132
The Controversy over Equal Representation in the Senate 135
The Controversy over Asylum.. 138
Honoring our Men and Women in the Armed Services.. 139
Tinian's Military Land Lease.. 142
National Guard Unit for the Northern Marianas... 146
The Retirement Fund Program 147
The Fiscal Condition of the Government in 2002 149
Highway Improvements 151
ENMU Alumni Distinguished Service Award 153
Telecommunications and the Sale of Verizon... 153
Meeting with the Philippines President 158
Meeting with Japan's Prime Minister 159
Meeting with Fiji's President.. 160
Pacific Basin Development Council.. 160
Chaba and a Trip to the Northern Islands.. 162
The Role of the Media.. 163
Perspectives on the Covenant 165
The Judiciary: Appointments, Pardons, and the Commemorative Celebration..... 167
Federal Territorial Policy.. 169

Chapter 8: The People Who Shaped Me 180

Important Dates and Events in NMI History 185

Addendums 201
Close Up Foundation letter on board membership. 202
In recognition of Juan N. Babauta and his work with the Close Up Foundation. 203
Statement before the Navajo Code Talkers.. 204
Letter from U.S. Pres. William J. Clinton... 205
Use of General Headnote 3(a). 206
Statement at the Marianas Marine Scouts Induction/Discharge Ceremony. 208
Luncheon invitation from their Majesties, the Emperor and Empress of Japan. 211
Presidential Proclamation 5564, November 3, 1986. 212
Japan Airlines October 26, 2005 letter to Gov. Juan N. Babauta. 214
Presidential Proclamation 8335, January 6, 2009. 215
Executive Order 12572, November 3, 1986. 216
Letter from Former Lt. Gov. Francisco C. Ada. 217
Letter from A. Kerry Strong. 218
Letter from R.E. Parker, Jr... 219
Inaugural Address of Gov. Juan Nekai Babauta... 220

References 223

Acknowledgments

Gratitude is extended to my wife, Charlene Tudela Babauta, for her unconditional support in the writing of this book. My wife served as advisor and sounding board that shaped the formulation and outline of the manuscript during the writing period. She insisted on the logical and consistent flow of the subject matter. Without her support, this book would not have been possible, for sure.

Gratitude is extended to Frank Sobolewski for his contribution in the editing of this book from the initial drafting, and in the verification of information. Frank is a native of Washington, D.C., and grew up in Suitland, Maryland. He graduated from George Washington University in Washington, D.C., with a bachelor's degree in political science and from the University of Hawaii at Manoa in Honolulu, Hawaii, with a Master of Arts degree in Teaching English as a Second Language. Frank lived on Rota for 15 years, taught at the Rota High School and at Northern Marianas College (NMC) Rota. He moved to Saipan and taught at NMC Saipan for four years. After teaching at NMC, he taught at Marianas High School until 2012. Frank retired from the CNMI government in 2012.

Gratitude is extended to Jan S. N. Furukawa for the editing of this book through its final draft. Jan is a native of Guam. She, too, graduated from the University of Hawaii at Manoa, with a B.A. in journalism. Throughout her career, she has worked with all of Guam's daily newspapers, and as well, *The Saipan Tribune* and *The Marianas Variety News & Views*. She has published several periodicals, and has taught English and Chamorro courses at public and private schools, the Japanese School of Guam, the Guam Community College and the University of Guam. She is now working with writers, artists, and publishers on various projects as a free-lance editor.

Appreciation is extended to Ron and Mary Castro, a husband-and-wife team who provided valuable technical and artistic advice for the book. I thank Ron for the creative design, and to Mary, I extend my sincere thanks for her excellent layout work and formatting of the book.

Special Appreciation is extended to David J. Sablan, Jr. for his unselfish and untiring volunteer work in taking on the role of coordinator in the publication process of this book. He personifies the true spirit of volunteerism and invaluable contribution in providing guidance throughout the editing, formatting, and cataloging of the book in the Library of Congress.

Introduction

For years, I've wanted to write about my experiences in public service, and I knew that that time would come. That time is now. Public Service in and of itself is an opportunity and an honor, especially in an elected capacity that is bestowed upon a person by the voters. Looking back at having been a public servant for more than two decades, I am enriched beyond expectation. Thus, I call this book "In Retrospect."

This book documents my background from growing up in the village of Tanapag, Saipan, and journeying to Enosburg Falls, Vermont, for high school, a move that changed my life's path. This book documents the beginning of my career in public service as a health planner, then as an elected official in the evolving government of the Northern Mariana Islands. This book also takes the reader to Washington, D.C., where I served 12 years as the CNMI's Resident Representative to the United States, and presents my record of service as Governor of the Commonwealth of the Northern Mariana Islands.

It is my hope that readers find insightful, and interesting, my experiences at home on the shores of Tanapag and at my adopted home on a Vermont dairy farm, and thereafter, at the service of my beloved Northern Mariana Islands and people. All my time, energy and efforts were dedicated to advancing the causes which I was elected to pursue. My views on issues are intended to provide the reader with additional insight on the critical policies which I initiated, debated and supported during my tenure as a public servant.

Included in this book is a Timeline which lists recent historic events in the NMI. It will be helpful in providing a clear, objective perspective on the political development of the Islands.

Finally, I also hope readers find interesting, as I do, the ongoing contentious discussion on the relationship between the CNMI and the U.S. governments. It takes center stage as the most prominent of all public policy debates in which I was engaged. All U.S. territories are but an afterthought in the formulation of federal policies. It's a view so common in Washington that it has transformed into an institutionalized norm. To be part of the U.S., rather than belong to the U.S., is what we in the territories want to accomplish, but this pursuit continues to be frustrating and fruitless to this day. I do remain hopeful, however, that the United States of America will someday end its colonial legacy.

Chapter 1: My Youth

I was born on Saipan, in the Northern Mariana Islands, on September 7, 1953. My parents were Santiago Miyasaki Babauta and Carmen Nekai Babauta. My father died on January 23, 2011, and my mother much earlier, on January 2, 1982. I am married to Charlene Tudela Babauta, and we have six children: Tiffany, Vanity, Nikki, Brent, Matthew and Charley. My sisters are Victoria, Margarita, Ana, Janet and Cecilia, and my brothers are Felipe, Luis and James. My mother was a descendant of the ReMauritius families originated by Alfredo Peter, a whaler from the island of Mauritius off the east coast of Africa. Her mother, Gregoria Nekai, was of Carolinian descent. Little is known about her father. To this day, my siblings and I are still asking one another questions and wondering who he was and where he came from. My mother was a nurse during the Naval Administration. My father was born on Saipan to Maria Manibusan Miyasaki and Juan Cruz Babauta. He grew up in the village of San Roque. He later moved to Tanapag, where he spent much of his adult life. He was a farm hand for his father. My father worked two jobs. Primarily, he was a farmer planting fruits and vegetables for family consumption. For selling and trading, he raised pigs, chickens and cows. He later worked as a mechanic and a carpenter. I cannot remember my father ever working for the government. I do remember, however, going to the farm in As Denni. My parents met in their teens, got married, and had nine children.

Farming was hard, as was paying the bills, so my father left farming and went to work as a carpenter, mechanic and fisherman. I remember going to Guam with him to work as a carpenter in the aftermath of Super Typhoon Karen in 1962. My father's carpentry work in Guam earned him enough money to return to Saipan to engage in other jobs. He and my mother opened a small family retail store in Tanapag. Goods were sold using a calculator and a log book where sales records were kept. The small income from the store paid the bills and bought school supplies for their children.

After my mother passed away at age 56, my father remarried to a Japanese woman he met on Saipan. He adopted a son and a grandson from her. Together, they opened a Japanese restaurant they called "Tokyo En," which thrived until the rent for the building grew beyond their reach. They closed the restaurant on Saipan, moved to Rota, and opened another "Tokyo En." My father also served as a Marine Scout who, like the rest of the scouts, held the rank of Corporal in the United States Marine Corps. When my father died at the age of 86, nearly 30 years after Mom's death, my siblings and I decided to reunite our parents. We exhumed my mother's skeletal remains at the San Roque Cemetery and reburied her with my father at the Veterans Cemetery in Marpi.

My Childhood

During the time I was growing up in the small village of Tanapag, my parents were my inspiration. They instilled in me the importance of education.

Historical note: National Security in the Back Yard December 1, 1952 – nine months before I was born – President Harry S. Truman ordered the return of the islands of Saipan and Tinian to the Department of the Navy as the Administering Authority. This transfer under the Trust Territory of the Pacific Islands to the Navy took effect on January 1, 1953. The reason for the transfer was to use the islands as military training areas. This was not just any training; the Central Intelligence Agency (CIA) trained Chinese Nationalists to fight against mainland Chinese Communists. The training was conducted by a group called the Naval Technical Training Unit (NTTU). This program was stopped by President John F. Kennedy on June 30, 1962.

Later, they encouraged me to leave Saipan to continue my education in the U.S. mainland. They understood the importance of education even though neither had completed high school.

Tanapag is a small and somewhat secluded village that enjoys a nice stretch of beautiful beach facing the Philippine Sea to the west. Our house sat less than 150 yards from the shoreline. The ocean inevitably became so much a part of my life. As a child growing up in this village, I quickly learned how to swim and fish. My fishing was purely recreational – an activity that my mother was totally against. I suppose it was because of my very young age at the time.

Tanapag is near the island's main seaport, where a lot of boys would land jobs as stevedores, loading and unloading cargo ships. One day, without telling my parents, I went with the older boys to work as a stevedore. I was barely 15 years old, a minor, and I wasn't supposed to be anywhere near the seaport, let alone work there. Stevedoring is a very dangerous job, and minors were prohibited from working as stevedores. But somehow I was hired and I worked for a whole afternoon. My mother, however, found out about it almost immediately. My stevedoring career ended that afternoon. The point of it all is that it was fun. We looted the ship of the foodstuffs on board, and ate canned goods and other goodies while unloading it.

Fifth grade class of Mr. David Babauta of San Roque Elemetary School. Juan N. Babauta second row, 2nd from the left.

I am the oldest son in our family of eleven. I have three older and two younger sisters, along with three younger brothers. Being the oldest son comes with certain responsibilities and expectations. I had to emulate the work of my father as the breadwinner of the family by working at the farm and being a protector of the family. For the most part, my early childhood days were spent at the farm in As Denni. There, I learned how to butcher a pig and cook locally raised chickens fresh from the cage. The use of a machete was a must at the farm. This knowledge and skill has served me well during my lifetime. I say that because can still cut open a coconut with a machete in one hand and the coconut in the other.

My father needed my help at the farm, but he would rather see that my time and energy were focused on education. My mother felt the same way, perhaps more so than anyone else, including my father. I was a very studious child, and I made sure that my homework was done before the next school day. In those days, getting an education was largely more expected of the boys than of the girls.

I attended Tanapag Elementary School for the first three grades, and then I was sent to nearby San Roque Elementary School, just north of Tanapag, up to the sixth grade. For intermediate school, I attended Chalan Kanoa Elementary and Hopwood Junior High School, about nine miles away. My schooling on Saipan stopped after 9th grade, when it was time for me to take the giant step of leaving my family, at the age of 15, to go to Vermont.

On May 28, 1969, the Trust Territory of the Pacific Islands (TTPI) Trial Division of the High Court ordered the appointment of Dwight C. Ovitt as my legal guardian. This action was necessary in order for me to be under Dwight's care, which he later delegated to his parents. Dwight, a Peace Corps volunteer who had been living and teaching on Saipan for about a year and a half, had gotten my parents' permission: I could go to Vermont with him, where I would live with his parents on a dairy farm with about 200 milking cows. The guardianship was not an automatic pass for me to go to Vermont, however, because at the time, I was not a United States citizen. Nonetheless, by August of that year, Dwight and I were on our way to Vermont. My mother cried her heart out when I left home; she feared I would not come back.

Our journey took us by way of Rota, Guam, Truk, Ponape, the Marshall Islands, Hawaii, Los Angeles, Washington, D.C. (to see Sen. George Aiken of Vermont) and on to Burlington, Vermont. Dwight had sought the assistance of the senior senator from the state in obtaining early residency for me. To become a resident in the states, I would have had to file for an immigrant visa through Guam, which would have taken at least six months before the visa could be granted. If, and when, "my number comes up," I would have had to go to Guam to be sworn in. Dwight asked Sen. Aiken to "persuade" the State department to give me special consideration so that the immigrant visa could be issued without me having to go back to Guam. Within two weeks, Sen. Aiken was able to obtain the requested special consideration. When we arrived in Burlington, Dwight and I took the bus to St. Albans, where his parents were waiting to pick us up for the 20-minute drive due north to my new home, Enosburg Falls.

High School in Vermont

My new home wasn't exactly located in the town of Enosburg Falls. It was due south and sat nearly on the town line that separated Enosburg Falls and the town of Bakersfield. The Ovitt family did most of their business transactions in Bakersfield. There they shopped for groceries, attended Granger meetings, played softball, attended church services, and buried their dead. There was no high school in Bakersfield; that is why I was enrolled at Enosburg Falls High.

Enosburg Falls, in Franklin County, had a population of 1,500. It was a dairy farm community considered the dairy capital of not just Vermont, but of the whole United States. Dairy farming was king in Vermont. Small, family dairy farms could be found throughout the state.

Juan with foster parent Evelyn Ovitt.

I lived with the Ovitt family (Wendell, Evelyn and their son, Duane, just one grade ahead of me) for three years. My adopted family owned and made their living off a relatively small dairy farm. It was an experience I was always proud to say, all the years thereafter, that I had lived on a dairy farm. I helped milk about 200 cows twice a day: every morning at 5 a.m. and every afternoon at 4 or 5 p.m. My other chores included helping with the hay in the summer, cutting corn for cow feed, and cutting wood in the fall for the wood furnace to keep us warm in the winter.

Mr. Ovitt was a very quiet and reserved man. At the barn, when going about our chores, there was very little conversation between us. When our chores were completed, we took the five-minute walk from the barn to the house. Every summer when the weather got really hot, he would speak to me in French, saying only: "Il fait chaud?" "It's hot, isn't it?" "Oh, yes," I would reply. End of conversation.

I learned a lot from Mr. Ovitt, not so much in words, but in action. To him, hard work is a virtue. Hard work is life. That's who he was. He taught this young boy from Saipan when and how to milk cows, cut hay, cut corn for cow feed, and cut wood to heat the house in the winter. The house we lived in had only recently (1970) put in an oil heating furnace, but for a long time, the house was heated only by burning wood the old-fashioned way. It was a dramatic change from the life I was used to on Saipan. In this completely different and foreign environment, I was scared, I was homesick, I missed my parents terribly, and I wanted to go back home. Fortunately, I didn't do that.

I had to keep reminding myself that I now lived with a new family, and that I had to do my share of the work around the house in addition to milking cows. But I knew that someday I wouldn't have to get up at 4:30 every morning to milk and clean up after the cows. While I struggled with this challenge on the farm, I was also struggling in adjusting and making the grades at school. I was counseled, tutored and coached before I was able to pull through. I learned that hard work, dedication and perseverance build character and give you a new outlook on life.

I studied at Enosburg Falls High for three years, in grades 10 through 12. I was on the college preparatory track with every intention of going on to college thereafter. My junior high and freshman years on Saipan, however, had not prepared me sufficiently for my sophomore year at Enosburg Falls High. I was at least two, perhaps three, grades behind. It was a struggle I knew I had to overcome no matter the odds.

In addition to the challenges at school, I faced two other challenges: homesickness and the cold winters. My first year was immensely difficult. When my mother got word of my homesickness, she tried everything she could to have me return to Saipan. Dwight, who was away doing work at the University of Vermont, refused to honor my mother's demand and saw to it that

Juan Nekai Babauta as a high school senior in Vermont.

I remained at Enosburg Falls with his parents. A one-way airplane ticket my parents sent me was promptly returned to Saipan with a message to them that I was not returning until I finished high school. Dwight clearly saw the value of education, and that the difficulties I was experiencing could be overcome. He stood his ground, and he prevailed.

My first winter in Vermont with temperatures dipping below zero contributed to the challenge. When the mercury dipped to ten-below in the dead of winter, it was brutal, bone-chilling, and this island boy couldn't understand why he had to stay. Having survived the first winter, my second winter wasn't so bad. I actually enjoyed the subsequent winters, making the best of the circumstances. I picked up ice skating, skiing and snowmobiling.

Enosburg Falls High School in Enosburg Falls, Vermont, in 2003.

At school, I tried my hand at basketball, but I couldn't do a layup worth anything. I turned to varsity baseball, and having played the game on Saipan, I was comfortable enough to sign up. I pitched and played second base for the team all three years. In addition, I was elected student body president my senior year, having run against three other candidates.

My participation in sports, on the student council, and in the National Honor Society opened up a whole new world for me. The school, the student body, and in large measure, the entire community, had taken me in as one of their own. I was the only student of color, brown. I was from an unheard-of island in the middle of the Pacific Ocean, which spurred curiosity and gave me a sense of mystique. Having survived the cultural and social barriers, I entered into another world: I started dating.

Living on a dairy farm was a unique experience for a boy from Micronesia, and what a contrast it was from what I was used to. Vermont was so far away from Saipan, and I was always mindful of that. There were times when I thought I would never return to Saipan. I got along very well with my new family. They were all very good to me. I even addressed Mr. Ovitt as "Pa," and Mrs. Ovitt as "Ma."

Back on Saipan, my parents had a daily routine, like clockwork, going to the post office to check if there was mail from me. Years later, my brother-in-law, Frank DLG. Camacho, gave me a detailed account of what was happening, especially during the first year I was gone. Frank told me that, whether my Mom got a letter from me or not, she would cry all her way back home from the post office in Chalan Kanoa to Tanapag. And because my Mom did not read English well enough, she assigned Frank to read and translate all my letters for all three years I was in Vermont. She trusted only Frank to give her a full account of what the letters said. In the beginning, Frank gave her a full and honest translation, but after a while, he had to bend his readings a little to keep her from crying and at times, not eating all day because of a simple line like, "Yesterday, I was feeling homesick."

I graduated from Enosburg Falls High on June 11, 1972. I was the recipient of the Principal's Award on that special day. The award, which brought praises from my adopted family and friends, was a total surprise. I must admit, deep down, I sensed that I was given special consideration for the award, simply because of who I was. I was the "Island Boy" who came from far away to get an education.

It was on that date that we took our last steps together as the Class of '72. The graduation ceremony was held outdoors, just yards away from the school in Lincoln Park. As we marched through the park, I looked ahead to a future filled with dreams and hopes. It was also a day to reflect upon the previous three years with fond memories of good and not-so-good times. I was filled with mixed emotions being so far away from home with no one from my immediate family in attendance to witness my graduation. My Vermont family, however, were all there to cheer me on, for which I am eternally grateful.

Living with the Ovitt family was a very heart-warming experience. They took me in as one of their own. When I first arrived, Duane, the youngest of the children, and I rode the bus to school every day. The following year, Duane drove his Chevy pick-up truck to school, and I rode with him. In the summer months, the entire family would go to Bakersfield to play softball. We did that only after the cows were milked. The days were longer in the summer months until darkness settled in around nine. After the cows were finished being milked around 6, we were off to play softball. The team was gender-mixed, so even Mrs. Ovitt got to play. Age also did not matter. If you could swing the bat, you were on a team.

The summer I graduated, I worked in Burlington as a laborer at the Coca-Cola Bottling Company. I shared an apartment with a University of Vermont graduate student from Ethiopia, who let me off the hook paying my share of the rent. He was a very kind and considerate person. I have lost track of him over the years. I wonder where he is and what he's doing.

Two years after I left the farm and the Ovitt family, Mr. Ovitt passed away. I was in college at Eastern New Mexico University at the time, and couldn't attend his funeral. I have always felt a sense of guilt about my absence because Mr. Ovitt played an important role in my life, transforming an island boy into a dairy farmer and introducing him to a whole new meaning of life from a perspective that could only come from a lifelong dairy farmer from Vermont.

Although I was not there to personally pay him my last respects, Mr. Ovitt lives on in me. His teachings will forever stay with me. Mrs. Ovitt had an even greater influence on me. I was impressed at how well-read she was. She was always reading. She did not have a college education, but she understood the Classics and also, more contemporary literary writers. She undoubtedly played a major role in my graduating from high school. She helped me with my schoolwork all through those years. If she were still alive and you saw her today, she would tell you how she read my English assignments to me and then explained what the stories were about. By the second year, I was reading on my own.

Eastern New Mexico University

After graduating from high school in Vermont, I went right to college. I had a choice between going to college on the East Coast, or go west. Somehow, I ended up in the southwest, at Eastern New Mexico University (ENMU) in Portales, New Mexico.

I flew from Burlington to Amarillo, Texas. I took the Greyhound bus from Amarillo to Portales. I remember waiting for my bus inside the Amarillo bus depot. The time was 1 a.m. I knew no one. I was frightened and unsure about going to Portales. I could just take the easy way out and return to Saipan. I'm glad that I didn't, though, because I had a great time my first year at ENMU.

I returned to Vermont after my freshman year at ENMU and enrolled at Johnson State College for the summer. Johnson State is a Teachers College located in Johnson. There, I picked up four credit hours for a history course entitled "Gods, Graves, Obelisks and the Ancient Near East." I drove a 50cc motorcycle for transportation. Driving around northern Vermont on a 50cc motorcycle in the summer was an awesome experience. I met wonderful and kind people. I appreciated the great outdoors of Vermont, the greenery, the vegetable and fruit stands along the country roads, the rich history, and the covered bridges.

At ENMU, I earned my bachelor's degree in American History and my master's in Political Science. For some reason, I was naturally attracted to history, especially American History. And being a campus activist, I picked up political science for my graduate degree. Money played a major role in my going to ENMU. In contrast to most other schools, the tuition there was very reasonable and affordable.

All through my college years, my parents continued to be my inspiration. But along the way, others also inspired me. My English teacher in high school played a significant role. He believed in me and had no doubt whatsoever that I would make it through college without a problem. I studied hard, harder than most.

College life was great. I would not trade it for anything in the world. It was a wonderful maturing process. I had to fend for myself, because there was nobody else to look out for me. I got involved in a number of campus organizations. During my senior year, I was elected president of the Political Science Association, and I joined the cross-country team. That was when my love for running began. I stayed away from the fraternities. My view of them did not match with my incessant appetite for studying. The fraternities on campus were not good role models. Often, they were associated with excessive alcohol drinking and pot smoking that was rampant on and off campus. The temptation to indulge was never there for me, and has remained that way to this day. The work-study job I held as an undergraduate helped me pay tuition for all four years. I held a teaching assistantship during my last year of graduate school. I graded papers and substituted for my professor in the undergraduate classes he was teaching. That, too, helped with tuition. And like a lot of students I knew who were far away from home, I had only soba at times for dinner.

I graduated from ENMU on April 30, 1976. I earned my Master of Arts degree eight months after acquiring my bachelor's. I started accumulating graduate credits after my third year as an undergraduate, thereby accelerating the time I would have otherwise spent as a graduate student. Graduate school was less stressful than my previous years. Much more, I enjoyed teaching during my last year. I truly enjoyed college, and I did not allow anything to distract me from it. Not the pot-smoking or alcohol-drinking, or even the girls.

After graduate school, I returned to Saipan to look for a job. I landed one at the hospital as a health planner, doing research. But it was not my field. My employment with the government began during a transitional period, that is, when the NMI officially separated from the Trust Territory of the Pacific Islands government. My job took me on a monthlong health survey throughout Micronesia, including Guam. Palau was the most memorable; surveys were conducted on remote islands such as Kayangel. A couple of hours' boat ride was the only way to get there, where there was a health dispensary to serve the residents. Although I was enjoying my job, I didn't feel comfortable because it was not what I was trained to do. Part of my job was planning for a new hospital on Saipan, now the Commonwealth Health Center. I worked in that job for almost a year before going back to school again. This time, I packed my bags and went to the University of Cincinnati.

University of Cincinnati

There is no doubt that my job as a health planner motivated me to go back to school. I had to be at peace with myself doing a job that would have a great impact on the community. In the end, it was my interest in health planning that led to my return to graduate school. Before leaving, I applied for educational leave. That was necessary to secure my financial obligations as a student. For the entire time I was at the University of Cincinnati, I was on educational leave from my job.

I was also offered admission at the University of Idaho for a postgraduate (Ph.D.) degree in Political Science. Classes were to begin on August 29, 1977. My bags were packed with the option of taking either path. But on August 23, the University of Cincinnati offered me admission to its graduate program in Community Health Planning/Health Services Administration. I chose that program.

I left Saipan and headed to the University of Cincinnati in September. A University Graduate Scholarship was assigned to me for two years after a review of my academic achievements and academic needs. The scholarship paid for my tuition and fees. It was a tremendous help. I couldn't have afforded it otherwise.

Historical note:
Portales, New Mexico at the time was considered the peanut capital of the United States. It is located 18 miles from the Texas border, 19 miles from Clovis, and 90 miles from Roswell. Agriculture is the major industry, with peanuts leading the way in crop production, followed by cotton, wheat, corn and potatoes. Like Vermont, dairy is also a major part of the economy.

Eastern New Mexico University is the third largest university in the state. It is located on a 400-acre campus with about 4,000 students.

My core courses were Primary Care Planning, Organization, and Administration; Hospital/Health Services Administration; Financial Analysis; Quantitative Analysis in Administration; Health Program Evaluation; Research Methods; and Legal and Ethical Issues in Health. For two grueling years, I studied like I had never studied before. It was a change. But because of it all, I gained a Master of Science degree in Health Planning/Health Services Administration.

In the evenings after classes, I practiced Taekwondo in downtown Cincinnati. It was a stress reliever from the rigor of classes and homework. I stopped after earning a brown belt.

On August 18, 1978, Gov. Carlos S. Camacho approved an extension of my leave so that I could complete my studies in Health Planning/Health Services Administration. His approval was based on the expectation of the Commonwealth Government that I would, upon completion, return to the Northern Marianas for appropriate employment.

One quarter of my studies landed me in Santa Fe, New Mexico, as an intern with the New Mexico State Health Planning and Development Agency. I served as an Area Health Planner. My job took me to every corner of the state, reviewing the State Health Plan and the Annual Implementation Plans for Emergency Management and Mental Health systems, and coordination of Rural Health Clinics and hospitals in remote areas.

While still an intern, I applied for a health planner position with the agency. I was interviewed for the job in Albuquerque by the agency's director on November 10, 1978. During the entire process, I had in the back of my mind that Gov. Carlos S. Camacho had extended my educational leave, and that I was still officially on the payroll with the NMI Government. I felt guilty going through the job interview, but I wanted it to be a test to see if I could really get the job. When I was offered the job, I felt very good about it. However, I turned down the offer two weeks after the interview, when I received a call from the Governor's Office on Saipan offering me the position of Deputy Executive Director of the Commonwealth Health Planning and Development Agency.

Upon completion of my internship, I was conferred the degree of Master of Science on August 24, 1979, in absentia. My only wish was for my parents to be in attendance to celebrate what turned out to be my last graduation from college. But it was not meant to be. I received my degree in the mail weeks later.

I returned to Saipan in December 1978, feeling good and very comfortable about taking my job as the Deputy Director of the Commonwealth Health Planning and Development Agency. It was an agency that was federally funded on an annual basis. I served in my capacity as Deputy Director for three months, after which I assumed the position of Executive Director in April 1979. Planning activities for a new hospital to replace the aging Dr. Torres Hospital were seriously getting underway.

Historical note:
In April 1972, the Northern Mariana Islands asked the U.S. for separate political status negotiations from the rest of Micronesia. Negotiations with the U.S. began on December 13, 1972.

Chapter 2: Public Service During the Trust Territory Period

Commonwealth Health Planning and Development Agency

Although I had just received my degree in this very field, there was still a lot of learning to do. Working with politicians was one of them. This was the hands-on part of the job that was never taught in college. As Executive Director of the agency, one of the things I had to do was go to the Legislature to justify why Saipan needed a new hospital. There were many issues the Legislature was interested in, like the size of the hospital, how to finance it, and the required health professionals to staff it.

What I thought would be the easiest part of the job turned out to be the most difficult: the location of the new hospital. The politicians fought over this, putting the project in jeopardy because of long delays. For the life of me, I couldn't understand what all the fuss was about. I found out later that it involved personal interest, having to do with the property on which the hospital would later be built.

For six years, I served as the Executive Director of the NMI's health planning agency, the equivalent of those in the 50 United States and the Territories. I served in that capacity from April 1979 until the time I was sworn in as Senator on January 13, 1986. At least 25 employees were under my direct supervision, ranging from clerical staff to Chief Health Planner, who I recruited from the States. By law, I reported directly to the governor, and I was advised by a 16-member Health Coordinating Council. Father Jose Garrido Villagomez served as chairman of the council for the entire life of the Agency.

Father Villagomez was an inspiration. His natural ability to bring people together to participate in the planning process contributed largely to its success. Although most of the council meetings were held on Saipan, Father Villagomez conducted meetings on Rota and Tinian, as well. One advantage of having a priest as chairman of the council was that our meetings were always blessed with a brief prayer before each and every one.

Part of my job was to make sure that funding for the agency came every year from the U.S. Public Health Service Region IX Office in San Francisco. I had to prepare a grant application every year, justifying the funding over which the Regional Office had authority.

My role as Executive Director, but more so as a health planner, led to the completion of a modern, 74-bed, medical/surgical acute hospital. This was the most significant professional contribution I made to a community early on in my life. The actual planning time took four years, as it involved not only a new hospital, but a new health care delivery system that was expected to meet the needs of the community, including on Rota and Tinian. I was charged with the responsibility of developing a comprehensive health planning document

Historical note: *On March 24, 1976, President Gerald Ford signed into law House Joint Resolution 549. This Joint Resolution became U.S. Public Law 94-241, "The Covenant to Establish a Commonwealth of the Northern Mariana Islands in Political Union with the United States of America." The Covenant is now found in 48 U.S.C. Sections 1801-1805. With President Ford signing into law House Joint Resolution 549, the parts of the Covenant that are listed in Section 1003(a) of the Covenant came into effect.*

which dealt with facilities, manpower, financing, and the operational start-up cost requirements of a new hospital.

The construction of the Commonwealth Health Center was funded by the U.S. Congress. The funding was initially authorized by Congress to be followed by an appropriation upon full justification for the need for a new hospital. It was this job that sent me to Washington, D.C., to appear before the U.S. Congress for the first time. Having to repeat my appearances on several occasions to request for funding was one of the aspects of the planning process that greatly enriched my experience.

Meeting of the Commonwealth Health Coordinating Council on Rota in 1982. L to R: Leslie Beck, Health Planner; Juan N. Babauta, Executive Director; Father Jose G. Villagomez, Chairman of the Council; Dr. Francisco T. Palacios, Director of Health Services.

Initially estimated at $24 million, the hospital ended up costing $30 million.

The significance of my role was that, for the first time since World War II, health care for the people of the Northern Mariana Islands had greatly improved. With a modern hospital facility and expanded services in public health, the health status of the people underwent considerable change. Death rates and the incidence of intestinal parasites, respiratory infections and tuberculosis all dropped. Infant deaths, in particular, dropped dramatically due to improved public health programs in maternal and child health services. Other health programs like mental health, dental services, and vocational rehabilitation services, all benefited from having a new facility, along with an increase in the number of doctors and nurses and other health care professionals staffing the hospital.

Today, the health status of the people of the Commonwealth is good by Pacific standards, whatever that means. Comparatively speaking, it could mean that the health profile is not too dissimilar from that of low- to medium-income rural America.

An inadequate database was a major setback in our planning and evaluation efforts. Our data collection and analysis were all done manually. The ability of the CNMI Government to satisfactorily fund, staff, operate and maintain the hospital remains a tremendous challenge to policymakers. Even with the facility now being enjoyed by the people, it suffers from its inability to generate enough revenue to be self-sustaining. Approximately 90% of its funds came from government appropriations. In my health planning days, I held the view, and still do, that the government must find a way to make the hospital financially solvent and operationally efficient. Otherwise, the cost of health care in the CNMI will continue to rise out of reach for so many.

Historical note: *On January 9, 1978, Dr. Carlos S. Camacho and Francisco C. Ada were sworn in as the first Governor and Lieutenant Governor of the Northern Mariana Islands.*

Historical note: *On January 10, 1981, Pedro P. Tenorio and Pedro A. Tenorio were sworn in as the 2nd Governor and Lieutenant Governor of the Northern Mariana Islands.*

As a Senator, I proposed that a mandatory health insurance program be instituted by creating a Commonwealth Health Insurance Corporation to operate and manage the program. The Corporation was to be governed by a Board of Directors to regulate the program. Insurance coverage would be mandatory for everyone in the Commonwealth. Funding would be provided, initially, by the Legislature on a declining scale until such time that the Corporation was self-sustaining. Self-sufficiency was expected five years after the initial implementation of the plan. One of the objectives of the program was to provide quality care for everyone who walked into the hospital, including those who could not afford to pay for the care they received. Critics said that regulation would stifle innovations. In health care, I say that conventional types of health insurance do not encourage efficient use of medical resources. My program was designed to facilitate coordination among all stakeholders of health care. Health care is not your normal commodity; it can't be substituted, and you can't send it back if you don't like it.

An analysis of the current and future health care needs and services capabilities of the Commonwealth is required. The most crucial element is determining the costs involved. The timing of the implementation of the insurance program also would be extremely important for these reasons: It would impose strict utilization on health services. It would ensure appropriate maintenance and inventory control. It would improve the billing and collection system (Revenue Cycle Management). It would obligate the government, at both federal and local levels, to develop an indigent program to cover their health care costs. It would improve the internal operations of the hospital from a fiscal standpoint. It would require a certain level of quality control, patient care, and patient safety. It would ensure a certain level of expected revenue per year. Finally, it would provide financial relief to the government. These measures, if implemented at that time, would have revolutionized the health care delivery system in the Commonwealth by ensuring that all persons had access to medical care, and the rising cost of health care would be contained.

Another contributor to the success of the health care planning process was Gov. Carlos S. Camacho. The National Health Planning and Resources Development Act of 1974 (P.L. 93-641) created and funded the Health Planning Agencies across the United States, including in the Northern Marianas and the territories. It was perceived by many states as infringing on their roles in managing the delivery of health care, but not so in the NMI. Gov. Camacho embraced this law and by so doing, made a profound difference. His appearance at the Section 1536 (P.L. 93-641, Section 1536) Health Planning Agencies Conference on November 19, 1980, on Saipan, set the stage and the tone for the health planning process in the NMI. He did so without trepidation, outlining the apparent need to utilize public input in the planning process, calling it "a device that was little known or utilized during my years of medical and public health practice." He added, "The introduction of health planning organizations has come at us with the impact of a tidal wave and has overwhelmed all resistance." It was a departure from the old ways that physicians like him would have resisted.

Two years later, Acting Gov. Pedro A. Tenorio signed into law P.L. 3-49, establishing within the Office of the Governor, the Commonwealth Health Planning and Development Agency and the Commonwealth Health Planning Coordinating Council.

The two biggest achievements during my term as Executive Director were securing the funding from the U.S. Congress to build the hospital, and producing all the planning documents for what is now the Commonwealth Health Center. Many had a hand in the successes. Representatives of the CNMI government spent many days and a lot of money going to Washington, D.C., in attempts to secure the funding. I will never forget the words from the House Appropriations Committee chairman when he declared that the money was in the appropriations bill, and that Congress would approve the bill by the end of that year.

The Board of Education and the Board of Regents

In addition to appearing before congressional committees in Washington, D.C., one of my most rewarding and significant professional experiences was serving as a member of, and twice as chairman of, the Board of Education for public schools and the Board of Regents for Northern Marianas College from October 1982 to January 1986. Before separating its functions, the Board served the dual responsibility of being a Board of Education and a Board of Regents at the same time. Membership then was by nomination by the governor, with the advice and consent of the Senate.

I also served on numerous other boards and commissions, all during the same three years. They included the National Association of State Boards of Education, the Medical Profession Licensing Board, the Pacific Post-Secondary Education Council, the CNMI Committee on Health Insurance, the Allied Health/Nursing Committee of the Northern Marianas College, and the Commonwealth Youth Advisory Committee.

Rather than recount my day-to-day activities as a board member for the school system and the college, I present here a brief chronology focusing on their establishment and accreditation.

By proclamation on August 23, 1976, the Resident Commissioner for the NMI transitional government, Erwin D. Canham, established a Northern Marianas Community College (NMCC). Not long after its establishment, the NMCC encountered numerous obstacles and was never able to come together as a viable institution despite efforts to save it from shutting down. The NMCC lacked funding, staffing, and suitable facilities to function effectively. When the Constitution of the Northern Mariana Islands came into full force and effect on January 9, 1978, education was a subject in two of its articles, which detailed the future of elementary, secondary and post-secondary education in the NMI. The first was Article III, directing the Legislature to establish a Department of Education, to be headed by a Superintendent of Education nominated by the Board of Education and appointed by the governor with the advice and consent of the Senate. The second was Article XV, which mandated that post-secondary education programs be established.

In March 1981, Gov. Camacho issued Executive Order No. 25, placing the community college within the Department of Education and under the control and supervision of the Board of Education. The governor's order was intended to "strengthen the Northern Marianas Community College and to consolidate and achieve efficient administration of the various local and federal programs pertaining to training and adult vocational education by allocating and placing them under a single administration through the College."

By October 1982, NMCC applied to become a candidate for accreditation by the Western Association of Schools and Colleges (WASC). That December, the association's Accrediting Commission for Community and Junior Colleges made its first site visit to NMCC. It issued 17 tasks that required action by the college. In January, the WASC commission granted the college Candidate Status. That same month, Public Law 3-43 vacated Executive Order No. 25 and established the Northern Marianas College (NMC) as a public, not-for-profit corporation with the Board of Education as its governing body. Thus, the demand imposed on the Board of Education meant serving both the Department of Education and the college.

From 1983 through 1985, the most important issue to confront the Board of Education/Board of Regents was NMC's accreditation. To be accredited by WASC, the college would have to meet certain prescribed standards. Meanwhile, accreditation for the public school system also was being considered by the Board of Education.

In February 1984, NMC began a Comprehensive Institutional Self-Study. Two months later, WASC's Accrediting Commission made its second on-site visit to the college, which reported on the 17 tasks mandated by the commission during its previous visit. One year later, NMC's Self-Study was completed, and the college applied for full accreditation.

In March 1985, the enactment of P.L. 4-34, the Postsecondary Education Act of 1984, formally ended the responsibility of the Board of Education as a governing body for the college. It provided for the transition of duties from that board to the Board of Regents. The transition was to occur upon certification of a new Board of Regents. Just before the separation, members of both boards met with the visiting evaluation team on accreditation for the Northern Marianas College.

The following month, members of the Board of Regents met with the visiting evaluation team again, along with the governor, members of the Legislature, and students and staff of the college. The next month, a draft report from the evaluation team was received by the Northern Marianas College, and in June, the Northern Marianas College was granted full accreditation, for the first time ever.

Accreditation was also on the agenda for the Department of Education, but it did not move as quickly. The Board of Education, in the summer of 1985, directed the Superintendent of Education to explore accreditation for the public schools.

Approved in the Second Constitutional Convention and by the voters in the general election in November 1985, Amendment 38 established the overall policy governing elementary and secondary education, and higher and adult continuing education. The Amendment directed the Legislature to establish a Northern Marianas College – which it had done in P.L. 3-43 in 1983 – to be headed by a president chosen by the Board of Regents. Furthermore, the Constitution made clear that the College "shall be responsible for providing education in the areas of adult vocational education and professional development for the people of the Commonwealth."

Three years later, Public Law 6-10, the Education Act of 1988, which I authored and which was signed into law by Gov. Pedro P. Tenorio, repealed P.L. 3-43 to conform to Amendment 38. It provided for an elected Board of Education and the establishment of the Public School System as an autonomous institution. The law did away with the position of Superintendent, and replaced it with the position of Commissioner of Education. Other sections of the law directed the Board of Education to establish teacher and librarian requirements, to evaluate and assess performance, and issue or revoke employee certifications.

The Northern Marianas College, as with every other U.S. Insular Area land grant institution, should have been endowed with support since 1986, the year the college was designated a federal land grant institution by the U.S. Congress. Even the college in the Federated States of Micronesia had received such a designation and the grant funding. But Congress at the time said that NMC was too small to warrant support. A decade later, the growth of NMC and its important place in higher education in the NMI led to the authorization and appropriation of the endowment.

Had funding been appropriated, it would have meant a permanent source of funding for research in plants and farming techniques, helping the economy grow ever since 1992. The NMI tried, in vain, to get $3 million appropriated through the agriculture appropriations bill in 1992. Finally, in April 1996, Pres. Bill Clinton signed into law the appropriations bill giving NMC an endowment of $3 million. The president of the college, Agnes McPhetres, signed the agreement for the funds, and NMC and the Office of Insular Affairs in the Department of the Interior set up the Trust Account into which the money was deposited. Earnings from that account would be available year after year for ongoing educational programs at the college. I pursued this funding because I believe strongly that education is the most important investment we can make for ourselves and our community. It also helps the standing of the college financially. And finally, we were no longer the only U.S. jurisdiction without a land-grant endowment. It was a matter of equity and fairness for the CNMI.

The Northern Marianas College has great potential to be an effective institution of higher learning, but it needs an unwavering commitment from the community and its leaders, of both the public and private sectors. To reach that level of public support, the college must have effective leadership. The Legislature has an obligation to provide sufficient financial support to the college in order for it to be successful.

NMC fulfills its mission of investing in human resources by offering more educational opportunities to its students, while improving the quality of the courses being offered. In May 2002, NMC awarded its first bachelor's degrees, with 30 students earning their Bachelor of Science degrees in Elementary Education. Those new teachers were integrated into our Public School System, offsetting part of the need for the costly import of teachers from the U.S. mainland. This demonstrated that by pursuing higher education, individuals can benefit their own economic condition as well as the community at large.

The CNMI needs more homegrown teachers and NMC, with its accredited status, can provide the teaching degree programs. In addition, the college could also become a regional center for education in nursing, which is another essential professional skill that all of the Micronesian islands need. For students from Asia, the college could offer training in English in a native language setting. Opportunities also exist to offer preparation and testing for professional certification in nursing and accounting, and for graduate admissions and other requirements for studying in the U.S. mainland and Hawaii.

To market the college and the Northern Marianas in this way, as a center for education in the Pacific, requires that we build modern facilities and hire a teaching staff that will attract students from elsewhere. The truth is that while NMC's instructors are ever improving, the facilities they and their students work in are falling apart. Classrooms at the college are housed in the original Trust Territory hospital (built in 1954 and "renovated" by every passing typhoon).

My vision for the Northern Marianas' economy is to move away from low-skill, labor-intensive industry toward activities that require a smaller, but well-educated, workforce. Education is such an economic activity and has the additional benefit of putting us in a position of being able to continually upgrade our human resources using local capacity.

Chapter 3: Senator in the CNMI Legislature

The many activities I was involved in as a health planner and member of the Board of Education and Regents and others, led to my run for Senator in 1985. As an employee of the government, I was merely carrying out policies established by the Legislature. There is nothing wrong with that, unless you feel that you can contribute more effectively by being a policymaker yourself. It was that feeling that led to my seeking an elected public office, starting with being a senator.

On the campaign trail, one of the things I enjoyed doing was going door-to-door, meeting with voters face-to-face, not only to ask for their support, but also to discuss whatever issues they wanted to talk about. One thing I learned is that you cannot take anyone for granted.

One of the most memorable experiences I had was visiting an elder at his house. I was somewhat acquainted with him from my earlier years growing up in Tanapag. Keep in mind that I was a Republican and this elder that I am talking about was a diehard Democrat. A diehard is defined as one who stubbornly resists change or refuses to abandon a position. As I approached his house, I could see from his body language that I was not a visitor he welcomed. He knew I was from the wrong party. I identified myself and extended all due respect to him. The closer I got, the more restless he became. I told him that I was a candidate for senator, and that I had come to ask for his support. He rattled the machete hanging on his side that was tied around his waist and said, "Let me tell you something: If Lassie was running as your opponent on the Democratic side, I would vote for Lassie." When I heard that, I was devastated. I could not believe Lassie had just defeated me at this household. I walked away demoralized. But I told myself that that incident could not and should not discourage me. It was a lesson to learn quickly that, although there are people like him in this world, I am glad there aren't very many of them around.

I won the election and served in the 5th and 6th Legislatures. I represented the 3rd Senatorial District of Saipan, the largest of all the islands in the Commonwealth. Legislators works full-time with an annual salary of $30,000. The salary of the legislators was increased to $39,000 in 1991 and has remained at that level to the present.

It was my first win as an elected official, and it felt good. It felt good to know that the people trust you enough to cast their precious vote for you. I was only 25 years of age when I entered public service in the CNMI Government in 1979, and although I was considered young for my age, it did not affect my performance at all. That is not to say, however, that I did not encounter any obstacles. There were many challenges, but I was excited, focused and determined to do the best that I could.

I wanted to make a difference in the area of education. I sponsored legislation that would forever change the educational system. Constitutional

Amendment 38 for an autonomous Public School System was approved by the 2nd Constitutional Convention and by the voters in November 1985. I followed through on this Constitutional provision by sponsoring legislation to implement it. I drafted and sponsored P.L. 6-10, transferring control of the Department of Education from the governor to the Board of Education and the Commissioner of the newly established Public School System.

My departure as the Executive Director of the Commonwealth Health Planning and Development Agency in order to begin my term as senator was a very gratifying moment in my new career as an elected public servant. The six years that I and my dedicated staff of 25 had spent planning for a new hospital were years of tremendous accomplishment. The planning process had come to an end; the next phase was the construction of the new Commonwealth Health Center (CHC). I was sad to leave the agency, but I was very excited to start my term as a member of the 5th Northern Mariana Islands Commonwealth Legislature.

My election to the Senate was an opportunity to work on even more challenging tasks in addition to the health issues that I had been working on previously. As my days at the Health Planning and Development Agency came to a close, I felt a sense of obligation, but more so gratitude, to formally notify Gov. Pedro P. Tenorio of my departure. I wanted him to know that it had been a privilege working under his leadership at a time when the CNMI was undergoing great transformations and challenges as the newest member of the American political family. The people of the Northern Marianas were engaged in an historic political development. They were putting together a whole new government, one with an experimental twist as a political entity that was different from other territorial governments. Our government was literally being built from the ground up.

Juan Nekai Babauta taking his seat as Senator in the Sixth Commonwealth of the Northern Mariana Islands Legislature on Capitol Hill, Saipan, on inauguration day in 1988.

On December 31, 1985, just two weeks before being sworn in as senator, I wrote Gov. Tenorio this letter:

Dear Governor Tenorio:

I would like to inform you of my impending departure from the Health Planning Agency as I will be serving the Commonwealth in the Senate come January 13, 1986.

I am extremely happy that I will be able to serve the Commonwealth in the legislative arena. However, I know that there is much to be done in your continuing effort to bringing our health care delivery system to standards. Two areas are especially important at this point. One is the establishment of a comprehensive health care financing plan. The other is a long range health manpower development program that would provide us with the local resources for generations to come. If I could be of any help, not just in health, but in other areas as well, please count on me for assistance from the Legislature.

In closing, I would like to thank you for the confidence you have placed in me to serve as Executive Director of the Commonwealth Health Planning and Development Agency for the past 4 years. I hope that I have contributed to satisfying your expectation in providing the best and most appropriate health care delivery system to our people.

As Senator, I look forward to working ever so closely with you.

Sincerely,

Juan Nekai Babauta
Executive Director, CHPDA

One of the first orders of business on inauguration day was the reorganization of the Senate leadership and assignment of chairmanship to its standing committees. I was privileged to have been assigned the position of Senate Floor Leader and chairman of three standing committees: the Committee on Fiscal Affairs, the Committee on Health Education and Welfare, the Committee on Rules and Procedures, and two Select Committees, on Water and Texas Road. As a customary practice on inauguration day, the spouse or a close family member of each of the newly sworn-in senators sat behind the Senate member during the entire swearing-in ceremony. Because I was not married at the time, my sister, Margarita B. Camacho, sat behind me.

Self-government?

After the officers were elected and the Senate was duly organized, Gov. Tenorio was escorted into the Senate chamber to give brief remarks. He called upon the Senate for a closer working relationship with his Administration. He was followed by each of the new Senate members also giving brief remarks. It became evident that one of the many issues that concerned the CNMI was its relationship with the U.S. Government; many in the room, on that day, viewed it as not going well. One senator remarked that some of the $140 million bond money, which the CNMI had secured for capital improvement projects and was already available for disbursement, was being held hostage by the Department of the Interior on technical grounds. That was just the tip of the iceberg on the untested relationship between the CNMI and the U.S. Government.

For the newly elected leaders of the CNMI, the ongoing formulation of their government, the Commonwealth of the Northern Mariana Islands, was still the order of the day. It was a time in CNMI history that was unlike any other. The people of the CNMI were excited and had hopes of great opportunities that were still ahead. However, it was also a period in which the leaders of the CNMI took issue with the federal government over matters concerning the Covenant that were not clearly defined, or even mentioned, in the Covenant.

The applicability of the U.S. Constitution's Territorial Clause is an example. The CNMI argued that the clause does not apply to the CNMI. The CNMI took the position that the Covenant was negotiated and approved by the people of the Northern Mariana Islands and the U.S. Government as a negotiated agreement, not as U.S. Public Law.

Another issue was the interpretation of Section 703 (a) of the Covenant, which commits the United States to "make available to the Northern Mariana Islands the full range of federal programs and services available to the territories of the United States." The interpretation raised many questions pertaining to: (1) statutes which mandate programs applicable to all U.S. territories, but not the CNMI; (2) statutes which apply to one or more territories (but not all), and not to the CNMI; and (3) still other statutes which apply to all areas, including the CNMI, but the formula for financing is applied differently to the CNMI.

A persistently more controversial issue that continues to concern the CNMI was the contrasting definitions of "self-government" by the U.S. and CNMI governments. The CNMI took the position that the right of self-government, as provided in Section 103 of the Covenant, is absolute and plenary, and that it therefore confers on the CNMI the exclusive right of legislation with respect to all of its internal affairs. In its view, this includes virtually everything except foreign affairs and defense. The CNMI, therefore, asserted that federal legislation is subject to the mutual consent requirement of Section 105 of the Covenant if that legislation in any way affects what the CNMI considers to be its internal affairs.

A Full Agenda

Protecting our precious environment was on the agenda during my term in the Senate. To that end, I sponsored legislation calling for the closure of the Puerto Rico Dump. This was followed by the Litter Control Act and the Solid Waste Management Act, imposing fees and penalties for littering and the illegal dumping of solid waste. In addition, I sponsored a resolution opposing nuclear waste dumping in the Pacific Ocean by the government of Japan. In the area of natural resources, I sponsored legislation controlling the disposition of public lands by what was then the Marianas Public Land Corporation. I chaired the Senate Select Committee on Texas Road, and spearheaded a move to reopen the old Texas Road that stretches from San Jose village in front of Oleai Elementary School, to Susupe and Chalan Kanoa villages. I held a number of public hearings, obtained approval from landowners who would be affected, had maps drawn up of the road, and had legislation drafted for introduction in the Senate to officially open the road as a main artery. However, all those efforts ended

Historical note: *After the election of the first constitutional government on December 10, 1997, the first elected members of the NMI Legislature, consisting of the House of Representatives and the Senate, were sworn into office on January 9, 1978.*

when the new administration of Gov. Lorenzo I. Deleon Guerrero in 1990 opposed the project. The reason stated was that Beach Road was sufficient.

During my time in the Senate, I authored the following Public Laws:

P.L. 5-33, "The Public Purpose Land Exchange Authorization Act of 1987."
P.L. 6-2, "The 24-hour Evaluation and Treatment Act."
P.L. 6-10, "The Education Act of 1988."
P.L. 6-12, "The Groundwater Management and Protection Act of 1988."
P.L. 6-18, "To Provide for Exemption to the Five Year Compliance Statute for Certification of Authority to Transact Insurance Underwriting in the CNMI."
P.L. 6-30, "The Commonwealth Solid Waste Management Act of 1988."
P.L. 6-37, "The Commonwealth Litter Control Act of 1989."

While a member of the Legislature, I also taught at Northern Marianas College. I taught evening classes in Government and Politics in the Spring and Fall semesters of 1986, and again in the Fall semesters of 1987 and 1988. There is one thing that I don't talk about very often. As my term as a senator entered its third year, I decided that I would not seek re-election so that I could return to academia. But having made that decision, I found myself making yet another. I was at a crossroads in my career, and could have easily taken one or the other. I applied to several colleges, mostly on the East Coast. The John F. Kennedy School of Government at Harvard University was one of them. I had decided, in effect, to put off public service for a while. However, while waiting

L to R: Members of the CNMI Senate, Sixth Northern Mariana Islands Commonwealth Legislature: Juan T. Guerrero, Jose P. Mafnas, Herman M. Manglona, Benjamin T. Manglona, Joseph S. Inos, Paul A. Manglona, Manuel O. Villagomez, Juan N. Babauta, and Herman R. Deleon Guerrero. Photo was taken on January 11, 1998.

to hear from the various colleges, the Northern Marianas Republican Party asked me to be a candidate for Resident Representative to the United States.

At that particular juncture in my life, I decided that I would make a run for Resident Representative and if I lost, I would go back to school. If I won, I would go to Washington, D.C., to represent the people of the Northern Marianas. A few days after I submitted my letter of intent to the Republican Party to run, Harvard University offered me admission to the John F. Kennedy School of Government's Lucius N. Littauer Program in Public Administration.

In applying for admission to Harvard, applicants were asked a number of essay questions on their background and contributions made, if any, to the community where they were. We were asked by the admissions committee to describe our most substantial professional contribution and the reason(s) we viewed it as such. I told the committee that as Executive Director of the Commonwealth Health Planning and Development Agency, my involvement as a health planner led to the successful completion of a modern, 74-bed medical/surgical acute hospital. This, I told the committee, was the most significant professional contribution I had ever made to a community.

I placed myself in a predicament that would haunt me for the rest of my life. I had to decide whether to pull out of my candidacy in the 1989 election and go to Harvard. Do I pack my bags and go to Harvard or do I run for Resident Representative to the United States? The Harvard option did not go as planned. Instead, I ran for the office, and with the trust and goodness of the people of the CNMI, I served three terms for a total of 12 years in Washington, D.C.

Chapter 4: Resident Representative to the United States

In November 1989, I was elected to the Office of Resident Representative to the United States, a position created by the CNMI Covenant and the CNMI Constitution. Originally, the term of office was two years, but it was amended to a four-year term by the 2nd Constitutional Convention and ratification by the voters in the general election in November 1985.

In January 1990, I was sworn in to a four-year term in Washington, D.C. I was re-elected to a second term in November 1993, and to a third term in November 1997. The position of Resident Representative in Washington, D.C., was virtually unknown and unheard of. To participate directly in the national legislative process, you have to have standing as a member of Congress. The elected Resident Representative was not a member of Congress, making it very difficult to participate in the legislative process. For 12 years, it was an uphill struggle. The only way then to move legislation for the CNMI was to lobby Congress.

Moving legislation through the Congress is difficult enough, members will admit, let alone lobbying for legislation as an outsider. My job in Washington, however, was not limited to lobbying the Congress; I also lobbied the White House and the various federal agencies and departments. Much of my lobbying effort was directed at the Department of the Interior, which is the designated federal department for administration and coordination of matters affecting the Insular Areas, including the CNMI.

Office in Washington, D.C.

My arrival in Washington, D.C. as the third Resident Representative found the 120-year-old, three-story townhouse building that had been utilized as the Washington office by the two previous Resident Representatives attractive and welcoming from its outside appearance. However, the inside of the building was in a state of deterioration. In heavy rain conditions, the basement would be entirely flooded with up to six inches of water, which caused rutting of the interior wall structures beyond repair. Water leaked through the cracked cement wall that served as a retaining wall against the earth eight feet below ground level. The drainage system had been plugged up, and was poorly designed and poorly maintained. The plumbing system of galvanized pipes had rusted and was holding on by the skin of its teeth, ready to burst. The old, Victorian-type windows that opened by sliding them up and down, guided by ropes inside the walls, were no longer operable.

I had to act quickly by requesting the Legislature for funding on top of the regular budget for the Office of the Resident Representative for the urgent repairs that had been waiting for years. Fortunately, the first wave of

The Office of the Resident Representative at 2121 R St., Washington, D.C., in December 1995.

visitors to the Washington office were members of the CNMI Legislature, and they were firsthand witnesses to the sad physical condition of the building at 2121 R Street N.W. The lack of space at ground level of the office was always an issue, especially when large groups of CNMI students visited the office, the Close Up students in particular, who numbered 50-60 at a time. Hosting of special events for important people from Capitol Hill was always met with inconvenience, because of the lack of space. The same conditions existed when the governor and CNMI legislators were in town on official business. To solve the problem, during my first term in office, I contracted for renovation of the office basement and exterior surfaces, and construction of a deck. The deck, which was an outdoor space behind the office, was a welcomed feature. An entire wall had to be taken out, replacing it with a sliding door for access to the added space for visitors. The cost for the entire renovation, including taking out part of the first floor for a doorway access to the basement – which was later turned into a library – was approximately $175,000. The townhouse building had been purchased by the CNMI Government in 1981 and by 1990, the value of the building had appreciated, based on the latest appraisal report, to $500,000. The renovation was necessary for the safety of the building occupants and to keep the value of the building at par with the rest of the neighborhood.

The four elected Resident Representatives to the United States. L to R: Edward Dlg. Pangelinan (1978–1983), Froilan C. Tenorio (1983–1990), Juan N. Babauta (1990–2002), and Pedro A. Tenorio (2002–2009)

Property Tax-exempt Status

The CNMI Government had purchased the townhouse building on R Street in 1981 for the Resident Representative's office. When the property was acquired by deed and recorded at the government of the District of Columbia's Department of Finance and Revenue, the CNMI was exempted from assessment of the property tax under the District of Columbia Code, Section 45-922 (3). The code exempted properties belonging to foreign governments and used for legation purposes. For six years, the CNMI office was exempted from paying the property tax. The tax-exempt status, however, ended on December 30, 1988, when the D.C. Department of Finance and Revenue determined that the CNMI property was entitled to a tax exemption, pursuant to the D.C. Code, only for the period prior to the full implementation of the Covenant by Presidential Proclamation 5564 of November 3, 1986. For all subsequent tax years, therefore, the CNMI had to pay the property tax, beginning with the tax year that commenced July 1, 1987. On July 13, 1989, Resident Representative Froilan C. Tenorio had presented to the District of Columbia government a detailed memorandum in support of a request for reconsideration of the denial of continued exemption from the property tax starting on July 1, 1987. The D.C. government refused, and demanded that the CNMI office commence payment of the tax.

The CNMI had two options. One was to petition the D.C. Superior Court for reconsideration of the tax-exempt status; the second was to seek a legislative remedy from the U.S. Congress. The CNMI, through its Resident Representative office, exercised both options. For two years, in 1988 and 1989, the CNMI lobbied Congress for tax-exempt status in letters written to members of Congress and key Congressional staff. At the same time, the Office of the Resident Representative petitioned the D.C. Superior Court, referenced as Tax Docket Nos. 4111-88, 4337-89 and 4339-89. On November 21, 1989, the Congress passed House Joint Resolution 175, containing this provision: "Real property owned by the Commonwealth of the Northern Mariana Islands in the capital of the United States and used by the Resident Representative thereof in the discharge of his representative duties under the Covenant shall be exempt from assessment and taxation." The resolution was signed into law as P.L. 101-219 by President George H. W. Bush on December 12, 1989, without a retroactive provision covering Tax Years 1987, 1988 and 1989. In the meantime, the petition in the Superior Court seeking tax-exempt status for 1987 and the succeeding tax years was still pending.

Upon taking office as the Resident Representative in January 1990, I found myself actively involved in the petition before the Superior Court. I sought written testimony of support from key Congressional staff familiar with the CNMI and the Covenant. The testimonies were the only remaining pieces of evidence that the Superior Court needed before making a decision. On August 3, 1990, the court issued an order stating that, "The Petitioner (CNMI) was entitled to an exemption of real property taxes for the Tax Year 1987 and the succeeding tax years, on the property known as Lot 16 in Square 2514 in the District of Columbia."

The political and legal status of the CNMI was central to the position taken by the D.C. Department of Finance and Revenue. In granting real property tax-exempt status to the CNMI office prior to the November 3, 1986 Presidential Proclamation, the D.C. Government considered the CNMI as having "foreign" status for tax purposes, and therefore granted real property tax-exempt status to the CNMI office. After the November 1986 Presidential Proclamation, the D.C. Government viewed the CNMI differently – no longer "foreign," but "domestic" – and therefore assessed the real property tax. The CNMI, at the time, argued that the status of the CNMI had been a matter of controversy before the Trusteeship Council of the United Nations and that, regardless of the November 1986 Presidential Proclamation, the CNMI retained its "foreign" status for tax purposes.

Following the granting of CNMI representation in the U.S. House of Representatives, the first delegate being elected in November 2008, the CNMI Government sold its property at 2121 R Street.

Historical notes: *On January 9, 1986 Pedro P. Tenorio and Pedro A. Tenorio were sworn in for a second term as the Governor and Lieutenant Governor of the Commonwealth of the Northern Mariana Islands.*

On January 14, 1986, the Compact of Free Association Act of 1985 was signed into law by President Ronald Reagan. The 1986 Compacts of Free Association granted the people of the Federated States of Micronesia and the Republic of the Marshall Islands the right of entry into the United States for employment and to establish residency as non-immigrants.

Historical note: *President Ronald Reagan issued Presidential Proclamation 5564, declaring that effective November 4, 1986 (Marianas time), (1) all parts of the Covenant were in full force and effect, (2) the Commonwealth of the Northern Mariana Islands officially came into existence, (3) the legal residents (domiciliaries) of the Northern Mariana Islands who were citizens of the Trust Territory of the Pacific Islands, and those persons who had been legal residents (domiciliaries) of the Northern Mariana Islands continuously since before January 1, 1974 but who were not citizens of the Trust Territory of the Pacific Islands and who were not already United States citizens, became U.S. citizens pursuant to Section 301 of the Covenant, and (4) the Trusteeship Agreement for the Trust Territory of the Pacific Islands was terminated for the Commonwealth of the Northern Mariana Islands, the Republic of the Marshall Islands, and the Federated States of Micronesia. (Termination of the Trusteeship for Palau came later).*

The Close Up Foundation

The Close Up Foundation is a nonprofit, nonpartisan organization that encourages responsible participation in the democratic process through educational programs in and publications on government and citizenship. Since its founding in 1970, Close Up has been committed to developing new and better ways for young people, teachers, and a widening circle of citizens of all ages to gain a practical understanding of how public policy affects their lives and how individual and collective efforts affect policy. The foundation's headquarters are located in Alexandria, Virginia. Throughout the school year, the organization conducts a Washington-based seminar program that brings high school students, teachers, and chaperones to the nation's capital for weeklong on-site learning experiences. During their stay in Washington, D.C., the students have the opportunity not only to see the outside appearances of the buildings and monuments they often see on television, but to actually see the inside of the buildings and meet the people who make and direct policy. Many CNMI students also participate in sessions on the Pacific Basin, which are held in Honolulu or in Philadelphia and New York.

Since the Close Up program was introduced in the Northern Marianas in 1985, high school students and teachers have been involved with increasing and active participation. In addition, Close Up provides training and materials for teachers throughout the Pacific Basin. Teachers, like the students, are participants in the program. Special seminars are conducted to help teachers gain access to the vast educational resources of Washington, explore special interest issues, and enhance professional development. Close Up participants may also take part in weekly televised seminars broadcast over the Cable Satellite Public Affairs Network (CSPAN). Companion curricular publications are provided to complement the experience during the program and later, for classroom use. Staff and curricular resources are also made available for the development of school-based and community-based courses and programs utilizing Close Up's citizenship education technology. From these intensive program experiences in Washington, D.C., Close Up participants return home with newly developed participatory skills and a deeper understanding of, and appreciation for, the need for informed and responsible citizenship.

An important component of the program experience centers around the way participation is organized by what is known as the "CLOSE UP community concept." Each year a representative cross-section of schools from each selected geographical region of "communities" is invited to participate. The Close Up communities range in size and scope from counties to metropolitan areas, and the entire country and its territories. In any given year, more than 2,400 public, private, and parochial high schools in urban, suburban, and rural settings from 54 communities in 50 states participate in Close Up between November and May. Each invited school or school system is commonly awarded a set of fellowships by the Foundation to support the participation of a teacher and to provide some financial assistance to students in need. Many schools initiate fundraising drives and seek local business assistance to support the participation of their students.

As the Resident Representative, I actively supported the Close Up program and the hundreds of CNMI students who came to Washington, D.C. as participants. This resulted in an invitation to become a member of the foundation's Board of Advisors in 1993. (See Addendum A., Letter from the Close Up Foundation.)

As a member of the Board of Advisors, I joined more than 400 members of Congress, U.S. governors and other state officials, and leading American educators and business owners, to help guide the Foundation's educational programs for young people across the country and in the U.S.-affiliated insular areas. Sitting as a member of the Board of Advisors gave me the opportunity to be at the forefront of efforts to promote the programs for the youth in the CNMI. It gave me the platform to actively pursue an increase in the number of students who participate. I set as my goal to increase the CNMI quota set by the program so more of our youth could reap the benefits of participation. Slots for CNMI students were quite small in number, prompting some of the students to pay for their own expenses just to be able to participate. Working with the Close Up program and the Interior department, which pays for the slots allowed for students from the U.S.-affiliated insular areas, the department agreed to cover all ground expenses for any number of students from the CNMI who paid their air fares to participate in the program.

For 12 years, I had the opportunity and privilege to host hundreds of CNMI high school students to a hearty lunch at my residence, and at the Office of the Resident Representative, followed with a question-and-answer session about the U.S. government and its political relationship with the CNMI. When the opportunity presented itself, I sought for a change in the pre-arranged schedule and took the students to places like the Civil War battlefields at Gettysburg, Pennsylvania, and other locations of historical significance. (See Addendum B., In recognition of work with the Close Up Foundation.)

Historical note: *On January 10, 1990, Lorenzo I. Deleon Guerrero and Benjamin T. Manglona were sworn in as the 3rd Governor and Lieutenant Governor of the Commonwealth of the Northern Mariana Islands.*

Environmental Health Issues (PCB Contamination)

Other than the Polychlorinated Biphenyl (PCB) contamination issue involving the village of Tanapag, the CNMI and the U.S. Environmental Protection Agency (EPA) had a very good, cooperative working relationship for many years. In addition to providing funds for the CNMI's environmental programs for water and wastewater projects, EPA also provided technical assistance to staff and agencies of the CNMI Government.

The relationship between the CNMI and EPA was challenged when the PCB contamination issue in the village of Tanapag reached the "high-water mark" level. After the many letters and meetings and at times fierce debate that ensued between EPA and Tanapag residents who were joined by officials of the CNMI Government, the federal government conceded and took responsibility for the clean-up of the PCB contamination.

Polychlorinated Biphenyl is a manmade chemical used as a coolant and lubricant in transformers, capacitors and other electrical equipment. Hundreds of capacitors containing PCB were brought into Tanapag by the U.S. military for use as radio or radar components. PCB was produced in the U.S. from 1929 until production was stopped in 1977.

The clean-up effort turned out to be one of EPA's biggest projects ever in the CNMI. Collaboration among Tanapag residents, the Office of the Resident Representative, and the CNMI Government was instrumental in convincing the U.S. Department of Defense (DOD) to make this a priority issue. The EPA and the Army Corps of Engineers (ACE) were assigned to oversee the clean-up. Others involved in the effort were the CNMI Division of Environmental Quality (DEQ) and the Office of the Mayor of Saipan. All were committed to ensuring that the clean-up effort was completed in a timely manner, and that the PCB contamination was removed, resulting in a safe environment for the village residents. But there were issues of distrust in EPA's handling of the clean-up and its commitment to the project. Tanapag residents challenged EPA from the day the contamination was discovered on November 29, 1988, to the completion of the clean-up in 2000.

The Tanapag Village Cemetery during the polychlorinated biphenyl contamination clean-up in Tanapag, Saipan.

The PCB contamination in Tanapag was a long and tightly-kept secret by the Department of Defense. It was perhaps the most challenging and difficult health issue that I was ever faced with as a public official, and it involved two of the most powerful federal bureaucracies – the EPA and the Department of Defense.

As Resident Representative, I placed this issue at the very top of my list of priorities. Given how difficult it can get at times to get any real answers from a huge federal bureaucracy like the Department of Defense, I knew I had to go to the very top of the chain of command for answers. I wrote a letter to the Secretary of Defense, informing him of the presence of the capacitors scattered throughout Tanapag in a state of deterioration, discharging PCB. In the same letter, I also asked that the Pentagon take responsibility for the presence of the capacitors and take immediate steps to clean up the contamination in the soil and in plants, fish and other animals like the swamp crabs that the villagers had been consuming for many years. Most important of all, I wanted an explanation for the many mysterious deaths of residents arising from what health officials considered unusual cancers, for the abnormal numbers of chromosomes, for the high rates of congenital heart disease, stillbirths and other negative reproductive effects, and for damage to the liver and impairment of the nervous system.

The frustration over the PCB contamination controversy came to a head at a village public hearing held in Tanapag on October 21, 1999, and attended by representatives of the EPA and the Corps of Engineers, and the residents of Tanapag, along with representatives from the CNMI Government, including the Office of the Resident Representative. I attended the public hearing as both the Resident Representative and a member of the community, having lived in Tanapag as a child. The hearing was held at the village social hall, right on the beach and next to one of the "hot spots" contaminated with PCB. Attending from the CNMI Government were the Secretary of the Department of Public Health, Joseph Kevin Villagomez; the Director of the DEQ, Ignacio V. Cabrera; DEQ's Environmental Planner and Public Health Specialist, Ray Masga; and the Special Assistant to the Resident Representative, Francisco I. Taitano. From the federal government were representatives from the Army Corps of Engineers and Formerly Used Defense Sites Program Manager, Helene Takemoto; U.S. Army Corps of Engineers Archaeologist, Charles Streck; EPA Region IX Toxicologist and Risk Assessor, Dr. Patrick Wilson; and EPA Pacific Islands Program Manager, Norman Lovelace.

The agenda sheet for the public hearing was circulated with the following format.

This 1988 photo shows CNMI Division of Environmental Quality and U.S. Environmental Protection Agency personnel removing discovered electrical capacitors containing polychlorinated biphenyl (PCB) found scattered throughout Tanapag Village on Saipan.

    I.   Review of PCB studies and findings.
          a. Review of Site History, Remedial Efforts, and sampling results.
          b. Review of PCB/Dioxin Toxicology, Community Exposure, Results of the Army Corps of Engineers Human Health Evaluation, and Community Medical Options.
          c. Review of Exposure Risk from the Cemetery and options for future use.
    II.   Site History and Chronology by Ignacio V. Cabrera, DEQ Director.
    III. Presentation of the Army Corps of Engineers Remediation Activities: Remedial Work since the Army Corps of Engineers Initial Involvement in 1992; Recent Remediation Activities and Sampling, including Cemetery Sampling Results; Future Remedial Work including the Cemetery; Schedule for Completion of Tanapag PCB Remediation. Presentation by Helene Takemoto, Formerly Used Defense Sites Program Manager, U.S. Army Corps of Engineers Pacific Division, Honolulu, Hawaii.

IV. Presentation of Toxicology of PCB's Dioxins, Human Health Impacts, Risk Factors, Exposure Levels. Presentation by Dr. Patrick Wilson, Ph.D., EPA Region IX.
V. Presentation of Results of Human Health Evaluation Study, by Charles Streck, Archaeologist, U.S. Army Corps of Engineers, Honolulu.
VI. Community Health Exposure Concerns from Cemetery Usage and Methods to Avoid Exposure during Visitation. Presentation by DEQ, CNMI Department of Public Health, and EPA (Dr. Wilson).
VII. Public Health Services/Options, including Medical Evaluations. Presentation by Joseph Kevin Villagomez, Secretary, CNMI Department of Public Health, and Gwen Eng, Agency for Toxic Substance and Disease Registry, EPA.
VIII. Questions and Answers.
IX. Summary and Closing.

The presentation by Helene Takemoto of the Army Corps of Engineers triggered a negative reaction from a Tanapag resident and community leader, Benigno M. Sablan, who said that Ms. Takemoto was very patronizing and condescending in her remarks by making it sound like she was doing the CNMI a great favor for the work she was doing on the PCB contamination issue. Her remarks were that the Defense Environmental Restoration Program for Formerly Used Defense Sites (FUDS) was working on 9,000 other sites across the country and that the Tanapag contamination was a miniscule part of the whole program, and that we in the CNMI should consider ourselves lucky that the Corps was doing remedial work. She also informed those present that the Defense Environmental Restoration Program for FUDS was not just for PCB contamination, but also for hazardous and toxic waste and unexploded ordnance, and we should be grateful that a decontamination project was funded, rather than other priority projects.

As the Resident Representative, I waited to hear what Mr. Streck, the archaeologist from the Army Corps of Engineers, had to say about the study commissioned by the Corps of Engineers entitled, "Human Health Evaluation of PCB Contamination, Tanapag Village, Saipan, Commonwealth of the Northern Mariana Islands," by Usha K. Prasad, Ph.D., June 3, 1997. Mr. Streck took five minutes to, in effect, brush through the 27-page report, with no one in the audience understanding what the report had to say. Mr. Streck did state, however, that "Health records and data obtained and used in the study are not useful in determining the contamination of PCB in Tanapag."

The final report of the effects of the PCB contamination, entitled "Human Health Evaluation of PCB Contamination," stated that the monthlong field study involved extensive interviews with village residents, community elders, health care practitioners, and other observers who could provide ethnographic and ethnomedical information needed to supplement the medical data being gathered. Particular effort was made to locate the families who resided near soil sampling sites identified in earlier studies. Medical records were reviewed for a total of 47 residents, and death records were reviewed for the entire village. (Ethnography is the descriptive anthropology of technologically primitive societies. Ethnology is the science that analyzes and compares human cultures. Ethnomedical refers to the comparative study of how different cultures view disease and how they treat or prevent it, and the medical beliefs and practices of indigenous cultures.) The report concluded that,

> "While the history of possible exposure extends over several decades, the results show little direct exposure to PCB as revealed in the medical records and interviews. With the exception of a couple of cases, morbidity data in general does not reflect the types of symptoms known or believed to be associated with PCB exposure."

However, in conclusion, even though the study showed little consequences from exposure, based on knowledge about the effects of dermal (of or relating to the skin) exposure, more information can be provided to people, such as the residents of Tanapag, about the possible consequences of exposure to PCBs. However, the report concluded that, "There appears to be no significant impact to human health." A headline in the October 19, 1999, issue of *The Marianas Variety* read, "Report: PCB contamination poses no health threat."

At the public hearing, I took to the podium and held up the newspaper clipping before the audience and called the report "garbage." I called it that because I knew, in my heart, that PCB contamination in Tanapag was real and was a health threat to the residents of Tanapag. The report said, "A direct relationship between the symptoms known to be associated with human exposure to PCB contamination and the exposure of the Tanapag residents to PCB could not be established due to the absence of such symptoms in the medical records of the Commonwealth Health Center." The report further stated, "While the history of possible exposure extends over several decades, the results show little direct exposure to PCB as revealed in the medical records and interviews." If the data from the medical records at CHC were not reliable, let alone verifiable, then how could one make any conclusion one way or the other? Yet the report concluded that there was little direct exposure to PCB. Finally, the report stated, "Knowledge about the effects of PCBs on human health is still a growing area." This meant that we had inadequate knowledge about PCB and its effects on humans. Yet the report concluded, "There appears to be no significant impact to human health." To a lay person, this just didn't make any sense.

While there was disagreement about the conclusions made in the report, I also pointed out at the hearing that the draft report made four recommendations which, at the time, I thought were excellent. The following recommendations were made on the basis of the data collected and analyzed.

    a. Provide the community of Tanapag an up-to-date, thorough background of the known effects of PCB contamination. This presentation

should be done by medical experts who have experience in diagnosis and treatment of PCB contamination.
   b. Establish or designate a locally-based medical expert who can be available to address the health concerns of the residents. Preferably, this should be a medical doctor on staff at the Commonwealth Health Center who can undergo special training on the effects that PCB contamination, as well as exposure to other chemicals/toxins, have on human health.
   c. Conduct a biologically-based health risk assessment of past and present residents of Tanapag who could have been exposed to PCB contamination. The assessment can be done on a segment/sample of the village population and needs to include individuals who have been identified as having had direct contact with PCB oils. Included in this assessment should be a review of health problems which may be symptomatic of long-term contact (dermal exposure), and if and how these may differ from exposure via consumption of contaminated foodstuffs.
   d. Monitor the continuing health status of the Tanapag residents who are known to have been exposed to or have come into contact with the capacitors and PCB oils.

These recommendations, however, were deleted from the final report issued in January 1999. At the public hearing, I pressed the EPA and the Corps of Engineers to reinstate these recommendations. I pressed them at least three times before they agreed, and only after someone from the audience wanted to confirm that they would do so. At that same public hearing, Ursula L. Aldan said that she had gotten information off the Internet about funding for the Defense Environmental Restoration Program for Formerly Used Defense Sites and wondered why the CNMI (Tanapag) was not on the National Priority Listing. Based on the information she had, she figured that if Tanapag were placed on the National Priority Listing, all kinds of funding would automatically follow. When the federal representatives did not react to her query, she turned to DEQ, the Department of Public Health, and me, and challenged us all to have the CNMI (Tanapag) placed on the National Priority Listing. As the Resident Representative, I returned to the podium and directly asked EPA representative Norman Lovelace if it were true that all kinds of funding would flow automatically if the CNMI was on the National Priority Listing. Mr. Lovelace responded that it was not entirely true, and that he felt it would be a long shot for Tanapag to be placed on the list. I took to the podium again and, with the support of the residents in attendance, verbally submitted our application to be considered. Mr. Lovelace verbally received the application and said that he would look into it when he returned to San Francisco.

Working with other community leaders, we went after EPA and the U.S. Army Corps of Engineers, demanding to not only rid the village of the contamination, but to conduct an on-site health screening of all the residents and test the groundwater supply for possible contamination. We battled the two federal agencies' excuses of lack of funding and lack of scientific proof that the mysterious deaths were caused by PCB exposure.

Working with then-Delegate Robert A. Underwood of Guam, we urged the EPA to develop permanent rules for the removal of PCBs from all U.S.-affiliated territories. The new rules allowed PCB-contaminated materials from outside the U.S. customs zone to enter the U.S. for disposal. This was necessary in order that contaminated soil from the village be shipped to the U.S. mainland. Because it took eight months for EPA to issue these new rules, the Army Corps of Engineers had to remediate, or treat the soil on-site, in order to comply with the demands placed on them by the residents of Tanapag and the CNMI Government.

With all the bureaucratic obstacles thrown our way to block our efforts, I was left with only one other recourse. I reported the matter to the White House in a letter to the president. Within weeks, mobilization for the on-site health screening was led by the U.S. Department of Health and Human Services in coordination with EPA, which included sending doctors and other highly trained health professionals to Saipan. Some 1,220 Tanapag residents underwent evaluation for presence of organic pollutants which included, but were not limited to, heavy metals such as lead, benzene, arsenic, chromium, furan, dichlorobenzene, dibenzene, ethyl bromide and dioxin. If any of these pollutants or chemicals were detected in our residents, appropriate medical treatments were to have followed.

In short, we did more than fight City Hall. We fought two powerful federal agencies with all we had. The end result was that PCB contamination was cleaned up and the residents of Tanapag were no longer exposed, according to the Department of Health and Human Services and the EPA. Many village residents were still skeptical whether or not the PCB contamination had been completely removed. They felt, however, that had it not been for the actions taken by the Office of the Resident Representative, and by a number of other community leaders, public health in Tanapag would still be at great risk from the PCB poison.

The funds used to pay for the clean-up of Tanapag came largely from the Defense Environmental Restoration Program (DERP). This program was first authorized in December 1983, with U.S. Public Law 98-212 providing for the Department of Defense to clean up hazardous substances and unsafe debris in Formerly Used Defense Sites (FUDS) on a year-to-year funded basis. The objectives of the program were to reduce, in a timely, cost-effective manner, the risk to human health, safety and the environment resulting from past Department of Defense activities. In 1986, the Superfund Amendment and Reauthorization Act authorized the Defense department to carry out its Defense Environmental Restoration Program, and created the Defense Environmental Restoration Account. In fiscal year 1985, its budget was $20.5 million. In fiscal year 2000, its budget was $238 million for use nationwide.

Historical note: *On January 10, 1994, Froilan C. Tenorio and Jesus C. Borja were sworn in as the 4th Governor and Lieutenant Governor of the Commonwealth of the Northern Mariana Islands.*

The DERP-FUDS Program in the Pacific Region covers Hawaii, American Samoa, Guam, the CNMI, and other U.S. island possessions. The allocation for the Honolulu District for use in the Pacific Region in fiscal year 2005 was only $4.5 million. The Department of Defense designated the Department of the Army as the Executive Agency for the program. The Army, in turn, designated the Army Corps of Engineers to provide program management and execution of the DERP-FUDS Program.

As of 2002, there were 502 properties in the Honolulu Engineer District's FUDS inventory. Of this number, 401 were determined to be eligible for the DERP-FUDS Program. However, only 114 were identified for action. The number of properties identified for action in the CNMI was 33. However, after the PCB contamination clean-up in Tanapag, and the removal of medical glass vials from the Chalan Kanoa Elementary School on Saipan, no sites in the CNMI are actively receiving funding under the program.

According to the U.S. Army Corps of Engineers, the Benefit/Cost standard (B/C ratio) cannot adequately accommodate the unique island needs. The national standard is not responsive to the unique geographic context of America's non-contiguous areas. The costs for island projects are higher than those for continental areas. This is reflected in low B/C ratios (or findings of "no Federal interests") for U.S. Army Corps of Engineers projects vital to island communities. For example, the outcome for the Tinian breakwater initiative of "no Federal interest" resulted in the breakwater not receiving any funding even though the need cannot be disputed.

Kennedy Center for the Performing Arts

Resident Representative Babauta presenting the CNMI flag at the National Cathedral of the Episcopal Church in Washington, D.C. Babauta is accompanied by staff members (L to R) Robert Schwalbach, Adam Turner and Francisco I. Taitano.

On February 5, 1992, I arranged and held a ceremony at the John F. Kennedy Center for the Performing Arts in Washington, D.C., to permanently display the CNMI flag in the Hall of the States. At the Kennedy Center, there are two Halls where flags are displayed: the Hall of States for the 50 states and the territories, and the Hall of Nations for all the national flags. Present at the ceremony were a number of members of Congress: Bill Lowery (CA), Ben Blaz (Guam), Ron de Lugo (Virgin Islands), and George Miller (CA). Also present were: James Ridenour, Director of the National Park Service; Lawrence Wilker, General Manager of the Kennedy Center; Stella Guerra, Assistant Secretary for Insular and International Affairs of the Department of the Interior; Guam Senator Marilyn Manibusan; Edward DLG. Pangelinan, former CNMI Resident Representative; and several others. The CNMI was represented by Gov. Lorenzo Deleon Guerrero;

me, as Resident Representative to the U.S.; Joseph S. Inos, Senate President; Thomas P. Villagomez, House Speaker; David M. Sablan, Planning and Budget Affairs Office; and Tim Bruce and Eric Smith, Legal Counsels to the Governor.

There was one special invited guest, Ambassador Fred Zeder. Also at the ceremony was Harold Lent, Jr., the person who made it all happen. Mr. Lent was a volunteer at the Kennedy Center who a year before came to my office wondering why the CNMI flag was not being flown in the center's Hall of States.

Resident Representative Babauta presenting the nine-by-fourteen-foot CNMI flag to James Ridenour, head of the National Park Service, to be displayed at the John F. Kennedy Center for the Performing Arts in a ceremony held at the Center on February 5, 1992, in Washington, D.C. Attending the ceremony were Lorenzo I. Deleon Guerrero, CNMI Governor; Joseph S. Inos, CNMI Senate President; Thomas P. Villagomez, Speaker of the CNMI House of Representatives; David M. Sablan, head of the CNMI Office of Management and Budget; Congressman George Miller of California; Manase Masur, representing Congressman Don Young of Alaska, representatives from the Department of the Interior, and numerous others.

The ceremony was about the displaying of the CNMI flag in the Hall of States as a fitting symbol of the political union between the CNMI and the U.S. The CNMI flag is one of the first that visitors see as they enter the Hall of States. Flags are arranged in order of entry into the Union. Because Delaware was the first State to enter the Union as it was the first state to ratify the Constitution, its flag appears first in the lineup. The CNMI flag is actually the very last, as the row of flags bends around at the end of the Hall and back to the front, hanging side-by-side with the Delaware flag.

A second main entry of the Kennedy Center for the Performing Arts building is the Hall of Nations, where the flags of nations around the world are on display. Both the Hall of Nations and the Hall of States connect to a grand foyer running the full length of the building, the equivalent of three football fields.

The flying of the CNMI flag was one of my priorities as Resident Representative. It is one way the people of the Northern Marianas can express their pride in being part of the U.S. It is a sign of our strength that the CNMI flag flies in the Hall of States, along with the flags of other states and territories. When I first arrived in Washington, D.C., virtually nowhere was the CNMI flag being flown. By the end of my first term, more than 50 were on display all over Washington, D.C., including in the National Cathedral, the sixth-largest Gothic cathedral in the world. After nearly a century of construction, the cathedral was dedicated by President George H.W. Bush in 1992. The cathedral is still not finished, because it is undergoing repairs for damage that was caused by an earthquake in Virginia in 2011.

Other official flag presentations were held at the following locations: Union Station (the railroad station near the U.S. Capitol), the National Police Memorial, the Department of the Interior, the Pentagon, Georgetown University, the Federal Bureau of Investigation, and the Department of State. Flag presentations were made to Congressman Morris Udall of Arizona, Ambassador John R. Haglelgam of the Federated States of Micronesia (who later became president of the FSM), Command Sergeant Major Martin A. Manglona, Command Sergeant Major Benjamin Palacios, the Marianas Association of Texas and Oklahoma, the Northern Marianas Club of San Diego, the CNMI Club of Portland, the Navajo Code Talkers, the President of the Navajo Nation, President Bush's Special Representative Mr. Lou Gallego, the U.S. Border Patrol Academy, and others.

Navajo Code Talkers

The Navajo Code Talkers, much like the Marianas Scouts, were recruited by the U.S. Marine Corps and served during World War II as radiomen who transmitted secret military orders in their native language. The code used by these Navajo men remained unbroken throughout the war. It was kept highly classified by the U.S. military years after the war's end. According to a 1993 article in *Smithsonian* magazine, the voice code, devised by an elite corps of Navajos in 1942, perplexed the Japanese and helped win the Pacific War. The article gave these as examples of the code used: Bombers were called *jaysho* – buzzards, and bombs were *ayeshi* – eggs. The commanding officer was *bihkehhe* – war chief, and each platoon was a *hasclishnih* – mud clan.

Resident Representative Babauta with the Navajo Code Talkers in Window Rock, Arizona, on March 10, 1994.

The Navajo Code Talkers played a major role in the American victories in the Pacific Theater, including the liberation of the Northern Mariana Islands from the Japanese Empire. Their recollections about the liberation of the Northern Marianas were about devastated homes and the loss of many lives on all sides. To this day, they remain silent over what they actually did in Guadalcanal, Okinawa, Guam and Saipan. The only stories they told were about the devastation of Garapan and Chalan Kanoa and the hikes they took in the terrain of Talofofo and in caves in Marpi in the midst of the fighting on Saipan.

The feats of these Navajo Marines and their unbroken code were not nationally recognized until 1982, when President Ronald Reagan proclaimed August 18 "National Navajo Code Talkers Day." To many, the *Smithsonian* article brought into focus the historical ties of the Mariana Islands and the Navajo people on the eve of the 50th anniversary of the fighting in the Marianas.

On March 10, 1994, I attended a ceremony in Window Rock, Arizona, to thank the Code Talkers for their sacrifices in Saipan. I presented a CNMI flag to Mr. Sam Billison, the President of the Navajo Code Talkers Association, and to Mr. Harold Foster, Vice President, as an expression of the CNMI's appreciation to the Navajo Code Talkers. The ceremony, which was largely organized through unofficial and private efforts, provided an opportunity for more than 40 Code Talkers and their families to be presented with an enlarged copy of the first U.S. postage stamp commemorating the Northern Mariana

Islands. The enlarged stamp was presented by me and the Navajo Nation President, Mr. Peterson Zah. In a brief statement, I thanked the men on behalf of the people of the CNMI for their individual efforts and sacrifices during the war. For some Code Talkers, it was through the ceremony that they learned that the people of the Northern Marianas had chosen to join the American political family. (See Addendum C., Statement by Juan N. Babauta.)

On March 21, 1994, 11 days after the Window Rock ceremony, Gov. Froilan C. Tenorio extended an invitation to the Code Talkers to participate in the 50th anniversary celebration of the liberation of the Northern Mariana Islands. The Code Talkers Association accepted, and agreed to raise funds to cover the cost of their trip to Saipan.

American Memorial Park Court of Honor

As Resident Representative and working with other CNMI leaders, we secured $3 million from Congress to develop the American Memorial Park in time for the 50th Anniversary of the World War II battles on Saipan. The American Memorial Park was designed to honor the Americans who died in the fighting on Saipan and Tinian and in the Philippine Sea.

Approximately 5,000 U.S. servicemen were killed during this fighting, but their identities were not known because there were no organized records kept by the Department of Defense, or by any other agency of the federal government, of the servicemen killed during the fighting in the Northern Marianas. The original design of the American Memorial Park called for a wall that would be partially surrounded with the U.S. flag and the Marine Corps flag, but without the names of those who were killed.

Governor Babauta and Lt. Governor Benavente, assisted by Command Sergeant Major Benjamin C. Palacios, lay a wreath at the American Memorial Park Court of Honor in June 2004 to honor and remember those who served in the Marianas during World War II and after.

I believe that those who gave their lives in past conflicts and those who risk their lives today defending our nation must not be forgotten. I felt strongly that a Court of Honor without the names would render that Court incomplete, and would not elicit the level of emotion and respect one must have when visiting such a place. To that end, the Office of the Resident Representative researched and published the only known listing of all the U.S. servicemen killed in the Northern Marianas Campaign during World War II. These names are now inscribed at the Court of Honor in the American Memorial Park.

The Court of Honor was made complete through the dedication of four members of my staff who researched all the names of the fallen and produced a memorial booklet. They were Alex M. Falig, Remedio N. Magofna-Pangelinan, Francisco I. Taitano, and Emeterio L. Saures. They scoured the archives at the Navy Annex in Arlington, Virginia, the Washington National Records Center in Suitland, Maryland, and the Marine Corps Historical Center in Washington, D.C. Thousands of war records on paper and microfilm were

Historical note: *On October 1, 1994, Palau's Compact of Free Association with the United States was approved. It permitted entry into the U.S. by citizens of Palau for purposes of employment and to establish residency as non-immigrants.*

pulled from the shelves of each of these archives. The records were examined, counted, cross-checked, verified, and authenticated. No one had ever before done this level of research, pulling together all those names of the servicemen killed in the Northern Marianas Campaign. (See Addendum D., Letter from Pres. William J. Clinton.)

The 5,000 names that the staff listed were sent for review and verification to a number of Marine Corps Associations that fought in the Pacific during World War II, and in the Northern Marianas Campaign, in particular. The names were also sent for review by the Department of the Navy and by the Commandant of the U.S. Marine Corps. In a number of instances, the Office of the Resident Representative communicated with immediate family members of those killed during the war for verification. The responses from the family members and from the Marine Corps Associations were extremely helpful. After the feedback period and after the information had all been received, my Office painstakingly compiled all the names and all the information associated with the names, and published it all in the first memorial booklet in 1994. After publication of the booklet, the American Memorial Park Court of Honor was modified so that the names of the war dead could be engraved in its marble walls. The booklet also prompted more feedback, more names, and the corrected spelling of some of the names. One person sent in a dog tag that had been found on Saipan for verification. Support letters and commendations were received by my Office from a number of federal agencies and officials, including the Departments of the Interior, Defense, and Veterans Affairs, the Chairman of the Joint Chiefs of Staff, and from the President and Vice President of the United States.

With the additional information received by the Office of the Resident Representative, it became necessary that a second edition of the booklet be published. Otherwise, the additional information would never be known, and the information in the 1994 edition would be incomplete. The updated edition was published by my Office and released to the public in May 1997. This memorial booklet became the authoritative document listing the names of those persons remembered, those names permanently engraved on the walls of the Court of Honor at the American Memorial Park on Saipan.

Resident Representative Juan N. Babauta with Jerome C. Deleon Guerrero at the Air Force Academy in Colorado Springs, Colorado, in June 1998. Representative Babauta had nominated Deleon Guerrero to the Academy in March 1997.

U.S. Armed Services Academy Appointments

My goal was to give CNMI students the same opportunity as other U.S. citizens have to enter U.S. military academies, reap all the benefits of a free top-flight college education, and go on to serve as officers in the U.S. Armed Forces. This goal was achieved in February 1996, with the passage of Public Law 104-106. This law allowed the Resident Representative to nominate CNMI students to the U.S. Military Academy at West Point, the Naval Academy in Annapolis, the Air Force Academy in Colorado Springs, and the U.S. Coast Guard Academy in New London, Connecticut.

Before this law was enacted, CNMI students did not have equal access to the academies as other U.S. citizens did. The normal route for admission is nomination by a member of Congress, but the CNMI had none at the time. Congressman Robert Underwood of Guam introduced the legislation we needed and helped move it through Congress. The proposal, giving the Resident Representative the authority to nominate CNMI students, was signed into law by President Bill Clinton. By January 1997, I had nominated the first three CNMI students to the U.S. military academies. They were Jerome C. Deleon Guerrero, nominated to the Air Force Academy; Rosalyn A. Ajoste, to the U.S. Military Academy (West Point); and Franicia Q. Tomokane, to the Naval Academy.

Interagency Group on Insular Areas

A constant challenge in Washington was working our way through the bureaucracy to keep federal attention on insular areas issues. Up to the time we were authorized a Congressional Delegate, the CNMI was utterly and completely disadvantaged over all the other insular areas. Working with those other areas, we were able to convince President Bill Clinton in 1999 to establish the Interagency Group on Insular Areas (IGIA) to coordinate through the White House federal policy regarding the territories.

For coordination purposes, the Secretary of the Interior usually sat as the chairperson of the IGIA. The Secretary coordinated the IGIA meetings with the appropriate White House and departmental officials, as needed, pursuant to the issues the insular jurisdictions brought to the table. The first meeting was held at the Department of the Interior on March 1, 2000. The main purpose of the meeting was to explore economic development objectives for the insular areas. Prior to that meeting, a series of preliminary staff-level roundtable meetings were held. Those roundtable meetings were structured around related "issue clusters," which brought together key federal agency officials and insular representatives with the appropriate expertise, working to gain a clearer understanding of the insular economic development proposals and to ascertain which issues were viable for immediate action.

Bishop Tomas A. Camacho with Resident Representative Babauta unveiling the CNMI flag at the Pentagon in Washington, D.C., in 1992.

The March 2000 meeting was attended by representatives from American Samoa, the CNMI, Guam and the Virgin Islands. The federal government was represented by the Departments of the Interior, State, Justice, Education, Defense, Treasury, Agriculture, Labor, Commerce, and Housing and Urban Development. Also in attendance were representatives from the Office of the U.S. Trade Representative, the Environmental Protection Agency, and the Federal Emergency Management Agency. Although there were many insular issues that were presented by the insular area governors and representatives that were present, the meeting focused more on establishing a closer and more effective working relationship between the federal government and the insular areas. Having that many people assembled in one room was a first step in achieving the objectives and purposes of the IGIA.

The assembled governors and other representatives were told by the federal representatives to expect a report on issues slated for immediate action by federal agencies in response to their concerns. Among the issues the island representatives had raised during the preparation for the IGIA meeting were:

1. Increased federal technical and financial resources to aid in economic planning and tourism promotion.
2. Inclusion of insular areas in U.S. trade missions.
3. Accounting for the special tax status of insular areas in tax treaty negotiations between the U.S. and foreign nations.
4. Expansion of U.S. visa waiver programs to facilitate tourism from Asian nations.
5. Targeting of job training programs to the needs of the insular areas.
6. Development of alternative, less intrusive approaches to Inspector General audits of local funds.
7. Reconfiguration of empowerment zone programs and the President's New Market Initiative so that the insular areas are not excluded.
8. Application of U.S. statistical collection systems completely to the insular areas.
9. Inclusion of insular areas in bilateral aviation negotiations.
10. Distribution of Coral Reef Initiative funding to increase local mitigation efforts.
11. Continuation of the lifting of Medicaid caps imposed on the insular areas.

The specific issues that Governor Pedro P. Tenorio and I raised were:

1. Clean-up of PCBs and other military hazardous waste in the Northern Marianas and Guam.
2. Establishment of an ongoing program of Compact Impact aid for Hawaii and the Northern Marianas, along the lines of that already established for Guam.
3. Resolution of land development issues between the U.S. Fish and Wildlife Service and Guam and the CNMI.
4. Funding for development of a strategic master plan and a consulting firm to help develop a seven-year strategic economic development plan.
5. The CNMI to be included in trade missions and promotional activities by the U.S. Department of Commerce and the Office of the U.S. Trade Representative. The decline of tourism and the anticipated decline of the garment industry highlighted the need to

revitalize tourism and promote new investment. Trade missions and promotional activities were to be undertaken with assistance from the appropriate federal agencies.

6. The CNMI also requested that the IGIA see to it that the CNMI achieve full implementation of the financial assistance provisions of the Covenant between the United States and the CNMI; undertake a comprehensive accounting of all categories of fees, taxes, and other collections to be remitted to the CNMI as provided for in the Covenant; and secure an agreement between the CNMI and the IRS on tax coordination.

The second meeting of the IGIA took place on September 10, 2003, at the Secretary of the Interior's office. Issues raised then were long-term projects on which the federal representatives said they would provide periodic updates to the insular areas. A follow-up meeting was held on February 24, 2004, at the Interior Secretary's office, and was attended by Mr. Toby Burke, the Special Assistant to the President for Intergovernmental Affairs. It was the first IGIA meeting that was attended by a representative of the White House.

Both the September 2003 and February 2004 meetings were attended by the governors of American Samoa, Guam, the Virgin Islands, and the CNMI. Representing the CNMI were me, as governor by then, and Resident Representative Pedro A. Tenorio. The issues raised at the meetings were:

1. Lack of consideration the insular areas receive when trade agreements are negotiated by the U.S.
2. For purposes of federal grant programs, that the Pacific insular areas be designated "rural" areas, particularly in order to qualify for FCC telecommunications subsidies designed to support rural health care.
3. The lack of VA facilities to serve the growing number of veterans in the insular areas. It was noted at the meeting that VA services on Guam had been upgraded.
4. Removal of the Medicaid funding cap or an adjustment of the federal-local cost share to 77-23.
5. Tax cover-over for the insular areas. Tax cover-over refers to taxes levied by Congress which are to be paid into the Treasury of the CNMI. This means that all revenues from the tax imposed by Title 26 of the U.S. Code upon residents, citizens, or entities of the Commonwealth, including military and civilian personnel assigned, employed, and/or based in the Commonwealth, are to be paid into the CNMI Treasury.
6. Lack of assistance on environmental issues concerning water supply, wastewater treatment, and solid waste management.
7. Air Cabotage rules and visa waiver policy. Exemptions from Cabotage regulations for foreign-flag airlines flying through the insular areas and visa waivers for tourists from China and the Philippines.
8. There is no permanent U.S. Coast Guard presence in the CNMI. The CNMI is served by the U.S. Coast Guard station on Guam.

Because of the vast ocean area surrounding the CNMI, a U.S. Coast Guard station and a detachment need to be set up in the CNMI.
9. Requested that when the U.S. negotiates international trade agreements, insular areas be included or consulted. The insular areas are often disproportionately affected, because they fall outside of the U.S. customs territory and are, therefore, considered foreign for U.S. trade purposes.

There are many challenges that the IGIA still faces. Many of those challenges are legislative issues that can only be resolved by amending existing laws or passing new laws. An example of such a challenge would be the increasing, or lifting, of the Medicaid funding cap. This is a universal issue for the insular areas, including Puerto Rico. Another example is the Compact Impact funding for the affected jurisdictions under the Compact of Free Association agreements between the U.S. and the Freely Associated States (FAS) that include the Republics of Palau and the Marshall Islands and the Federated States of Micronesia. The CNMI has incurred costs for health, education, public safety, and other services for the citizens of the FAS who have migrated to the CNMI. The current funding level of $5.2 million a year is wholly inadequate for the CNMI. Thus, without legislative remedy, the federal agencies that do want to help find it difficult to do so. A greater challenge is that Congress is known to take its time to enact legislation in times of immediate need by the insular areas, and federal agencies are barred from lobbying Congress. Thus, the insular areas find themselves on their own when it comes to the legislative process.

The Garment Industry, Immigration, Minimum Wage and Labor

The first garment factory opened on Saipan in October 1983. The second garment factory opened two months later. After the two factories began production, and because of a repeal of government regulations that limited the number of garment manufacturers, 34 more factories opened up over the next 10 years. Garment manufacturing became the CNMI's second-largest industry. According to the *2003 Bank of Hawaii Economic Report*, annual garment sales (market value) between 1999 and 2002 peaked at $1.06 billion, and economic indicators for that period showed that the garment industry actually surpassed the tourism industry to be No. 1 in the Commonwealth.

The garment industry came to Saipan for a number of reasons. The industry came because federal immigration laws and the federal minimum wage did not apply to the CNMI. This meant that the manufacturing companies could easily bring in laborers and pay them the prevailing local minimum wage. Another reason for coming to Saipan was that the CNMI is not within the customs territory of the U.S. This means that articles imported into the Northern Marianas are not subject to duty, as provided in the Harmonized Tariff Schedule of the United States, General Note 3(a)(iv). The purpose of Headnote 3(a) is to promote the economic development of insular possessions.

(See Addendum E., Use of General Headnote 3(a).) Another compelling reason for coming to Saipan, perhaps even more so than the open immigration and low wages, was the privilege of exporting finished garments to the U.S. under Headnote 3(a), a provision in U.S. customs law that allows for importing garments into the U.S. duty-free when half the value of those garments is added in the Commonwealth.

The factors described above laid out the ideal environment for investing in garment manufacturing on Saipan. The CNMI government allowed Asian manufacturers to set up shop on Saipan and hire workers from Asia, primarily from China and the Philippines. As the number of garment factories grew, so did the number of alien workers. One of the first of many warnings that would later come about the growing number of alien workers being brought to the CNMI and the possible consequences of the CNMI's alien labor policies came in a May 7, 1986, letter addressed to Gov. Pedro P. Tenorio from Richard T. Montoya, the Interior department's Assistant Secretary for Territorial and International Affairs. Mr. Montoya warned Gov. Tenorio that, "The recent news reports on the tremendous growth in alien labor in the Northern Mariana Islands are extremely disturbing." Mr. Montoya added, "The intent of Congress in providing the privilege of Headnote 3(a) to the territories is to benefit local, and not alien, job and business growth. The extensive and permanent use of alien labor in Headnote 3(a) industries is an abuse which cannot be tolerated by the Administration." Based on a Government Accountability Office Report issued in February 2000 on the CNMI garment and tourism industries, by 1999, the size of the workforce in the garment industry alone was about 16,000, while total employment in the CNMI was about 43,700. This number was 58% of the entire CNMI population.

Increasing production and meeting quotas were the operative phrases for every garment factory that opened. Increased demands for exports put manufacturers under pressure to meet their production quotas in order to satisfy U.S. buyers. This pressure forced garment manufacturers to increase productivity by making factory workers work longer and produce more. The workers were placed on alternate shifts and required to work overtime, including weekends. The workers were required to live in barracks and their movement was restricted. Security guards were posted so that no one could leave the compound without permission. Local law enforcement agencies would later discover that living conditions in many of the barracks violated local and federal health and safety standards.

Meanwhile, the CNMI Government did not have the necessary resources to monitor, let alone enforce, local laws and regulations pertaining to manufacturing. Because of the government's general lack of enforcement capabilities, and the lack of political will, reports of mistreatment of many of the factory workers began to surface in the local and national media. Allegations of human rights violations, such as beatings, rapes, illegal detention of alien workers, nonpayment of wages, substandard living conditions, prostitution, forced abortions, confiscation of employees' travel documents, and threats of deportation led to a series of Congressional oversight investigations in Washington. As the Congress got increasingly involved, calls were also being made to federalize control of immigration and control of the minimum wage in the CNMI.

On March 18, 1992, I spoke publicly in my State of the Washington Office Report to the 8th Commonwealth Legislature about the labor abuses on Saipan that were being reported, especially in the garment industry. I spoke of the unfortunate situation about our Commonwealth suddenly becoming infamous for conditions that Martin Luther King, Jr. and John F. Kennedy would have deplored. I said that over the previous few weeks, I had watched with embarrassment as *The Washington Post* and NBC-TV portrayed our home islands as a place where workers were cheated out of their wages, imprisoned in barracks, and forced to work slavish hours. I also told the legislators and the listening public that I supposed I could say nothing – that it was for the courts to decide the truth of the U.S. Department of Labor's allegations of slave labor in the garment industry on Saipan. Instead I said, "But I have seen the fences around the barracks, and I have heard the stories and in my heart, I know. And in your hearts, you know." I said that this was a matter of moral concern. If human beings were being abused in our islands, we simply could not tolerate it.

The allegations of human rights violations drew media attention both at home and abroad. On September 16, 1992, CBS News aired my interview with them in which I stated that human rights abuses were taking place on Saipan in the garment factories, in the construction industry, and in domestic household work, and that I was ashamed of what was happening on my island. The next day, Congressman George Miller wrote me a letter in which he said,

> "Your statements on CBS News last night were right on target. You are virtually the only political leader in the Commonwealth of the Northern Mariana Islands who has had the courage to speak against an intolerable situation and stand up for the principles on which this country is based."

In a September 30, 1994 interview by *Pacific Star*, I denounced the labor system in the CNMI as a system that exploits the poverty of foreigners for the enrichment of a few businesses in the CNMI. I was quoted as saying, "It is a system that justifies itself by saying that labor conditions that are unfair in the Marianas are permissible because they are less unfair than conditions in the countries where the workers come from." I believed then as I do today, that the economic convenience of low-wage workers, because of their availability under CNMI immigration law, created a new demand for these workers, which was unrelated to the needs of conventional economic development. Therefore, it should come as no surprise that under a system in which immigrants are maintained as an economic underclass without political rights and with severely limited legal rights, acts of individual exploitation will occur.

In the January 22, 1997 issue of *The Marianas Variety*, a headline read, "U.S. Labor sues club." The suit was filed by the U.S. Secretary of Labor against the owners of a nightclub on Saipan for allegedly employing underage exotic dancers, believed to be only 15 years old. Other complaints included nonpayment of wages, including nonpayment of required overtime pay, and child labor for employing a minor.

On February 22, 1997, *The Washington Post* ran a news story on the garment factories as "sweatshops" where the workers were being oppressed. The story also alleged that Willie Tan, a major garment factory owner on Saipan, had financed a recent trip to the CNMI by several members of Congress and their staff to validate that the factories owned by Mr. Tan were among the very best in the world. A February 26, 1997, *Marianas Variety* article reported that the CNMI Government had paid for that trip. Mr. Tan's attorney, Steven Pixley, called *The Washington Post* story "irresponsible, and unprofessional."

Congressman George Miller of California, who was considered the most vocal critic of the CNMI in Congress, led the charge. He authored federal takeover bills on immigration and the minimum wage in the CNMI, and took on the Commonwealth's leaders at every congressional hearing on human rights violations in the CNMI. Miller railed against the garment industry for putting the "Made in the U.S.A." label on garments made by alien workers in sweatshop conditions. Congressman Miller's anti-CNMI crusade included his opposition to granting the CNMI a nonvoting Delegate in the Congress based on charges that the labor abuses were still rampant in the Commonwealth.

A June 28, 1996 (Guam) *Pacific Daily News* article reported that Sen. Frank H. Murkowski of Alaska, at a Senate hearing, slammed the CNMI on working conditions in the garment factories, calling the industry a "sweatshop" and warned the CNMI officials to "clean up their act or face drastic changes" in how Congress treats the CNMI Government. Murkowski went on to say that "Americans are not going to stand for the kind of working conditions [on Saipan] under the American flag." In 1997 alone, three federal takeover bills were introduced in Congress: S. 1100, introduced by Sen. Daniel Akaka of Hawaii, along with seven co-sponsors; S. 1275, by Sen. Frank Murkowski, and H.R. 1450, by Congressman Miller.

From December 29, 1996, through January 3, 1997, Republican Congressmen Brian Bilbray, Dana Rohrabacher, and John J. Duncan, Jr. were on Saipan on a fact-finding visit to the factories and on immigration and minimum wage issues. They strongly opposed any effort to federalize immigration control and the minimum wage. All three were against giving the CNMI a congressional delegate, adding that having a nonvoting delegate in Congress "is more of an ego thing" for the people than it is an actual benefit. They came across as actually perceiving themselves to be representing the CNMI and knowing what was best for the people of the Northern Marianas by defending the garment industry, in spite of the widespread allegations of human rights violations.

On April 16, 1997, the Hay Group, a Washington, D.C.-based consulting firm, released its study, "CNMI Minimum Wage Analysis," which recommended that minimum wage hikes in the CNMI be deferred for at least three years. As Resident Representative, I felt that the wage study was an attempt to shield the garment industry from efforts by the CNMI Government to increase the minimum wage. My position was supported by Rep. Stanley T. Torres of Saipan, when he stated that the wage report was an excuse to protect the garment industry's magnate, Willie Tan. An increase of the minimum wage by five or ten cents per hour would cost the industry millions of dollars. Many others viewed the study as an attempt to buy time for the industry. Less than two months after the report was issued, the governor of the CNMI, Froilan C. Tenorio, not only opposed an increase, but wanted it rolled back. Nonetheless, on June 15, 1996, he signed a law requiring that the local minimum wage be increased by 30 cents, from $2.75 to $3.05 per hour, effective two weeks later.

As Resident Representative, I supported a gradual and steady increase in the local minimum wage, and I lobbied the Legislature not to roll it back. I recommended that a federal-local wage board be established to set the minimum wage by industry or by sector. My position was viewed as anti-garment industry, and as being aligned with Congressman Miller's, who many in the CNMI viewed as an enemy of the CNMI. U.S. Congressman Dana Rohrabacher criticized me, saying, "Mr. Babauta is apparently playing footsies with the liberals in Congress." He added, "But I have news for Mr. Babauta – the liberals don't control Congress." The spokesman for Gov. Tenorio also took a jab at me, saying, "We certainly felt that perhaps the Washington Representative was conspiring against us for a while now, and it has always been perplexing to us."

Clearly, the CNMI Government had been lobbying hard in the conservative Republican-controlled House of Representatives to invoke the spirit of free trade to help fight off a federal takeover. The powerful network of conservative lawmakers, led by Majority Whip Tom DeLay, defended the garment industry as a free-market success story that should be left alone. In the meantime, lobbying efforts led by Jack Abramoff had collected more than $6 million in fees from the CNMI Government and businesses on Saipan, according to a *Washington Post* article. A February 2, 1998 *Time* magazine article entitled, "Give Me Your Tired, Your Poor," told the story of a young Chinese woman recruited to work in a Saipan garment factory. The first paragraph of the article told the story:

> "The young Chinese woman believed she had come to America. But how could this be the American dream? Li Li, 26, found herself working 18-hour days in a factory cutting textiles. At night she and 700 other workers were locked up in a company barracks infested with rats and equipped with just one outside toilet for every fifty people. The residents were allowed out only on Sundays for a maximum of one hour. When she complained

about conditions, according to her account, she and another female worker were beaten by a factory foreman wielding heavy dressmaking scissors."

In April 1998, Republican Congressmen Don Young of Alaska and Elton Gallegly of California co-sponsored a bill aimed at reforming the CNMI labor and immigration laws and policies. Congressman Young chaired the House Committee on Resources, which had jurisdiction over the territories and other insular areas, including the CNMI. Provisions in the bill included imposition of a 50% local hiring requirement in the garment industry, creation of an industry-sensitive committee to review the CNMI's wage policies, and creation of a CNMI nonvoting delegate seat in Congress.

The conservative magazine *National Review*, in its September 4, 1998 issue, published an article entitled "Slave Trade." The article compared the CNMI to Kuwait on what it called, "The most sobering look at the development of the captive-worker model of immigration." The article further stated that, "The captive workers are subjected to all the indignities one would expect, including withholding of pay, sexual exploitation, coerced abortions — the Chinese are even prohibited by their contracts from going to church." The article concluded with the statement: "But many conservative lawmakers, staffers, and journalists have touted the islands as a phenomenal economic success and an experimental laboratory of liberty."

On May 24, 1999, ABC News 20/20 aired a segment called "The Shame of Saipan." It opened with:

> "Tonight, a 20/20 investigation looks into a shameful violation of human rights on American soil – the U.S. territory of Saipan, an island in the Pacific. In Washington today, human rights activists asked the Attorney General to investigate allegations first raised in an award-winning report by our chief investigative correspondent Brian Ross – allegations that some young Asian women have become virtual indentured servants on the island."

Bills introduced in Congress in 1997 (S. 1275) and 1999 (S. 1052) by Sens. Murkowski and Akaka sought to impose U.S. immigration laws on the CNMI. Their proposals included "a transition period not to exceed ten years" for full application of those laws in the CNMI to lessen any adverse impact on the economy.

The State of Hawaii Legislature got involved by adopting two House Resolutions (H.R. 123 and H.C.R. 140) condemning the "Hundreds of cases of rape, forced prostitution, kidnapping, torture, assault and battery, and violations of labor rights committed by employers and local government officials in the CNMI." Both Resolutions requested the U.S. House of Representatives to "Speedily pass S. 1052 relating to the Commonwealth of the Northern Mariana Islands."

As a person, as well as an official representative of the people of the CNMI, I stood for what I believed in. I lost many political friends in the process, but I gained a few as well. One was Mr. Jose C. Tenorio (Joeten), the founder and owner of Joeten Enterprises, Inc. He and I communicated regularly, whether I was in Washington or on Saipan. Whenever I called in the morning and missed him at his home, the housemaid would tell me, "He just left and he wants you to call the office." Joeten wanted me to call him first thing in the mornings; that was when he wanted to talk to me about issues like self-government, the economy, and the controversies surrounding the garment manufacturing industry. He would tell me, "John, the garment industry is like a big cancer in our economy. Keep up the fight, I am behind you." That was all I needed to hear from Joeten, and he made sure to remind me every time I spoke to him.

Punishment from Congressman Tom DeLay and Jack Abramoff for Not Conforming

During the Covenant negotiations in the 1970s, the Northern Marianas delegation was especially concerned about the U.S. immigration laws and their application to the NMI. The delegation was worried about how the U.S. immigration laws would affect their island culture. They feared that their Chamorro and Carolinian heritage would be overwhelmed by an influx of Asian laborers. They wanted protection from this happening, and also from the possibility of war refugees entering the NMI from Southeast Asia. These were important matters among many that I discussed, while still the Resident Representative in Washington, with Ambassador F. Haydn Williams, the president's Personal Representative for the Micronesia and Marianas Future Political Status Negotiations.

After the Covenant was approved by President Gerald Ford on March 24, 1976, it was expected that the Trusteeship Agreement would be terminated once the Compacts of Free Association with the other districts in the Trust Territory were finalized. But those negotiations dragged on over a much longer period than anyone had anticipated. It took an additional 14 years for the United Nations Security Council to terminate the Trusteeship on December 22, 1990. It was during this transition period that the CNMI Government and the business entities interested in the Northern Marianas began to institutionalize opposition to any federal implementation of Sections 503(a) and (c) of the Covenant, which deal with control over immigration and the minimum wage. With the advent of the garment industry on Saipan and an unrestricted immigration policy, the CNMI was committed to blocking, with the help of hired Washington lobbyists, any federal action on minimum wage and immigration in the CNMI.

The Covenant and the interpretation of it created a political tug-of-war in the 1990s between Democratic Congressman George Miller of California and Majority Whip and later, Majority Leader, Tom DeLay of Texas. Both these men, reflecting their opposing political philosophies, had different visions of the Covenant and the CNMI. Mr. Miller was on the hard left, while Mr. DeLay was on the hard right. They were working against each other over the CNMI. While the CNMI was being used as a political football in Washington, it also was getting trashed in the mainstream U.S. media over labor abuses and mistreatment of alien workers in the garment factories, the construction and hospitality industries, and in private residences as domestic workers.

Mr. Miller saw violations of human rights, lack of enforcement of federal and CNMI labor laws, and foot-dragging by the CNMI Government and private businesses to correct failed policies. Mr. DeLay praised the CNMI for the economic miracle and successes it had created and because, in his view, the laboratory of liberty and free enterprise was alive and well in the Northern Marianas. The tug-of-war had started before I got to Washington, and it continued well beyond the 12 years I served as Resident Representative.

According to Ambassador Williams, at the core of this debate were the reports of the serious social, economic, and environmental impacts of the CNMI's labor and immigration policies on life in the CNMI. Encouraging uncontrolled population growth through abuse of immigration control, and turning the indigenous citizens of the Commonwealth into a minority were the consequences of such policies.

Four U.S. administrations, beginning with President Ronald Reagan, voiced deep concern over these developments. The Congress, too, recognized the need to act on CNMI immigration and labor policies in the 1980s and 1990s. On October 6, 1998, the U.S Attorney General and the Secretaries of Interior, Labor, and Commerce, in a joint letter to the U.S. Vice President (as President of the Senate), the Speaker of the House, and seven other Congressional members, urged them to enact legislation extending federal immigration and minimum wage laws to the CNMI, as originally anticipated by the Covenant agreement. The Covenant Implementation Act called for the extension of U.S. immigration laws to the CNMI with proper transitional measures and exemptions. This bill had been introduced in the Senate in three successive Congresses: as S. 1275 on October 8, 1997, as S. 1052 on May 13, 1999, and as S. 507 on March 9, 2001. S. 1052 was passed by unanimous consent of the Senate on February 7, 2000, but died in the House without a hearing, because of the influence of Congressman DeLay and Jack Abramoff.

In the years that I served as Resident Representative, I was an outspoken critic of the immigration and labor policies in the CNMI. When I publicly criticized the garment industry in the CNMI in my 1993 State of the Washington Office Report, I was perceived as having aligned myself with the policies of Congressman Miller and the liberal left against the policies of Congressman DeLay on the right. My positions on immigration, labor and the minimum wage were not based on whether they were to the left or to the right; they were about putting a stop to the deteriorating conditions in the CNMI, including high unemployment, low wages, failure to pay wages, and poor living and working conditions. My positions on these issues were widely known in the CNMI and in Washington.

In the early 1990s, Mr. Abramoff tried to persuade me to change my position on these issues. He came to my Washington office several times and to my residence in McLean, Virginia. He even invited me to a round of golf at an exclusive resort in the D.C. area in his attempt to convince me to change my position. I tried to impress upon him that, because of his close ties to Tom DeLay, he could do a lot of good for the CNMI by directing all his energy and influence towards correcting the problems rather than fighting Congressman Miller. I even told Mr. Abramoff that Tom DeLay was not going to be leader of the House majority forever, and that federalization of immigration control and the minimum wage in the CNMI was inevitable. Realizing that he couldn't win me over, he turned to the leaders in the CNMI to convince them that the way to go was to block any attempts by Congress at a federal takeover.

I felt Mr. Abramoff's influence in the CNMI, because key leaders in the CNMI Government and in the private sector would turn against my positions, even with the knowledge that the refusal by the CNMI Government to increase the minimum wage was driving U.S. citizens out of the labor market. Certain human rights groups argued that the booming garment industry fostered an exploitive working environment. These problems had become so severe that U.S. officials received formal complaints from three countries concerning the treatment of their citizens as foreign workers in the CNMI.

During this long, dragged-out tug-of-war between Congressmen Miller and DeLay, nobody benefitted financially more than Mr. Abramoff, who served as the chief lobbyist for the CNMI solely to block all attempts by Congress to federalize control of immigration and the minimum wage. The lobbying contracts between Mr. Abramoff and the CNMI Government amounted to millions of dollars, especially during the 1990s, all of which has been well-documented. At one point, Mr. Abramoff was paid a staggering $4 million in one year. He was successful in his efforts because of his close ties with Mr. DeLay. Mr. Abramoff went so far as to have Mr. DeLay order his staff to stop any and all legislation in Congress that had to do with the CNMI and was initiated by me, even if that legislation was about health or education. Sadly, all of Mr. Abramoff's efforts were about money and greed. The more money he made, the more he wanted. Much of the money that he received went to political fund-raisers for conservative Republicans. It was not about what was good public policy for the CNMI; rather, it was about the CNMI being the cash cow for political contributions, trips to a tropical paradise, and golf tournaments to raise even more money for Congressman DeLay and for the right-wing Republicans allied with Mr. Abramoff.

The last of the CNMI Government's contracts with Mr. Abramoff's original lobbying firm was on September 3, 2000. The CNMI Government then rehired the lobbying firm of Preston Gates Ellis & Rouvelas Meeds to fight the imposition of U.S. labor, immigration, and minimum wage laws on the

CNMI. Preston Gates had picked Mr. Abramoff, because of his close ties with Mr. DeLay, to lobby against H.R. 1621, the House proposal that would take away the "Made in the U.S.A." label on all CNMI products. That would mean the denial of duty-free and quota-free treatment of all products made in the Commonwealth that were then imported into the customs territory of the U.S. Gov. Pedro P. Tenorio argued that omitting the "Made in the U.S.A." label would cost the CNMI Government $85 million in annual revenue and have a devastating impact on the economy. H.R. 1621, and an identical bill in the Senate, S. 922, were introduced in April 1999. H.R. 1621 was a bipartisan bill, with seven Republican and 21 Democratic co-sponsors. However, neither house of Congress passed the bills.

Towards the end of the year 2000, Mr. Abramoff left Preston Gates and transferred to the law and lobbying firm of Greenberg Traurig. In order to continue to benefit from Mr. Abramoff's services, expertise, and connections, Gov. Tenorio in February 2001 signed a contract with Greenberg Traurig for $600,000 ($100,000 per month) for the first six months of 2001. Gov. Tenorio later that year signed two three-month extensions of the contract, at the same monthly rate. This was the last contract of the CNMI Government for Mr. Abramoff's services, because I became governor in January 2002 and refused to sign any lobbying contracts.

The global economy is here: the North American Free Trade Agreement (NAFTA), the General Agreement on Tariffs and Trade (GATT), and the World Trade Organization (WTO). These are agreements that affect U.S. commerce, and therefore, affect related provisions of the Covenant. The competitive advantage of tariff-free access to the U.S. market for insular area markets eroded under NAFTA and GATT. NAFTA brought tariff-free trade to the U.S., Canada and Mexico. GATT reduced tariff and non-tariff barriers. These two agreements alone reduced the significance of Headnote 3(a), and imperiled the garment industry in the CNMI. The issues were no longer just about immigration and the minimum wage. The global trade issues in international agreements went beyond Tom DeLay's reach and political influence. Mr. DeLay played with fire and it went out of control.

The end results were that the CNMI lost control of both immigration and the minimum wage, and Jack Abramoff made off with millions of dollars in lobbying fees. Four years later, Mr. Abramoff was sentenced to more than five years in jail for fraud, tax evasion and conspiracy to bribe public officials. It was, after all, all about money and greed.

Recognition for the Marianas Marine Scouts

While Resident Representative to the U.S., I and my staff also set out to achieve the recognition of the Marianas Marine Scouts. This recognition had to do with the men who served as Scouts with the U.S. Marine Corps (USMC) in World War II. Obtaining recognition for these men was to honor them for risking their lives for America. The goal of recognizing these men was accomplished in January 2000, when the men were discharged as Marine Corps veterans with the rank of corporal.

Now for Then: The Marianas Marine Scouts is a publication that was made possible by my Office through a grant provided by the Interior department's Office of Insular Affairs. The Marianas Marine Scouts was a select group of about 60 Chamorro and Carolinian men placed under the command of the USMC's 6th Provisional Military Police in July 1945 to assist in the Northern Marianas mop-up operations. Even though the islands were declared secure by U.S. forces, several hundred Japanese soldiers remained hidden in the jungles of Saipan and the Northern Islands, killing American soldiers in sniper attacks.

The men were issued Marine Corps uniforms, trained to use rifles and grenades, and instructed in hand-to-hand combat. Once on duty, they came to be known as "Marine Scouts." The Scouts took part in military expeditions on Saipan and on the island of Maug, and some other Northern Islands. Incredibly, none was killed during these highly dangerous operations. After completing their mission, the men saw no discharges, no campaign ribbons, and no veterans' benefits. The Marine Scouts were relieved of their duty and forgotten for more than 50 years.

The Scouts wanted nothing more than to be recognized for their service. For many years, this oversight bothered me and Edward DLG. Pangelinan, the first Resident Representative to the U.S., who later served as my Office's advisor and legal counsel. Both Mr. Pangelinan and I are sons of two of the Scouts. For more than five decades, the men spoke of their wartime experiences to family members and friends at social and political events, and from one generation to the next, and each year, residents of the Northern Marianas remember them in veterans' ceremonies. Mr. Pangelinan and I both felt that if the Office of the Resident Representative did not pursue this matter to the end, it would be forever a lost cause.

Efforts by my Office requesting the Department of Defense to give official recognition to the Marine Scouts were ignored and ostensibly denied. Attempts to get information from the Central Intelligence Agency by phone and letters were not successful, either. In one particular instance, the CIA even denied having received the several letters I had written them. All our efforts were stonewalled. I decided to take a different approach. It was a shot in the dark. For nearly two years, I dedicated three of my staff members, on a full-time basis, to research all World War II documents related to the Northern Mariana Islands for any reference or evidence that the Marine Corps had recruited and trained these men and sent them on a special mission. My staff labored through at least 50,000 pages of documents, sifting through box after box of unclassified documents at the National Archives, the Marine Corps Historical Center, and the Naval Archives. For nearly two years, my staff came up empty-handed. Exhausted and ready to give up, they unearthed a one-page document still stamped "Classified" – in one of the boxes labeled "Unclassified" – documenting the fact that the USMC had in fact recruited, trained, and sent the Marine Scouts on their mission. It was the document we needed to present to the Pentagon.

With the evidence in our possession, we began the application process provided in U.S. Public Law 95-202, which authorizes the review of civilians who provided service to the country for recognition. The effort resulted in a 100-page application filed on September 30, 1997, with the Secretary of the Air Force who, in this matter, was acting as the Executive Agent of the Secretary of Defense. The petition called for official recognition of the Scouts as U.S. veterans. It would take another two years before the Civilian/Military Service Review Board, which is responsible for responding to applications like ours, reached a decision.

I remember when the call finally came. It was September 23, 1999. James Johnson, who worked with the Service Review Board, was the one who actually gave us the great news that our application had been approved after its validity was confirmed, and declared the Marianas Scouts "active military." Shortly after the phone call, we received the Board's eight-page memorandum stating that the Marianas Marine Scouts' service "should be equated to active military duty."

However, the process still was not complete. There were some details that needed to be addressed. The most memorable one was the rank to be given each of the Scouts. Six officials from the Service Review Board came to my office and, after a lengthy discussion, recommended that the Scouts be given the rank of Private. I burst out in dismay and disgust, owing to the fact that after 50 years of abandonment and denial, all they would receive was the rank of Private. The officials retreated to a private room to discuss the matter. A few minutes later, they came back with the recommendation of the rank of Corporal. "Corporal it is!" I said.

On September 30, 1999, the forgotten Marine Scouts were formally recognized as Marine Corps veterans. In a special ceremony on January 31, 2000, the governments of the United States and the Commonwealth of the Northern Mariana Islands paid tribute to 64 Marine Scouts who became honored veterans of the U.S. Armed Forces. The men were inducted, and then honorably discharged, as members of the Marine Corps. The ceremony was held in the Multi-Purpose Center in Susupe on Saipan. (See Addendum F., Statement at the Marianas Marine Scouts Induction/Discharge Ceremony.)

A separate special ceremony was held for Cristino Dela Cruz at his residence on Capitol Hill on Saipan, where he was bedridden and gravely ill. His wife, Eugenia Demapan Dela Cruz, told me during the ceremony, "He's been waiting for this for so long, I know now he will pass." Cristino Dela Cruz, Miguel Tenorio, and Benedicto Taisacan were the first group of Scouts who served the Marines from June 19 until September 2, 1945. Another induction ceremony took place at the hospital for Marine Scout Jose C. Magofna, who also was bedridden. As with Dela Cruz, Magofna was sworn in by U.S. District Court Judge Alex P. Munson, accompanied by Marine Corps Brig. Gen. R.E. Parker, Gov. Pedro P. Tenorio, Edward DLG. Pangelinan and myself. Ten years after becoming a veteran, and age having taken its toll, Gregorio C. Cabrera of Saipan was the first veteran to be buried with full military honors at the newly constructed Veterans Cemetery on Saipan.

Astronaut Chiaki Mukai Visits Saipan

Dr. Chiaki Mukai, the astronaut from Japan who flew with John Glenn on his historic return to space in 1998, accepted my invitation to visit the Northern Marianas in June 1999. She arrived on Saipan on June 13 for her three-day visit to meet with CNMI leaders, students, and others. Dr. Mukai was the featured keynote speaker for the 1,200 nurses attending the American Pacific Nursing Leaders Council Conference at the time. She was also the commencement speaker at the Hopwood Junior High School and Marianas High School graduation ceremonies, and visited several elementary schools to speak to the students.

Astronaut Chiaki Mukai as guest speaker at Dandan Elementary School on Saipan.

Ms. Mukai is a Japanese doctor and an astronaut for the Japan Aerospace Exploration Agency (JAXA), which used to be the National Space Development Agency (NASDA) of Japan. She was the first Japanese woman in space, and was the first Japanese citizen to have flown in two spaceflights, both of which were space shuttle missions. Her first spaceflight was STS-65 aboard Space Shuttle Columbia in July 1994, which was a spacelab mission. Her second spaceflight was STS-95 aboard Space Shuttle Discovery in 1998. The Space Shuttle Discovery was a highly publicized mission due to former Project Mercury astronaut and U.S. Sen. John H. Glenn, Jr.'s return to space for his second space flight at age 77.

As Resident Representative, I first met Astronaut Mukai on April 20, 1999, in Washington, D.C. She had already received my invitation to visit the CNMI two months prior. With the assistance of a mutual friend, I received word from NASDA in March 1999 that it had approved my invitation. Plans were immediately put in place for her historic visit. Astronaut Mukai arrived on June 13, 1999, wanting to taste the local food and visit a local store. Her goal was to learn as much as she could about our islands' people and cultures.

Aside from being commencement speaker at two graduations and keynote speaker at the nurses' conference, Dr. Mukai also met with members and staff of the Legislature on Capitol Hill. The Legislature bestowed on her honorary citizenship and a token CNMI driver's license. A "Key to the CNMI" had been presented to her by Gov. Tenorio at the airport when she first arrived; in return, Dr. Mukai presented, as a token of her appreciation, a commemorative souvenir of her space exploration to the members of the legislature, to the governor, and to the graduating students at the commencement exercises she attended.

Dr. Mukai's most memorable message in speaking to the many students was, "If you can dream it, you can do it." One might ask, how did Dr. Mukai's visit benefit the CNMI? I would say that the schoolchildren of the NMI had an opportunity to meet with Astronaut Mukai, further inspiring them in their studies. Dr. Mukai's visit provided good publicity for our islands – a benefit to our tourism industry; and arranging her visit supported a good working relationship between the CNMI Government and that of Japan.

Veterans Cemetery on Saipan

The federal government provides many benefits that should be, but were not available to the CNMI, for instance, obtaining grant funds to establish a veterans cemetery. As Resident Representative, I worked closely with the CNMI Office of Veterans Affairs on Saipan, and with the U.S. Department of Veterans Affairs, to obtain the necessary funding for construction of a veterans cemetery on Saipan. During my first year in office in 1990, meetings were held between representatives of my Office, the U.S. Department of Veterans Affairs, and the CNMI's VA office who had traveled all the way from Saipan to participate in the meetings. The efforts put into the meetings paid off quickly when in 1992, the State Cemetery Grants Service notified the CNMI that the U.S. Department of Veterans Affairs would fund the cost of a veterans cemetery on Saipan. The State Cemetery Grants Service identified $1.5 million for the design and construction. As a condition to the awarding of the grant, the CNMI was required to match the $1.5 million in federal money, and to designate a site.

Resident Representative Babauta honoring our veterans at the Arlington National Cemetery near Washington, D.C., in Arlington, Virginia, with Command Sergeant Major Benjamin C. Palacios.

Initial efforts in identifying public land for a cemetery were challenging, due to several factors: Land restrictions to Northern Marianas descent only, availability and suitability of public lands, and coming up with the funding to match the federal dollars. On August 10, 1993, *The Marianas Variety* reported that the designation by the Marianas Public Land Corporation (MPLC) of a section of the Tanapag cemetery for veterans was countered by an individual claiming to own the property. Instead of looking elsewhere, MPLC took that individual to court, thus further delaying the process. In the meantime, the $1.5 million grant for the cemetery had a September 30, 1994, deadline. The CNMI would lose the money if matching funds were not identified. During this time, I worked closely with Joseph Palacios, the director of the CNMI Office of Veterans Affairs, and subsequently, with Vicente Deleon Guerrero as the new director. Both men are U.S. veterans themselves and worked tirelessly to secure the establishment of the cemetery. Together, we obtained a waiver of the matching requirement for this grant.

When the CNMI Government finally designated a new site in Marpi, the funding for the cemetery had gone through its fifth year of reauthorization by the U.S. Department of Veterans Affairs. However, even though the funding had been identified, it had not been awarded. Regardless of the status of the grant funds, there was a lot of planning already taking place. For instance, in anticipation of the construction of the cemetery, my Office had provided the CNMI VA Office information on granite headstones, and an application for each grave.

Honoring Our Soldiers: Command Sergeant Major Luis C. Palacios being presented the CNMI flag by Representatives Pete P. Reyes and Karl T. Reyes at the Open House Ceremony at Camp Frank D. Merrill, home of the 5th Ranger Training Battalion in Dahlonega, Georgia on July 30, 1994. Resident Representative Juan N. Babauta looks on.

When I took over as the new governor in 2002, I continued to follow up on the project. On June 24, 2005, the CNMI Office of Veterans Affairs submitted the formal application for federal assistance for the envisioned cemetery. Two months later, the U.S. Secretary of Veterans Affairs, Mr. R. James Nicholson, informed me that his department was awarding the grant in the amount of $1,666,980 for 100 percent of allowable costs associated with the cemetery. The Notification of Award was also sent to Mrs. Ruth A. Coleman, the Executive Officer for Military and Veterans Affairs on Saipan. With the notification, the CNMI quickly commenced the design and construction of the CNMI Veterans Cemetery. Later the same year, the newly constructed CNMI Veterans Cemetery was dedicated and opened for the proper burial – with respect, dignity and honor – of every departed veteran.

Telecommunications and Rate Integration

Prior to July 1, 1997, the Northern Mariana Islands and Guam, for purposes of making telephone calls, were treated as international destinations. The signing of the Telecommunications Act of 1996 by Pres. Bill Clinton guaranteed comparable domestic service for the insular areas, including the Northern Mariana Islands and Guam. This law, however, did not automatically assign area codes for these islands; that was a decision that the Federal Communications Commission (FCC) had to make.

The Government of Canada objected to the CNMI and Guam's bid for a domestic U.S. telephone area code. Canada's major telecommunications company, Teleglobe Canada Inc., and GTE, the parent company of Micronesia Telecommunications Corporation, filed a protest, igniting a vigorous lobbying effort by leaders from the CNMI and Guam for inclusion. Objection to a CNMI domestic area code was also filed by Micronesian Telecommunications Corporation (MTC), whose headquarters were located on Saipan. According to the October 20, 1995, issue of the *Marianas Variety*, MTC opposed the CNMI Government's petition for inclusion in the North American Numbering Plan (NANP), because it would be costly and useless for the Commonwealth.

MTC General Manager Robert Enfield at the time said, "It would benefit only people who place long-distance calls to the U.S." Enfield added, "Conversion to NANP is estimated to cost $2 million, and giving one the ability to dial 1 instead of 011 is the only thing that we will get for $2 million."

Despite MTC's and Canada's opposition, the leaders of the CNMI were united on the Commonwealth's inclusion. As the Resident Representative, I worked alongside Guam Del. Robert A. Underwood, Guam Gov. Carl T.C. Gutierrez, CNMI Gov. Froilan C. Tenorio and others in seeking support from the FCC, members of Congress, and a number of federal agencies on the matter. By March 1996, we were able to secure the necessary support. In May, Canada lifted its objection to the inclusion plan. As for MTC, there was no record of its objection being rescinded. With Canada's protest ended, the NANP administrator finally assigned the 670 area code to the CNMI and the 671 code to Guam. This resulted in a tremendous reduction in long-distance telephone rates for persons in the CNMI and Guam calling the U.S., or callers in the U.S. dialing the Marianas.

Voice of America Relay Station on Tinian

The Voice of America (VOA) relay station on Tinian was in the planning stages for several years before the construction contract for it was awarded on August 30, 1996. The U.S. Information Agency (USIA) chose a Kuwaiti firm to build the station. The Office of the Resident Representative for many years worked on behalf of the Tinian project by lobbying Congress. The project also received support from the leadership of Tinian. Tinian Mayor Herman M. Manglona and Legislative Delegation Chairman Joaquin Adriano both made contact with officials in Washington on this issue, with both leaders referring to the project's impact on local conditions and economic advantages for Tinian.

On 800 acres of U.S. Government-leased land on the island of Tinian, the Voice of America constructed a shortwave relay station consisting of four to eight high-powered (500 Kilowatt) shortwave transmitters and five to ten pairs of curtain antennas. Construction took about three years to complete, at a cost of approximately $100 million. VOA viewed the establishment of the station as the beginning of a long-term relationship with the residents of Tinian. The new relay station supplemented VOA broadcasts from the Philippines and Thailand, and eliminated language coverage gaps in listening areas in China, Southeast Asia, and Oceania. However, the broadcasts were not intended to be heard in the Mariana Islands.

At the time of construction, VOA was broadcasting more than 12 hours of programming weekly in 46-plus languages to an estimated 130 million listeners. Millions more hear VOA programs which are rebroadcast by local radio stations throughout the world. The around-the-clock news broadcasts are clear, accurate, and objective, presenting a balanced projection of American thought and policies. Programs are produced in VOA's Washington, D.C., headquarters and fed via satellite to 15 relay stations in the U.S. and abroad, which transmit the programs to listeners. The Voice of America has been broadcasting since 1942. It became part of the USIA in 1954.

The Gates Millennium Scholarship

At the announcement of the Gates Millennium Scholarship Program in 1999 by Bill Gates and his wife, Melinda, it was not clear that students of Pacific Islands descent were included in the category of Asian Pacific Americans, one of several established by the program. As Resident Representative, I contacted the Gates Foundation shortly after the announcement and explained why our Chamorro and Carolinian students should be eligible to benefit from the program aimed at increasing educational opportunities for minority students. The scholarship program is intended for eligible students with good records in mathematics and the sciences, and with commitment to academic study.

When the Gates Foundation informed me that Chamorro and Carolinian students would be eligible for its scholarship program, I announced the good news in the CNMI on February 10, 2000. The program also opted to include other Pacific Islanders, as well as persons of Filipino, Japanese, Korean, Chinese, and South Asian ethnicity, who are U.S. citizens or permanent residents under the broader category of Asian Pacific Americans. As Resident Representative, my goal was to make students and educators in the CNMI aware of the Gates Millennium Scholarship Program, and to confirm that Pacific Islanders can qualify for it.

Resident Representative Babauta as guest speaker at Kagman Elementary School on Saipan on October 22, 2001.

For selected students, the Gates Millennium Scholarship provides the needed funds for tuition and living expenses during their entire course of academic study. To qualify, students have to be nominated by teachers, principals, professors, individuals from community agencies, and others, in their personal capacities. During the first year of the program, 4,000 scholarships were awarded, and 1,000 per year thereafter.

Marianas Included in National World War II Memorial

When the American Battle Monuments Commission (ABMC) was completing its plans for a World War II Memorial on the Mall in Washington, D.C., the Marianas (The Northern Mariana Islands and Guam) were not included for recognition. The memorial walls were to honor the 16 million people who served in the U.S. Armed Forces during the Second World War, the 400,000-plus servicemen who died in the war, and all who supported the war effort from home. The commission is a small, independent agency of the U.S. Government that administers, operates, and maintains permanent U.S. military cemeteries, memorials and monuments, both inside and outside the United States, in carrying out the law that established it in 1923.

Pres. Clinton had appointed Ambassador F. Haydn Williams to serve on the commission, and he was subsequently named chairman of its National World War II Memorial Committee, with the primary responsibility of determining the site and design of the memorial. Mr. Williams had previously served as the president's Personal Representative for the Micronesia and the Marianas Future Political Status Negotiations with the rank of Ambassador. These negotiations ended the U.S. Trusteeship over the islands.

Planning for the national memorial on the Mall had been in progress for five years before the ABMC realized that the Mariana Islands were not mentioned on its walls. In June 1997, Congressman Robert A. Underwood of Guam and I requested that the commission recognize the wartime role of the people of the Marianas in its final design. With the support and urging of Chairman Williams, it was agreed that the Mariana Islands would be incorporated before the plan was submitted to the White House for approval. The memorial was formally dedicated in 2004. World War II is the sole 20th-century event commemorated on the Mall's central axis, according to the ABMC.

Historical Note:
On January 9, 1997, Pedro P. Tenorio and Jesus R. Sablan were sworn in as the 5th Governor and Lieutenant Governor of the Commonwealth of the Northern Mariana Islands.

Other Accomplishments

Additional accomplishments during my 12-year tenure as the Resident Representative include:

- Securing $5.5 million for the construction of an Air Traffic Control tower at the Saipan International Airport.
- Assuring that the CNMI received more than $49 million in Covenant Section 702 funding from FY 1993 to FY 2003.
- Including the CNMI in legislation to receive the Robert Byrd Scholarship. Forty college-bound students from the CNMI to receive $1,500 each, annually.
- Making the CNMI eligible to participate in the Junior Statesman Scholarship for two students to receive $5,000 each, annually.
- Procuring a $3 million Northern Marianas College Endowment fund, ensuring year-after-year income for the college.
- Obtaining $1 million for local efforts to prevent brown tree snakes from being brought into the CNMI.

- Fighting for and winning the redistribution of insular area funds worth approximately $6 million annually for construction and repair of CNMI roads.
- Fighting for and securing Pentagon approval for the CNMI to institute the Junior Reserve Officer Training Corps (JROTC) in public high schools.

Lessons Learned

There were hard lessons learned from working in Washington as the Resident Representative to the United States. Many of them brought great satisfaction and a sense of accomplishment. Others brought pain and at times, disdain, at the bloated egos that reign over Washington.

Resident Representative Babauta and Guam Delegate Robert A. Underwood as guest speakers at Yale Law School, March 2, 1998.

Territorial issues in Washington are a low priority. They do not produce excitement in the halls of Congress. In the grand scheme of things and under the weight of a huge bureaucracy and big egos, the territories are an afterthought, simply because they don't show up on the Washington radar screen. My good friend, former Guam Del. Robert A. Underwood, told me that a Washington insider once told him that, "No one in Congress is going to bleed for the territories." Fundamentally, there is a lot of truth to that. U.S. representatives and senators have their own constituency to answer to, and will not risk their political careers to champion others' causes.

Washington is rarely bipartisan. Territorial issues, therefore, must not bear any party affiliations lest you achieve no results. As a Republican, I pushed every NMI issue I had on its own merit, not on mine or any other political persuasion or affiliation. Those I dealt with in Washington knew my party affiliation, but ironically, I had more Democrats helping me than Republicans.

Now that the people can elect a Delegate to represent them in the U.S. Congress, and given the partisan political environment that prevails in Washington, it is incumbent that the voters put the right person in office to represent the CNMI. That person must possess a respectable level of education, articulate clearly and convincingly NMI issues, and have the ability to work both sides of the political divide.

After four years as Senator and 12 years as Resident Representative to the United States and having worked with four governors, I decided it was time to get back home and run for governor. First, I had to win a primary election to become the official candidate for the Republican Party. Then, I ran in a four-way race in the general election, which pitted the Republican Party, the Democratic Party, the newly formed Reform Party, and the newly formed Covenant Party against one another.

Running for governor was an experience I will never forget. First, I had to pick a running mate. I picked then-Representative from precinct 2 and Speaker of the House Diego Tenorio Benavente. Together, we produced and campaigned on a platform which became the Republican Party Platform. It consisted of six major priorities:

- First was Educational Excellence: To strive for excellence in our schools and provide everyone the opportunity for learning. Our main focus was to stake our economic future on becoming the most well-educated population in the Pacific Islands.
- Second, Economic Progress and Diversification: Maintain free, competitive markets with a minimum of government interference. We believed that jobs would go to countries with a developed high-tech infrastructure and an appropriately educated workforce.
- Third, Our Environment: Protect and enhance our islands and waters for our people, our economy, and our future. Protection of our environment is critical to our No. 1 industry, tourism. Tourism involves more than just marketing. It also involves making destinations more appealing. This means conserving and enhancing a destination's assets. It is, after all, the unique heritage and culture, wildlife, and natural beauty of a community or region that attract sightseers in the first place.
- Fourth, Performance Government: Our government must provide equitable, efficient customer service. We believed that government should focus on providing goods and services not adequately supplied by markets, chiefly in education, public health, public safety, environmental protection, and a reliable regulatory system that encourages and supports growth in the private sector.
- Fifth, Healthy Communities: Encourage healthy lifestyles and improve delivery of health care. We believed that it wasn't enough to give everyone access to health care; we felt that we actually had to work at keeping everyone healthy.
- Sixth, Public Safety: Establish a safe and orderly community environment. The greatest respect we can show to the men and women who

Resident Representative Juan N. Babauta and Speaker of the CNMI House of Representatives Diego T. Benavente at a Congressional hearing in Washington, D.C.

risk their lives to keep us all safe is to provide them the tools and training and leadership they need themselves to be safe.

To get our message out, my running mate and I decided to walk the streets and visit as many people in their homes as possible, an experience I recommend to anyone running for public office. We learned firsthand how people were feeling about their government, the education system, and about who is, and who is not, benefitting in the economic system that we had built in the CNMI. We heard about what to do with sewer overflows, littering, solid waste disposal, junk cars, unpaved roads, the lack of streetlights, stray dogs, street signs, the cost of health care, medical referrals, jobs for local residents, scholarships for our students, and of course, about our relationship with the federal government.

In the November 3, 2001, election, it was difficult to ascertain who our biggest supporters were. I can only say that in that four-way race, Diego and I garnered about 45 percent of the votes cast. Our base support came from the Republican Party; members worked tirelessly to put together a campaign that won support from voters throughout the Commonwealth. One of the many challenges we had faced was holding rallies and pocket meetings on all three islands (Saipan, Rota and Tinian).

Winning the election was a combination of tremendous feelings. One was the feeling of achieving a life-long goal. Achieving this goal didn't happen overnight; it took years to lay the foundation that led to my becoming the governor. On Election Day and through the night, I was in the presence of many of my closest supporters awaiting the election returns. It was an evening that I wanted to spend with only the people who had worked extra hard all through the campaign, and who shared my vision for the CNMI. Winning was indeed, a dream come true. If there was anyone I wished could have been there the moment I was declared the winner, that person would be my mother, who had died on January 2, 1981. (Similarly, my running mate, Diego, lost his mother not long before the election.) I wished my mother had been present when I was elected senator, Resident Representative, and more than anything, when I was elected governor. My only consolation was that my father was there in her place. And though my mother was not there in person, I could feel her presence, in spirit.

Chapter 5: Governor

I was elected governor on November 3, 2001. CNMI Supreme Court Chief Justice Miguel S. Demapan administered the Oath of Office on January 14, 2002.

Being governor of the CNMI was a tremendous honor. The job, however, came with a huge responsibility unlike any other. I left my house every morning, excited about my tasks ahead. Lt. Gov. Benavente shared the same sentiment and commitment. Diego and I worked hard and performed the best that we could.

When you are in public service, especially as an elected official, you are an open book. You are subject to scrutiny and ridicule. Every once in a while, you might get some praise. It is a demanding job, because people expect a lot from you. There is a saying that goes, "All politics is local." This is very true in the CNMI. By and large, people vote for you because you have reached out and touched them by doing something for them. The power of the executive is vested in the governor, whose job is to execute the laws of the CNMI. In order to be governor, you have to be a qualified voter of the CNMI, 35 years of age or older, and not have been convicted of a felony. And yes, you have to campaign and be elected by the people.

I have two sons, both of whom were born on Saipan: Brent Babauta and Matthew Sablan. Brent went to school in Oregon and lives there now. Matthew is in Washington State in college. Brent attracted the local media one year into my term as governor when reporters asked him what advice you would give your dad about his job. He said, "To take it easy and not work so hard so that he could spend more time with me." In politics, spending 100 percent of your time with family is not possible without neglecting your job. For me, the challenge was finding a balance between the two.

The governor has many responsibilities. One of the most important is to submit to the legislature a proposed budget for the following fiscal year. Another is to report annually to the lawmakers on all affairs regarding the CNMI. The Constitution gives the governor the power to grant reprieves, commutations and pardons. The governor appoints the heads of the executive departments, judges, the public auditor, and members of numerous boards and commissions. Under his emergency powers, the governor may declare a state of emergency in cases of invasion, civil disturbance, natural disaster, or other calamity. There are many other powers vested in the governor. The most exercised one is the veto power. It is, as they say, where the buck stops. As far as my personal life is concerned, well, I didn't have one.

There were fun moments, and there were also frustrating moments. I had the most fun rappelling, for the very first time, off a 70-foot cliff at Obyan Beach during officers' training by the Department of Public Safety and the

Historical note: *On January 14, 2002, Juan N. Babauta and Diego T. Benavente were sworn in as the 6th Governor and Lieutenant Governor of the Commonwealth of the Northern Mariana Islands.*

Juan with his father, Santiago M. Babauta, at his inauguration as Governor of the CNMI in January 2002.

Governor Babauta with Vermont Governor James H. Douglas.

Office of Emergency Management. It made me appreciate the difficult and dangerous job our police officers must perform to save lives. It was an experience I will never forget. On the other hand, one of the most frustrating things involved working with the National Weather Service in issuing bulletins before and during a typhoon. The frustration was that the forecasts were issued one to two hours late. An hour is a long time between bulletins in view of the possible rapid movement of a typhoon. Often, we would already be in the throes of a storm before the actual bulletin was issued out of Hawaii, where the National Weather Service's Pacific regional headquarters are located. In the meantime, there was nothing the CNMI could do, because it cannot issue its own bulletins. This is frustrating because the safety of the public is put at risk.

Public Security, Public Safety, and Emergencies

My first year as governor was a difficult recovery period from the impact of 9/11. The CNMI faced the same challenges as did everywhere else. *The New York Times* reported that 36 of the 50 states faced budget deficits then, and health care and education programs had to be cut. We were hit by two typhoons in 2002, the West Coast port lockout, and the threats of war and SARS continued to squeeze our economy even tighter. Our tourism industry had taken a nosedive. The lieutenant governor and I worked personally to promote our island destination by going to Japan, Korea and China. I built a secure visa system, which allowed charter flights to come from China. With these efforts, tourist arrivals went up by more than 16% in just that one year.

The challenge in getting our tourism back on track was obtaining consensus from all the major players, public and private. The least difficult decision I had to make was raising the minimum wage to the U.S. level for all new government contracts for construction that was federally funded. When you believe strongly about something, your decision to do something about it comes easy. I still strongly believe that CNMI wages have to be increased.

Seven months into my term, I spoke before a joint meeting of the Legislature about the fiscal condition of our government. I wanted to inform the lawmakers about what I had done, and what we all would have to do in the days and months to come. I told them that the government was spending more than it was taking in. When I took office, the government, in its first quarter of the budget cycle, was spending at an annual rate of $225 million, even though revenues had been projected at only $179 million. We were facing a $28 million deficit. To address this, I issued an expenditure control directive: reduce travel, eliminate overtime except for essential services, and reduce costs for utilities, office space and cars. In the second quarter, I cut the budget 12% across the board, except for the Public School System. These efforts paid off by reducing government-wide spending by $1.5 million per month. I accelerated the drawdown of federal funds in the amount of $16 million. So, instead of the

$28 million deficit that we were looking at earlier in the year, we were foreseeing an $11 million deficit.

Just as challenging as the budget was the outlook at the Commonwealth Utilities Corporation (CUC). The corporation was not generating enough revenue to be self-sustaining, and this situation was compounded by the sudden increase in fuel costs, which forced CUC to impose a fuel surcharge of 3 cents on top of the 11 cents per kilowatt hour being charged for electricity. The issue surrounding the decision to declare a state of emergency was that CUC was unable to pay for its fuel, and without fuel, there would be no power. Without electricity, the CUC water and wastewater pumping systems would not operate. If this were to happen, we would be facing an imminent and extreme emergency.

My job as governor was to ensure the continued provision of electricity to public health and public safety facilities, and to our schools, homes and workplaces. In order for me to do this, I had to assume full control by suspending the CUC board of directors' powers and reprogramming all necessary funds for CUC to address the emergency conditions. CUC was not only in the red, its engines were breaking down. Money was a major factor in fixing the problems at the time, even after reducing the cost of managing and operating CUC. The restructuring of CUC was necessary in order to keep it under the broader control of the governor and to impose the appropriate power rates to be able to pay for fuel, management and operations.

The world has changed significantly since 9/11. In 2002, the U.S. Congress created a new government department, the Department of Homeland Security, exclusively related to homeland defense. A component of the Department of Homeland Security is the Transportation Security Administration, which has as its primary task the securing of our nation's airports. Along with everyone else, the CNMI was faced with a major new focus managing the security of our three airports (Saipan, Rota, and Tinian). In terms of our Saipan airport, we anticipated enclosing the entire entrance to the terminal. We had to delay the opening of our new Tinian airport for several months to gain federal approval.

Securing our airports was one thing, but securing our borders was totally another matter. There was no permanent United States Coast Guard presence in the CNMI. We were served by the Coast Guard Station on Guam. In the meantime, tourism took a beating. The number of tourists dropped dramatically world-wide, including in the CNMI. We scrambled to keep our visitors from Japan coming by increasing our promotion dollars, and we began destination enhancement work to counter the effects of 9/11. Investors looking to the CNMI were concerned about safety, thus further affecting our economy. The Legislature worked on legislation to ease up on the requirements for investing so that we don't lose current and potential investors. As governor, I was required to develop a homeland security strategy plan for the CNMI. I did this by designating the CNMI Emergency Management Office (EMO) as the State Administrative Agency for Homeland Security Assessment and Strategy programs. Our goals were to ensure that the CNMI promoted protection of all critical infrastructure facilities, to respond to any terrorist attack, and to recover from it.

During severe typhoons, many of our government employees were involved in manning the Emergency Management Office, the Department of Public Safety, and the Commonwealth Ports Authority. These employees worked around the clock to monitor and disseminate information about the typhoons. I often took the role of support staff. I helped answer incoming calls to EMO on the status of the weather, and conducted onsite visits in areas where there was devastation caused by winds or flooding. I also visited the various typhoon shelters all over Saipan, mostly at school sites. Keeping communications open with Rota, Tinian and the Northern Islands was essential in order to assess the destruction and damages.

Relations with Other Countries

Reaching out to leaders and heads of state in our Pacific region was one of the most important functions a governor would have to perform. I was honored to have met a few of them during my term as governor. One such meeting was with the President of the Philippines, Gloria Macapagal-Arroyo, in Manila on July 31, 2002. The meeting was historic as this was the first time a sitting president of the Philippines and a sitting governor of the CNMI met. The goal of the CNMI Government in this meeting was to assure the Philippine Government that its overseas workers in the Northern Marianas were being treated well. I

An historic moment in CNMI history is captured in this photo taken in January 2003 on Saipan of the first five CNMI governors with the Governor of Guam, Felix Perez Camacho. L to R: Froilan C. Tenorio, Juan Nekai Babauta, Felix Camacho, Lorenzo Iglesias Deleon Guerrero, Carlos S. Camacho, and Pedro P. Tenorio.

noted to President Arroyo that the CNMI had experienced some difficult labor problems involving non-resident workers. The problems involved working conditions, non-payment of wages, and others. While the NMI was challenged in that respect, I indicated to President Arroyo that the workers from the Philippines had made positive contributions to the NMI. (See Meeting with Philippine President.) It was important to note this because President Arroyo herself had visited Saipan when she was a senator at a time when she was critical of the CNMI because of labor conditions.

Two months later, in September 2002, I traveled to Japan to have a similar meeting with the Prime Minister of Japan, Junichiro Koizumi. Tourism was the main focus of my meeting with the Prime Minister. Japan was our mainstay for our tourism industry as close to 85% of our visitors then came from Japan. The challenge was that the NMI was only getting 300,000 visitors per year out of 17 million Japanese who traveled abroad. We needed to go after them, because they were not going to come on their own, given the competitiveness of the tourism markets.

My Medical Examination

In June 2002, at the age of 48, I presented myself for a complete medical history and physical examination at the Commonwealth Health Center hospital. I did this to set an example of the importance of regular medical exams as a preventive measure. I never smoked, though I have been around it. I have never used drugs of any kind, including marijuana. I drink caffeine, and lots of it. I had had no alcohol for 13 years, all during my tenure as Resident Representative and as governor.

With regards to exposure to environmental agents, I was raised in Tanapag, which has been associated with Polychlorinated Biphenyl (PCB) exposure. I was never tested for PCB exposure. I jogged regularly. As governor, I had very limited time to spare. In this job, I was able to retire around midnight. This was a concern the doctor raised, associated with stress. The doctor noted that my "hours spent for job-related duties" were excessive, and did not permit a healthy balance with leisure time, essential for continued good health. Further, the doctor did not consider a "business dinner" as a leisure activity, as "business" is the operative word. Although the doctor was happy when my evaluation suggested overall good health, he said "silent killers," such as hypertension and stress, are often overlooked. My job could easily contribute to either one of the two, or a combination of them. He was of the opinion that in order for me to preserve and protect my health, I would have to reduce my evening and weekend work-related hours and simultaneously increase the time spent in "stress-reducing" activities. Finally, the doctor gave this final warning: "I do feel that we should not ignore the preponderance of literature warning us of the long-term illness which may befall you."

Tort Reform to Save the Insurance Industry

Prior to 2004, insurance companies were leaving the CNMI due to an increase in the monetary awards for non-economic damages. They were also leaving because the insurance laws of the CNMI had not been updated to meet the needs of existing businesses and new investors.

In 2004, I worked with the insurance industry (Pacifica Insurance Special Counsel Joe Iacopino) and the CNMI Legislature (Rep. Martin B. Ada, in particular) to push for protective legislation. I also worked with consumer advocates and members of the CNMI Bar Association to ensure that the proposed legislation mandated that insurance companies live up to their responsibilities.

In 2005, I signed into law three measures that accomplished my goal of tort reform: Public Laws 14-39, 14-49 and 14-70. P.L. 14-39 limits the instances in which a "direct action" can be brought against an insurer. P.L. 14-49 establishes limits on liability for non-economic damages. P.L. 14-70 prohibits a third party from bringing a "bad faith" claim against an insurance company. These three laws effectuated the fundamental changes that were necessary to make certain that insurers could continue to do business in the CNMI. These laws not only benefit the insurance companies, they also help consumers by reducing costs. This ensures that the people of the CNMI, its existing businesses, and prospective investors, have access to the insurance coverage they need to sustain themselves and grow, with increased economic development.

Adult Correctional Facility

Before construction of the new Adult Correctional Facility began in 2002, the old Commonwealth prison was located in the Susupe Civic Center. It had been built in 1981 to hold 32 inmates. All of the beds were in two-person, maximum security cells. There were no single isolation cells to house individuals who might require such separation from others. Based on 1999 and 2000 in-house reports by the CNMI Department of Public Safety and a 1996 report by the U.S. Department of the Interior, the prison population was averaging between 58 and 74 inmates, which was in the range of 181% to 231% of rated capacity. Inmate overcrowding and increased population projections underlined the critical situation contributing directly to tensions and threats to public safety and the welfare of prisoners and prison guards.

After the Northern Mariana Islands achieved Commonwealth status in 1978, police and corrections facilities were required to meet federal standards and U.S. constitutional guarantees. Reports and survey results from the National Institute of Corrections and the U.S. Bureau of Justice Assistance indicated that the Commonwealth was not meeting standards in the specific areas of detention, corrections and prison facilities. Funding for construction of a new facility had been the main obstacle, and the CNMI faced the possibility of civil liability if the noncompliance issues were not corrected. The local courts were faced with the possibility of refusing to commit convicted felons to the old facility, because doing so would have constituted cruel and unusual punishment.

In the absence of clearly identified funding for construction of a new prison, the Department of Public Safety retained a consulting firm from 1995 to 1998 to prepare the architectural and engineering design for a new corrections facility, with construction costs estimated at the time at $11.7 million. That estimate would nearly double by the time construction began four years later. Before the Babauta-Benavente Administration came into office in January 2002, decisions had been made about the future of the CNMI penal system that presented serious problems for the Commonwealth. The planned prison facility was vastly larger than needed, providing space for 586 inmates when, at the time, there were only 151. The design did not include classrooms and other facilities necessary to rehabilitate, rather than just house, prisoners. The new estimate for the construction was $19 million, twice what the Legislature had appropriated. And because of its size, the prison also was going to result in considerably greater costs of operations, utilities and general maintenance.

It was important to note that, contrary to common belief, none of this was required by the U.S. Department of Justice under the provisions of the 1999 Consent Decree issued against the CNMI Government. My Administration worked diligently to deal with these issues. We developed plans to eliminate half the prison space in order to reduce the operational costs. Facilities for rehabilitation were added, and we worked with the 13th Legislature to obtain bond funds to pay for it all. We worked to improve relations with the Justice department as part of our overall policy of cooperating with, rather than fighting, the federal government. We wanted to make it easier for the CNMI to comply with, and as a result end, the Consent Decree.

Construction of the new correctional facility, also located in Susupe, began in March 2002 and was completed in the fall of 2004. It consisted of 110,000 square feet of operational areas on two levels, and provided a 344-bed facility with functional areas such as administrative offices, open dormitories, medical suites, cells, a booking and release center, kitchen, open exercise yards, and the central plant. Fifty percent of the funding for the project was provided by federal Capital Improvement Project grants under Section 702 of the Covenant for fiscal years 1996-2002. The other 50 percent was provided through local sources. In September 2004, I signed a bill creating a separate Department of Corrections, previously under the Department of Public Safety, that would deal with the issues created by the decision to build this large prison. The new Corrections department would focus its efforts on running the facility in a way that maintained the highest level of security, so that the public was protected, the staff was safe, and the inmates posed no threat to one another. The department also would operate in a way that rehabilitated prisoners so that when they returned to society, they would have the skills to lead productive lives and avoid future criminal conduct. I gave the new department sufficient time – one year – to prepare to meet the goals of security, cost control and rehabilitation. The new Adult Correctional Facility opened in September 2005.

CNMI Integrated Fiscal Plan

The CNMI Integrated Fiscal Plan (2003) supported legislation that had been prepared to reduce government spending, enhance revenues, and stimulate economic activity. It was a three-pronged approach in the continuing efforts of my Administration to restructure the Commonwealth government and revitalize our economy, promulgated as a balanced response to the fiscal realities of the day.

By way of historical perspective, since the peak year for government spending, which was Fiscal Year 1997, government expenditures had been reduced 21%, from $268 million to $212 million, by FY2002. Even as revenues declined, the government in 2003 was cutting spending, while services were expanding. High-profile examples of these new services included five new schools, the Saipan solid waste facility, and the juvenile prison facility. Expenditures by the CNMI Government in FY2002 were far below the national average. Based on FY2002 unaudited accounts, the government spent $3,064 per capita, less than half the national average of $6,208, based on U.S. Department of Commerce data for FY2000. This comparison confirmed that the CNMI Government had inadequate resources to provide U.S.-standard services to its residents. (CNMI Integrated Fiscal Plan, 2003)

To reduce government spending and accommodate growing demand for public services, my Administration in 2003 proposed the cost-cutting legislation entitled the "Commonwealth Integrated Fiscal Plan and Responsible Act of 2003." It proposed:

Reductions in Government Spending:
1. Holiday Suspension, to suspend all 14 paid holidays for one year.
2. Differential Suspension, to suspend a generous system of differential pay.
3. Protection of Employee Benefits, in the event of a reduction in hours.
4. Suspension of Merit Pay, Within Grade Increases, 30% Retirement Bonus, for one year.
5. Annual Leave Suspension, also for a year, of lump-sum payments for any leave. All positions were to remain vacant while Annual Leave was being paid, and all accumulation of unused Annual Leave would be suspended.

Revenue Enhancement:
1. User Fee
2. Hotel Occupancy Tax
3. Vehicle Related Fees
4. Non-resident Worker Fee
5. Income Tax Rebate
6. Assignment of Excess Public Health Revenues

Estimates of increased revenues as a direct result of enactment were $15.1 million in one year. (CNMI Integrated Fiscal Plan, 2003)

The third portion of the fiscal plan comprised the immediate actions that the CNMI Government could take to stimulate the economy. According to the plan, the readiest means of stimulating economic activity was for the government to expend the $94.9 million in Capital Improvement Projects funding that the Commonwealth Development Authority said was available. Not only would this expenditure create business opportunities and jobs, but it also would result in an approximately 10% return in revenues for the government. Examples of such projects included the Garapan Revitalization Project and the expansion of the Public Health Building and Dialysis Center on Saipan.

In short, the economic stimulus component of the Integrated Fiscal Plan required no new funding, but rather released funds for quick

Juan N. Babauta as Governor.

expenditure that might otherwise languish, and most importantly, targeted these monies at projects that had the best chances of revitalizing the economy.

Iraq Defector

In February 2002, My Executive Assistant came into my office to inform me of an unscheduled meeting with six federal agents who had just arrived at my office, a meeting they said was very important. The agents were ushered into a small conference room that connected to my office. I entered the conference room and greeted the guests. The person identifying himself as the lead agent very calmly said:

> "Sir, we want to inform you that we have a guest on island from Iraq. This individual defected from Iraq to escape the Saddam Hussein regime, and Saipan was chosen as the most appropriate jurisdiction to debrief this person. Our guest is at an undisclosed location. The debriefing will take about two weeks, and then at that point he will be processed for relocation to a still unknown location. For security reasons, we ask that you do not disclose this information privately or publicly."

This meeting lasted 30 minutes, and ended with the understanding that I would receive regular briefings on the status of "our guest." I was not told the guest's location, his name, or whether he was alone or not. After the meeting, in a one-to-one conversation with the lead agent, I was informed that the defector had been involved in the development of weapons of mass destruction in Iraq for the Saddam Hussein regime. As a defector, his life was now endangered. A number of his immediate family members, who were still in Iraq at the time of his defection, had been executed.

On a trip to Washington in 2003 to attend the annual National Governors Association Winter Meeting, I was met by two high-ranking Pentagon officials at the Office of the Resident Representative to inform me that a meeting at the Pentagon had been arranged for me on the Iraq defector. Early in the morning the next day, I was picked up by the same officials at 2121 R St. and driven to the Pentagon. After going through unbelievably tight security at the Pentagon, finally I met with a four-star general who simply said to me, "On behalf of the president, I want to thank the CNMI people for their contribution to our national security by hosting our guest from Iraq." I told the general that I appreciated our meeting, and was pleased that the CNMI could play such an important role. Following the meeting, I was escorted back to 2121 R Street.

A week after returning to Saipan, I was visited again by the federal agents. This time, they had an embarrassing question to ask. The assigned agent asked, "Sir, do you do divorce?" As governor I can marry people, but I was not sure about granting divorces. A quick check with the Attorney General indicated I could not. The agents then asked for my assistance in scheduling a meeting between them and a judge at the judiciary building. I learned later that our special "guest" had to divorce one of his wives in order for his processing by the CIA to move forward. When it was clear that our "guest" had stayed longer than the two weeks I was told, I kindly asked the agents if I could possibly meet this person who not only had consumed a lot of my time, but remained a mystery guest to me. The agents said that I could, and that a meeting between the defector and me would be arranged.

Two more weeks passed before I was contacted by one of the agents at approximately 8 one evening and told to be at the airport at 9 to meet our guest when he arrived at the airport for his departure. When I got there, I was escorted through the security gate on the south side of the airport and onto the tarmac, where a C-130 military aircraft, with engines running, sat waiting. The scene at the airport was straight out of a James Bond movie, in which a plane is heavily guarded by military personnel armed with submachine guns, all on alert, covering all of a 100-yard radius from the aircraft. The C-130 was not the only aircraft standing by; there were at least two fighter jets, also sitting on the runway with engines running. When the guest finally arrived at the airport, the vehicle he was in had at least three escort vehicles following closely, with emergency lights flashing. The guest got out of his vehicle, and was escorted to where I and a number of federal agents were standing, waiting for him. We approached each other to be introduced in the dark, we shook hands, and he said, "Thank you very much for allowing me to stay on your beautiful island. Your island is very safe. Thank you." I saw that he was of medium build, and he was likely in his late 50s. He spoke in understandable English, with a heavy Middle Eastern accent. After the quick conversation we had, I walked him to the rear of the aircraft. At that point, everyone turned to exit the gates and proceed outside the secured area. Our guest left Saipan at approximately 11 p.m.

President Bush on the Iraq War: "It's a matter of time."

The annual National Governors Association Winter Meeting agenda in Washington, D.C., includes dinner at the White House, customarily hosted by the president and key Cabinet members. For most governors, this is a do-not-miss event, just because of the honor it bestows. March 2003's dinner was my second in two years.

That White House dinner, however, was different. As rare as it is for any governor to spend a lot of time with the Chief Executive at events like these, because of the formality involved, I actually spent more time chatting with him than I bargained for. After the formal picture-taking of each governor and his or her spouse with the president and the First Lady, we were all ushered into a holding area next to the dining room for cocktails and the opportunity to mingle with other governors and Cabinet members. During this 15-minute period, I had the rare opportunity to chat separately with President Bush and Vice President Dick Cheney. I spent more time with them than with any of the governors or Cabinet members. I caught Vice Pres. Cheney's attention by bringing up the topic of the Iraq defector still on Saipan being debriefed by federal agents. The vice president turned his slightly tilted head to a straight-up position, and gave me this "How did you know that?" look. He dodged the subject, and we continued our discussion on the growing number of people from the CNMI who were enlisting in the military, and the many already deployed to the Middle East. My chat with Pres. Bush was mainly about the CNMI and his father's visit to Saipan when he was vice president. But I got his attention for much longer once we were inside the dining room. As the guests were taking their assigned seats, I saw that the president was sitting alone at the head table. I walked over to speak to him one more time. I told him that we in the CNMI were doing our part in the war on terror by hosting the Iraq defector who was still on Saipan. He gave me the same look I got from the vice president just minutes earlier. Interestingly, the president asked, "How is he doing?" I replied, "He must be doing all right, Mr. President. I don't hear any complaints from him." The president then said, "That's good to know." By this time, all eyes were on the two of us; we were holding up the dinner ceremony. Yet I had to ask, "So, Mr. President, when are we going to war against Iraq?" And he replied, almost whispering, "It's a matter of time." "Thank you, Mr. President," I said, and retreated to my assigned seat. I knew then that the invasion of Iraq was imminent.

Governor Babauta with President George W. Bush and First Lady Laura Bush during President Bush's second inauguration as the 43rd President of the United States on January 20, 2005. Also in the photo is Amata Radewagen, now the Delegate to Congress from American Samoa.

Back in the CNMI, there was a great sense of an impending military conflict between the U.S. and Iraq. When I returned home, I was asked by the local media whether the U.S. was going to war. I promptly replied, "It's a matter of time." Two weeks later, on March 20, Pres. Bush announced the start of the war, with U.S. and allied forces executing airstrikes on military targets and efforts to kill Saddam Hussein.

My Education Initiatives

Appearing at Marianas High School on September 15, 2003, I announced plans for a series of education initiatives in the form of grant programs for students, teachers and schools throughout the Commonwealth. The purpose of the initiatives was to help us all reach our goal of becoming the most well-educated group of people in the entire Pacific Islands region by raising the level of academic performance. I believe strongly that no matter what your vision may be for the future of the CNMI, that vision will not be achieved without a highly educated population. I also believe that we have gone far too long expecting teachers and students to succeed without sufficient books and supplies in their classrooms. My education initiatives were an effort to change that.

One way to achieve excellence in education is to put more resources in the hands of teachers. One of the initiatives featured a reimbursement program for teachers. They would be reimbursed for up to $250 of the money they had spent out of their own pockets for classroom supplies. The second component was the Teacher of the Year Award. Cash awards would be provided for the first time to demonstrate our respect for good teaching. The teacher who was selected Teacher of the Year would receive a cash award of $2,000, and the first and second runners-up would receive $1,000 and $500, respectively. The third component was the grant program that came in three categories: the Development Director Pilot Program; the Healthy Students Pilot Program; and Computers in Classrooms.

On January 15, 2004, I announced the recipients of the grants for schools. The Development Director Pilot Program was awarded $62,000 to allow one school to hire a Development Director devoted full-time to raising money to provide students with the books and supplies, microscopes, computers, and all the other equipment students need to learn. The Healthy Students Pilot Program was awarded $125,000 to allow one high school to set up a program of health-related services so that students could more easily get help and advice about their physical and mental well-being. The Computers in Classrooms grant was designed to provide every single student in a particular grade with his or her own laptop. They could work with it at school and take it home. It would be theirs to use whenever and wherever they needed it. Each of Saipan Southern High School's 220 sophomores got one laptop that year.

First Western Micronesian Chief Executives' Summit

The Chief Executives of the CNMI, the Territory of Guam, the State of Yap in the Federated States of Micronesia (FSM), and the Republic of Palau held the First Western Micronesian Chief Executives' Summit in 2003 in Koror, then the capital of Palau. The meeting was organized by the four chief executives "with the recognition that their histories, economies, cultures, and people are intricately tied to one another and that each island government can only be strengthened by expanded interaction and mutual cooperation." (First Joint Communique of the First Western Micronesian Chief Executives' Summit, March 7, 2003.) This first joint communique by the four chief executives in recognition of their commonality and commitment to cooperation was signed by me, as Governor of the CNMI; Felix P. Camacho, Governor of Guam; Robert Ruecho, Governor of Yap, FSM; and Tommy E. Remengesau, Jr., President of the Republic of Palau.

Meeting of the Western Micronesian Chief Executives held July 13–14, 2004 on Saipan. L to R: Governor Robert Ruecho (Yap), Governor Felix P. Camacho (Guam), Governor Juan N. Babauta (CNMI), and President Tommy Remengesau, Jr. (Palau). Meeting focused on regional cooperation to address issues affecting the islands of the western Pacific.

The specific issues discussed during the summit included:
a. Regional Tourism: Inter-Island travel that would entail a comprehensive promotional effort to include discounts for citizens/residents of each jurisdiction.

b. Creation of a Regional Airline: Development of tourism is crucial in each of the four jurisdictions, and the development of a regional airline is essential to expanding tourism markets and guaranteeing a constant flow of visitors from major partners in the region.
c. Regional Health Care Initiatives: With regional drug and medical equipment procurement as a single entity, costs could be reduced. Medical Referrals outside the region could be significantly reduced by sharing resources and upgrading facilities throughout the four states. The center of this referral system would be Guam, due to its more advanced medical services.
d. Solid Waste Management: The four states could cooperate to take advantage of economies of scale to enhance opportunities for scrap metal and hazardous materials disposal, and for comprehensive solid waste management.
e. Renewable Energy: Cooperation, again, is essential to reducing the cost of energy consumption; we all agreed, therefore, to survey current energy sources and identify appropriate, eco-friendly, alternative energy technologies, such as solar, wind, and ocean thermal conversion.
f. Telecommunications: The four states recognized that the high cost of communications was limiting economic growth and contact with the international marketplace. They stressed the need to combine efforts to assess appropriate and alternative telecommunications systems, such as submarine cables (circle cable system to protect against system failures) and satellites.
g. Education: The Chief Executives proposed that a regional trades education capacity be developed in light of emphasis on college preparatory programs already in place.
h. Expansion of Regional Partnerships: In order to bring higher quality and lower cost services to the region, the Summit participants should also include the president of the FSM and all of its respective governors, and the president of the Republic of the Marshall Islands.

With regard to Item c, it is a known fact that every year, millions of dollars are spent by all the Micronesian islands for off-island medical treatment of patients in Hawaii, the U.S. mainland and the Philippines. The CNMI alone spent more than $7 million for off-island referrals in one year. In addition to government expenditures, families also spend a significant amount of financial resources on these referrals. With the advent of diagnosis via telemedicine, with growing populations creating economies of scale, and perhaps more importantly, with the increasing number of indigenous persons who are doctors or other medical professionals, new solutions for delivery of health care are feasible and must be explored.

My vision is to develop our own regional health care centers and, for example, direct all our tertiary care patients to Guam, rather than the Philippines or Hawaii. Guam would build on and strengthen the delivery of medical services in specialized areas so as to receive patients referred from the CNMI. With this support and understanding, the CNMI could turn its attention toward becoming the regional center for pediatric care. The FSM and Palau also would develop their specialized regional facilities. In short, my vision is simply to redirect part of our government and private expenditures to the development of our health care resources in a regional manner, a form of re-investment in the neighborhood.

My vision actually already existed, in the U.S. state of Alaska. As Sen. Frank Murkowski stated in his September 21, 2001, letter to Interior Secretary Gale Norton on this subject:

> "There are villages and communities in Alaska that are as remote from centers for specialized health care as the most isolated islands and atolls in Micronesia, yet we have taken advantage of technology to markedly improve the ability of the local communities to provide care. In the case of the government in Micronesia, that technology, as well as a better-focused use of facilities, could provide far better levels of care within the islands than is possible now even with off-island referrals. A coordinated approach could also relieve some of the local governments of the maintenance costs for facilities and services that are duplicated on neighboring islands."

We need long-term regional commitment from everybody. Goals must be clearly defined. We must think regionally. Health care costs have skyrocketed. We are spending more and more resources on health care, and projections are that costs will increase. I propose that united as a region, we can best address our individual needs as well as our neighbors'.

My Assistant for Carolinian Affairs

At the time of the inauguration of the first elected officials of the Commonwealth Government on January 9, 1978, Carolinians were still the minority population compared to Chamorros. In 1982, there were 11,000 Chamorros and 2,900 Carolinians in the Northern Mariana Islands (See Alkire, 1984). The Carolinians were considered more traditional and still, to some degree, held on to their clan system. But if the clan system has not totally disappeared, their navigational skills for sailing on the high seas have. According to Brower in *A Song for Satawal* (1983), the Carolinians are no longer building canoes, and are no longer the fishermen that they once were.

Most colonial efforts to develop Saipan along mercantile and industrial lines concentrated on training and providing jobs for Chamorros. They were also given preferences in the political realm. The Japanese also favored Chamorros over Carolinians by training them to fill skilled positions. (Leibowitz, 1989)

In acknowledgment of this historical background, the people of the Northern Marianas, in adopting their own constitution, included and established in Article III, Section 18, the position of Executive Assistant to the Governor for Carolinian Affairs. His role is to advise the governor on matters affecting persons of Carolinian descent. He also is authorized to review policies, investigate complaints, recommend budget items, and deal with matters affecting Carolinians, and in all cases report his findings and make recommendations.

Not specifically mentioned in Article III of the constitution is the role of the executive assistant in regards to Carolinian culture and traditions. The fear among Carolinians is that their culture is dying. Many in the Carolinian community are saddened by this, and at the very least, are looking for ways to maintain what they still have, and to preserve what they once had for future generations of Carolinians to discern.

During the Babauta-Benavente Administration, at the recommendation of Executive Assistant Victorino Nekai Igitol, the Office of Carolinian Affairs was tasked with coordinating the recording of the use of the Carolinian language – to include written, audio, and video formats – in traditional songs. To accomplish this task, the executive assistant was authorized to seek appropriate grants from the federal government, including from the Administration for Native Americans (ANA), to carry out the duties and responsibilities of his office.

Governor Juan N. Babauta with Master Navigator Mau Piailug in 2002.

Mr. Igitol also was assigned to identify land for acquisition for the expansion of his office and its capacity, as well to utilize the property for demonstration projects, such as the construction of traditional houses and the production of various arts and crafts. The Babauta-Benavente Administration, through the recommendation of the executive assistant, was able to identify and deed such land to the Office of Carolinian Affairs. The property is a prime beachfront property, in keeping with the inherent connection of the Carolinians to the ocean.

The ocean is a major part of the life and culture of both Chamorros and Carolinians. This point was made by Lt. Gov. Jesus C. Borja of the CNMI in his appearance before the U.S. Senate Committee on Indian Affairs at a June 1, 1995, hearing in Hawaii. He spoke in support of the Hawaiian Community Fisheries Act, which was the main subject of the hearing, but also about the protection of indigenous fishing rights in the Northern Marianas. He pointed out that the Covenant between the CNMI and the U.S., and the Commonwealth Constitution, similarly recognize special resource rights for our indigenous peoples. Lt. Gov. Borja tied this recognition of rights to a similar proposal entitled The Pacific Insular Areas Fisheries Empowerment Act, which also was presented at the hearing.

In recognition of the indigenous Chamorro and Carolinian right to fish in CNMI waters, the Congress should and must extend to us "traditional fishing rights," and the right to use modern techniques and equipment. This is a goal worthy of being pursued by the Office of Carolinian Affairs, in addition to those activities in which it is already engaged. This being a much broader and more complex issue, the Office of Carolinian Affairs should work jointly with the Office of Indigenous Affairs.

Keeping SARS at Bay

Close proximity to Southeast Asia exposes the Northern Marianas to potentially deadly diseases, a matter of enormous public health significance. The biggest threat to the CNMI was the Sudden Acute Respiratory Syndrome (SARS), which broke out in Guangdong Province in China, and spread from there in late 2002 and 2003. SARS infected more than 8,000 people worldwide, killing 774. As the governor at the time, I was faced with the challenge of protecting the public's health without adversely affecting the visitor industry. A single case of SARS reaching the Northern Marianas would have placed the population at risk, and would have had a devastating effect on tourism.

One of the ways SARS might have been brought here was through an infected tourist. Because of the many visitors who came from Southeast Asia – from Indonesia, the Philippines, Thailand, China and other countries – I had to act to prevent SARS from being brought in from areas that had confirmed cases. One of the decisions I had to make was to temporarily halt flights carrying tourists from these countries. I was criticized by the business community, including the Saipan Chamber of Commerce and others, for being too cautious. My feeling then was, I would have been criticized anyway had I done nothing. I made my decision in the best interest of the community.

Because of design and equipment limitations, the air within the hospital on Saipan is recirculated; if there were a SARS case, the entire hospital could be contaminated. I and a number of other elected officials went to Congress to ask the House Committee on Government Reform and Oversight, and the Subcommittee on Welfare and Human Rights, chaired by Congressman Dan Burton, for funding to upgrade the hospital's ventilation and air-conditioning systems. My goal was to keep our islands SARS-free, and I would have done anything to keep the deadly disease out.

The question remains, did I make the right decision? Did I prevent SARS from being brought into the CNMI that would have placed the people at risk, and would have ruined tourism in the CNMI? I believe I did. Perhaps I will never know. I can say, however, that the Commonwealth remained SARS-free.

Rota East Harbor Redesigned

Late in 2002, the Rota East Harbor was about to receive a long-overdue facelift. The whole facility was redesigned with a wider, safer boat ramp, a deeper harbor, and a larger breakwater. Construction was due to begin in January 2003. But on December 12, 2002, Supertyphoon Pongsona hit the harbor so hard that it changed the landscape. The concrete breakwater was completely destroyed, and enormous amounts of sediment were moved around, both on land and in the water. The whole facility had to be redesigned; in fact, this project almost didn't happen.

Delays due to the damage caused by Pongsona put a federal Economic Development Administration grant at risk of expiring. But teamwork saved the project. First, the Rota Legislative Delegation met and agreed to commit adequate funding. Then, I called all the signatories together and got them to sign the contract in record time. Guam Pacific Power Corporation began construction in November 2004, when funds became available from local and federal sources. The U.S. Army Corps of Engineers (ACOE) provided construction management.

Rota West Harbor, 2002.

The redesign had been completed in February 2003, with a much larger breakwater to prevent future typhoon damage. Besides the new dock and boat ramp, the harbor now features a concrete-paved entrance and parking lot, and a seawall in its interior. Knowing that the harbor is vital to the community, engineers designed the facility so that the public could use the existing dock as long as possible, right up until the time construction on the new dock started. The dock now sits on top of the breakwater, at 110 feet long and 24 feet wide.

Rota has a small docking facility on the western side of the island, built in 1984. It consists of an entrance channel 685 feet long, 300 feet wide, and 20 feet in depth, according to the U.S. Army Corps of Engineers. Goods and services arrive on Rota by small vessels – with no more than minus 16 feet of draft – with special maneuvering capability due to the narrow channel entrance and limited turning space.

The majority of goods and services arrive in Rota by barge. The size and limited nature of the current west harbor forces goods to be off-loaded on Guam and transferred to smaller barges capable of negotiating the west harbor. This adds time and cost to goods shipped. Any improvement of the harbors, either the west or east harbor, will result in significant economic improvement for the island.

Tinian's Harbor

Tinian's harbor, built in 1944, is in a state of disrepair. According to the U.S. Army Corps of Engineers, the inner breakwater is 1,210 feet long, made up of a single row of ½-inch-thick interlocking sheet piling. The outer breakwater is 3,594 feet long, consisting of ½-inch-thick interlocking steel sheet piles, which make up 120 circular cells. Each cell is 30 feet in diameter, and is filled with crushed and quarried coral. The cells have been deteriorating and now are in danger of collapsing.

The existing harbor size, its configuration, and its depth restrict larger vessels from entering the harbor. Rehabilitation of the breakwater and deepening of the harbor to accommodate larger vessels would save the people of Tinian millions of dollars in transshipment costs and could significantly improve the island's economic outlook.

While I was the Resident Representative and as governor, I put a great deal of energy into securing federal support to rehabilitate the harbor. A reconnaissance study needed to be done on the condition of the harbor, followed by feasibility studies to determine the cost and benefits of committing millions of dollars to the project. The federal response was that feasibility studies would be initiated if the reconnaissance report determined federal interest to be consistent with federal policy. I questioned that policy. Does it always have to involve federal interest? What about the community's interest?

The harbor is Tinian's lifeline to economic growth. Maintaining a marginal economy ultimately would not be in the federal government's best interest, because the suffering in the long term would cost more than the actual cost in dollars of rehabilitating the harbor. In principle, this applies to Rota and to Saipan, as well.

Council on Physical Fitness

After a hectic day, I enjoy jogging as a stress reliever. Jogging is something that I have been doing since my high school and college years. The sometimes bitter, cold weather the 12 years I was in Washington, D.C., was not an obstacle. In Virginia, where I lived, I jogged whenever possible from my residence in McLean to the Central Intelligence Agency headquarters in Langley, and back. When I was home on Saipan, I ran on the Beach Road pathway, a beautiful and scenic run, especially at sunset. After years of running only intermittently, I took it up seriously soon after my election in November 2001. I started out running two miles, and then extended it to three to five miles a day. Later, for a whole year, I was jogging up to six to eight miles a day. Then on December 7, 2003, I ran in my first-ever half-marathon, at the 1st Saipan-Korea Marathon Festival. The course started at the American Memorial Park in Garapan and went to the Pacific Islands Club in San Antonio, and back to the park. Running those six to eight miles daily proved too rigorous; my knees started to hurt. At the advice of three doctors, I reduced my running in Marpi to five miles every other day.

Improved health is what motivates me to run as I do. Running has become part of my life. I have no plan to stop. I get a natural high after each run, during which I am freed from life's everyday stressors. My body is rejuvenated with energy, and my mental state is ever-alert. I believe firmly that all individuals likewise would benefit from greater attention to physical activity, fitness and sports programs and issues. In keeping with that belief, I established the Governor's Council on Physical Fitness and Sports just two days prior to the 1st Saipan-Korea marathon. Its creation was intended to emphasize the importance of regular physical activity and promote active sports participation by people of all ages, genders, ethnicities and abilities. I am convinced that the lack of physical fitness, poor nutrition, and a lack of preventive measures to maintain good health have cost the Northern Marianas millions of dollars in lost productivity and in providing health care due to illnesses that could have been prevented.

Studies indicate that there is a direct relationship between good health and physical fitness and student performance, in the primary and secondary grade levels. The Governor's Council also was created to develop programs to reduce obesity, especially among younger persons, as well as to initiate regular fitness, sports and other physical activities for older persons and persons with disabilities. The permanent members of the Council were the governor, the four mayors, the Speaker of the House of Representatives, and the Secretary of Public Health.

On May 22, 2004, the Council kicked off its campaign to promote healthier lifestyles with a mass walk on Saipan's Beach Road. Government offices, private companies, nonprofit organizations, sports teams, schools, private citizens and others from all over the CNMI gathered in the Garapan area in the early morning hours to kick off the mile-long walk. I and the mayors of Saipan, Rota, Tinian and the Northern Islands led the way. Similar mass walks were held on Rota the following month, and on Tinian in July.

I continue to run about six miles every other day, at the northern end of the island, where there is a lot of shade in the late afternoon from the trees on both sides of the road. It's a quiet, serene location. My run starts at the Marianas Resort Hotel and Spa intersection and goes to the lookout above Suicide Cliff, and back. A portion of it is a grueling three miles uphill.

Japanese Royalty Visit Saipan

The visit of Emperor Akihito and Empress Michiko of Japan in June 2005 was an historical experience. It was the first visit ever to Saipan by the Imperial couple. The planning of their trip down to their minute-by-minute movement during their day-and-a-half tour was very impressive. Their plan included advance parties being dispatched to Saipan for a series of meetings with CNMI officials on the couple's activities and related security concerns. Senior-ranking Japanese Ambassadors to different countries also were sent to Saipan to affirm that certain protocols were followed while in the presence of, or in meetings with, the Imperial couple. The bowing of the head and body is the acceptable way to show respect. Another is not to extend your hand for handshaking unless they do so first.

The U.S. Government provided Secret Service protection for the Imperial couple during their brief stay. In addition to those assigned to protect the Imperial couple's every move, snipers were posted on the hillside facing the Nikko Hotel in San Roque, where the Imperial couple spent the night. Movement of all vehicles in and out of the hotel's front entrance had to be "sanitized," which meant a thorough inspection of every vehicle, inside and outside, including its underbelly.

Upon the arrival of the Emperor and Empress at the Saipan International Airport, I had the distinct honor of going inside the airplane (Japan Airlines) to welcome them. I introduced myself and thanked them for coming to visit. I escorted them out of the plane and into the terminal, where they were met by a long line of CNMI officials who joined me in welcoming them. I accompanied them on their site visits in Marpi, the Aging Center, and the American Memorial Park.

Governor Juan N. Babauta escorts Emperor Akihito and Empress Michiko of Japan upon the Imperial Couple's arrival at the Francisco C. Ada Saipan International Airport in June 2005.

In Marpi, their first stop was at the Japanese Memorial, the walkway carpeted in red to heighten the dignity of the shrine. The memorial is located next to the Japanese Command Post where Imperial Army soldiers stood their ground, refusing to surrender, and took refuge in a small cave until their capture by American forces. The Imperial couple then headed up the road to Suicide Cliff. There, they stood silently, bowing their heads in prayer for the many Japanese civilians who took their lives by jumping off the cliff rather than face capture by U.S. forces. The Imperial motorcade then headed down to the Banzai Cliff Memorial. There, the royal couple again stood silently, facing the open ocean, bowing their heads. The visit to Banzai Cliff was supposed to have been the last in the Marpi area before the Imperial couple was to drive south to the American Memorial Park in Garapan. However, the motorcade made an unscheduled stop in the middle of the road, across from the Korean Memorial, no more than 250 feet from the Japanese Memorial. The Imperial couple got out of their limousine, walked across the street to the Korean Memorial, and there they stood for several seconds in silent prayer, just as they did at the previous stops. It was an unexpected act of respect. The Secret Service agents appeared to have been caught off-guard, because they were jumping out of their tinted vehicles to see what was going on. At the American Memorial Park, the Imperial couple paid tribute to the U.S. soldiers, sailors and Marines killed in the wartime fighting on Saipan and Tinian, despite the sudden downpour of rain that got a lot of the people following the Imperial couple, including myself, soaking wet. The Emperor and Empress were unfazed by the heavy rain. When their limousine pulled up in front of the Visitor Center at the park, they got out of their limousine despite the heavy rain and proceeded to the designated spot for prayers and paid tribute to the war dead by laying a wreath. The Imperial couple displayed an amazing sense of courage and statesmanship. At the Senior Citizen Center in Garapan, the couple was greeted by a group of very enthusiastic senior citizens who had been looking forward to the Imperial visit. A number of them were seen hugging the couple, and some were conversing in Japanese with the Emperor and Empress. The senior citizens performed traditional dances and sang songs in their honor.

Following the tour, I joined the couple for lunch at the Nikko Hotel, where I had the once-in-a-lifetime honor of sitting between them. (See Addendum G., Luncheon Invitation.) I conversed quite a bit with the Emperor, but more so with the Empress. She was impressively smart and extremely knowledgeable about the history and culture of the people of the Marianas. She spoke English fluently. I had the honor of having dinner with them that evening and again, I sat between them for the most wonderful and graceful dinner. Throughout their visit, their every move was flawless and their every statement, stately. The visit was good for the CNMI because of the media exposure we received from it. It was indeed very memorable. I describe the entire experience in one word, "Excellent."

The NMC Pacific Gateway Project at La Fiesta Mall

The Pacific Gateway Project was conceived by the Northern Marianas College in an effort to advance to a new level of educational experience. It was an initiative that aimed to replace the worn-down As Terlaje Campus on Saipan, and to introduce a new education industry in the Commonwealth. However, NMC was faced with the great challenge of securing the necessary funding for the renovation of the existing campus buildings, as well as for new construction to augment those buildings. The NMC Board of Regents and the NMC Administration set out to explore alternative means of generating revenue. Increasing tuition and fees, among other things, was considered. NMC's search gave birth to the concept of the "Pacific Gateway Project." (Report of the La Fiesta Exploratory Team to NMC Interim President Antonio DeLeon Guerrero, July 27, 2004.)

The La Fiesta Task Force was composed of members from the CNMI business community, the NMC Board of Regents, the NMC Administration, faculty and students. The Exploratory Team was composed of NMC administrators, faculty, staff, and students. The difference between the Task Force and the Exploratory Team was that the latter did not limit its focus to a college campus, but looked at alternative uses of the La Fiesta Mall facility. NMC sought to establish a new direction by turning higher education into a major industry in the CNMI.

With that goal in mind, NMC (its Board of Regents, president, legal counsel and staff) sought funding from the Legislature, but could not come up with the money due to the hard reality of decreasing revenues and competing needs of the government. College officials then sought the assistance of the Governor's Office. For several weeks, the officials appealed to me to find them money for the purchase of the La Fiesta Mall to serve as the college's main campus, and to keep the As Terlaje Campus as a separate one so that the students would actually commute between the two. NMC even considered the idea of borrowing money for the purchase.

Members of the Board of Regents and the college's president gave me a complete briefing on their planned Pacific Gateway Project. After several meetings, NMC (specifically, Board Chairman Vincent J. Seman, the NMC president, legal counsel and staff members) essentially appealed to me to find them the necessary funds. As a supporter of the only postsecondary educational institution in the CNMI and as governor, I recognized and supported the project, in concept, and the economic potential of the plan. However, along with my support, NMC asked that I assist directly in helping them find $3.5 million as a down-payment for the $7.5 million sale price for the facility. This was far less than the original cost, and far less than the $30 million estimated cost to renovate the As Terlaje Campus.

I directed my Senior Policy Advisor to work with the U.S. Department of Interior's Office of Insular Affairs (OIA) in identifying funds for the down payment. This was the one source that came to mind immediately, knowing the support of the OIA when it comes to education. My office briefed the Deputy Assistant Secretary for Insular Affairs and, as a result, the Interior department decided to support the project by giving NMC, in the form of a grant, the required deposit amount of $3.5 million. The money identified was 100% federal funds. I turned the money over to NMC officials (the Board of Regents and Legal Counsel Jesus C. Borja, who also was present). The college negotiated the deal with the Nikko Hotel, which owned the facility, and with the down-payment secured, bought the La Fiesta Mall in its name and properly recorded the purchase at the land registration office.

Carried away by the excitement of it all, planners and others who supported the project overlooked some of its shortcomings. One was whether NMC could afford to transition into a new facility without jeopardizing operations at the As Terlaje Campus. After analyzing the costs, the accrediting Western Association of Schools and Colleges (WASC) raised some concerns. By the time the association's concerns escalated to a possible suspension of NMC's accreditation, the only way to get out of it was to dispose of the property. Under pressure that the college may very well lose its accredited status, NMC decided that it could no longer shoulder the costs of renovations and operations of the La Fiesta Mall. At that point, the Board of Regents and the NMC president turned to me and asked that my Administration accept a transfer of the La Fiesta Mall from the college to the CNMI Government. I was committed to doing anything to save NMC, in the face of being criticized for what had happened. NMC placed me in a predicament no governor wants to be in. Had I refused the transfer of the property, NMC's accreditation would have been taken away. It was an outcome I did not want to see happen. In a Memorandum of Agreement between the college and the Governor's Office, dated January 13, 2004, I agreed to transfer the property. It was a decision that would haunt me throughout my Administration. In the aftermath, the government was left with an annual lease payment of $200,000 and a facility that steadily deteriorated in the ensuing years. Beyond that, however, the

Commonwealth lost out on an opportunity for a much-needed new NMC campus on Saipan, an opportunity for much-needed new revenues for the college, and an opportunity for a much-needed new education industry in our islands. Indeed, had the Pacific Gateway Project succeeded, we would have a much healthier economy today.

With the failure of the Pacific Gateway Project at the doorstep of the government, the political blame game began. I was accused of being a landowner where the mall sits. It also was alleged that members of my immediate family also were property owners and that we benefitted from the transaction. When these accusations started hitting the airwaves, I requested the Public Auditor to conduct an immediate investigation on the allegations. The investigation was conducted, and it made clear that I was not a landowner at the mall site, nor were any of my immediate family members. With all the criticism I faced, I was extremely dismayed that no one from NMC (the Board of Regents, administration, staff, legal counsel or students) dared to stand up to defend the action I took on their behalf.

Secretary of the Interior Visits Saipan

On January 15, 2004, the CNMI had the pleasure of hosting Secretary of the Interior Gale Norton and a delegation of seven Congressmen, including then-House Resources Committee Chairman Richard Pombo. We gathered at the government house on Capitol Hill on Saipan, where Secretary Norton and I signed a grant that provided $5,171,914 to the CNMI to help defray the costs of migration under the Compacts of Free Association between the U.S. and the Freely Associated States: the Federated States of Micronesia, the Republic of Palau, and the Republic of the Marshall Islands.

In the Interior department's Notification of Grant Award, the stated purpose of the grant read as follows.

> "To provide funding for health, educational, social or public safety services, or infrastructure related to such services specifically affected by qualified non-immigrants, as Impact Assistance for the Commonwealth of the Northern Mariana Islands under section 104(e)(3) of Public Law 108-188."

In a brief statement, Secretary Norton said, "These funds will help the Marianas provide health, education, and other social services to the citizens who are permitted to migrate here under the Compacts of Free Association." The Secretary thanked Congress, directing her comments to the visiting delegation led by Chairman Pombo, for working to get the Compact Impact legislation passed. "Without the support of Congress, none of this would have been possible," she said. I was joined by Resident Representative Pete A. Tenorio, who helped coordinate the Secretary's visit. I thanked the Secretary for taking the time to personally sign the Compact Impact grant documents in the CNMI, and told her that those funds would be used to improve the lives of the people of the Commonwealth. The grant would enhance opportunities for education, job training, employment, and specific critical Capital Improvement Projects that were necessary to sustain and enhance our infrastructure.

The Compact Impact legislation provided that $30 million would be divided each year for the next 20 years among the CNMI, Guam, Hawaii and American Samoa. The funds were to be divided proportionately among the jurisdictions on the basis of the number of people in each that migrated from the Freely Associated States after 1986, when the original compacts went into effect.

Rota Judicial Complex

Construction of the new Rota Judicial Complex began in January 2004. The facility in Sinapalo cost about $3.1 million to build, and with other expenses such as design and engineering, the total cost of the project was $3.55 million. The architects and contractor had worked closely with the Mayor of Rota and the judiciary for more than a year to develop a building program that would meet current needs and serve the population of Rota well into the future.

The Rota Judicial Complex opened its doors in March 2005. In spite of two typhoons and several near-misses by other storms, the construction of the new courthouse was completed as scheduled. The new facility consisted of a Superior Court courtroom, a Supreme Court courtroom, supporting services, judges' chambers, staff rooms and office space for use by community groups.

Covenant Section 702 Funding Agreement

Lt. Gov. Diego T. Benavente in February 2004 negotiated an agreement with Deputy Assistant Secretary of the Interior David Cohen that provided long-term financial assistance to the Commonwealth. The agreement provided up to $13 million each year until 2010 for Capital Improvement Projects (CIP).

Lt. Gov. Benavente wanted a more stable source of funding so that the CNMI could plan its economic development with assurance that funding would be available. A compromise was reached that provided the CNMI a substantial amount of minimum funding, while also having a significant amount of funding up for competition among the CNMI, Guam, American Samoa and the U.S. Virgin Islands.

The compromise reached was that the CNMI would be allocated a baseline target of $11 million per year for the next six years, but the amount actually allocated could fluctuate between $9 and $13 million, depending on the CNMI's performance on its fiscal management and specific budget proposals compared with those of other insular areas. It was an agreement that created a competitive approach to additional funding, based on sound economic development plans in the insular areas.

The Commonwealth's CIP funding comes out of a mandatory annual appropriation of $27.7 million, which the CNMI once had all to itself, but which the Office of Insular Affairs now receives to fund infrastructure projects in Guam, the Virgin Islands, American Samoa, and the CNMI, along with certain other jurisdictions. Lt. Gov. Benavente summed it up by saying, "We came up with an agreement that will benefit both sides." He credited Resident Representative Pete A. Tenorio for his efforts in making matching funds optional for the funding received by the CNMI. The CNMI lost its mandatory annual appropriation at a 1996 Congressional hearing when Gov. Froilan C. Tenorio told Congress that the CNMI no longer needed the Covenant Section 702 funding. This statement made by Gov. Tenorio drew strong objections from me, the Resident Representative at the time, and from members of the CNMI Legislature at the hearing. Giving more weight to the governor's statement, Congress decided that the annual appropriation of $27.7 million that the CNMI alone was receiving would now go to all the insular areas for their infrastructure development needs on a competitive basis. The Department of the Interior's Office of Insular Affairs now receives the Covenant Section 702 funding, an annual appropriation of $27.7 million to fund infrastructure projects for the Insular Areas, which compete for the funds based on their baseline level funding of $11 million for the CNMI, $10 million for American Samoa, and $3.3 million each for Guam and the Virgin Islands. According to the Interior department, only a percentage of these funds supports water, wastewater and solid waste infrastructure, and each of the mentioned insular areas prioritizes portions of this assistance for projects such as schools, hospitals, roads and other critical needs. Interior also receives technical assistance funding from Congress, up to $10 million every year, as discretionary grants for infrastructure planning, studies and pilot projects. The Federated States of Micronesia, the Republic of Palau, and the Republic of the Marshall Islands also receive a portion of this funding for their infrastructure projects.

Stateless Persons

In April 1998, Jacinto A. Sabangan, Jr., Esther Hae Jin Sohn, and 26 other people claimed they were U.S. citizens by virtue of their birth in the CNMI, and applied for U.S. passports. Sohn was born on December 12, 1982, and Sabangan, on November 30, 1983 – prior to the November 1986 Presidential Proclamation conferring U.S. citizenship on the residents of the Northern Mariana Islands and placing into full force and effect their Covenant with the United States. (See Addendum H., Presidential Proclamation 5564.)

In 1999, the U.S. State department rejected Sabangan's claim of citizenship and his application for a U.S. passport. Three years later, Sohn's claim of citizenship and application for a U.S. passport also were rejected. Sabangan and Sohn took their case to the U.S. District Court for the CNMI, seeking a declaration that they were U.S. citizens, and for the Court to order the State department to issue them passports. On July 10, 2003, the District Court dismissed their claim, and on July 12 officially entered a judgment against them. Sabangan and Sohn appealed their claim of citizenship to the U.S. Ninth Circuit Court of Appeals. Nearly a year later, the Ninth Circuit Court reversed the judgment of the District Court and ruled that Sabangan and Sohn were citizens of the U.S. at birth under Section 1 of the Fourteenth Amendment, which was made applicable to the Northern Marianas on January 9, 1978 (before Sabangan and Sohn were born), by Sections 501(a) and 1003 of the Covenant.

In April 2004, while the appeal was still in the Ninth Circuit, I had issued a public notice of open registration of "stateless persons" for the purpose of compiling a comprehensive list of the names of individuals within the Commonwealth who could be classified as such. Individuals who were eligible to register as "stateless persons" were those people who were born and raised in the Northern Mariana Islands between January 1, 1974, and November 3, 1986, and who were not already U.S. citizens, due to the fact that Section 301 (c) of the Covenant granted citizenship to only those persons who were "domiciled continuously in the Northern Mariana Islands beginning prior to January 1, 1974" and continuing through November 4, 1986. The list of names that resulted was verified and authenticated by the CNMI Recorder's Office, and it was submitted to the Office of Congressman Dan Burton of Indiana, who was then the chairman of the House Subcommittee on Welfare and Human Rights. Congressman Burton indicated that legislation would be introduced in the Congress to address the issue of "stateless persons" in the CNMI, and that the proposal would have to include an accurate list of qualified persons.

Meanwhile, with the support of the Fourteenth Legislature, House Bill 14-97 was passed and transmitted to me for action. On May 27, 2004, to demonstrate further support, I signed into law House Bill 14-97 as P.L. 14-8 in order to allow these "stateless persons" to live and work in the CNMI. They had lived in the Commonwealth with their parents under "immediate relative" status, many having reached the age of 21 and no longer considered immediate relatives under the labor and immigration laws of the Commonwealth prior to the signing of P.L. 14-8.

It is unfortunate that these "stateless persons" had to endure the hardship of not being allowed to travel outside of the Commonwealth. They had remained in the CNMI their entire lives. They had no status other than being born in the CNMI in a time period not clearly defined in the Covenant, which eventually forced them to seek a judicial remedy.

Approved Destination Status – China

Tourism in the CNMI had been steadily declining since reaching its peak in 1997. That steady decline was raising concerns in the private sector, and news of the Japan Airlines pullout was expected to exacerbate the situation in the number of tourists choosing the CNMI as a destination. The emergence of China as a source to fill the vacuum attracted the interest of the CNMI, which had to act or face a continued decline in the number of tourists who came to the CNMI.

In 2003, on my invitation, He Guangwei, the chairman of the National Tourism Administration of the People's Republic of China, visited Saipan for preliminary discussions on the CNMI's request for Approved Destination Status (ADS). The CNMI had been seeking ADS designation since 2002, the same year it started receiving visitors from China. Based on the Marianas Visitors Authority (MVA) recommendation, Approved Destination Status issued by the government of China would help the CNMI establish a better relationship with visitors from that country, in addition to making the CNMI a destination of choice. The MVA opened offices in three cities in China to help tourists from there learn about the CNMI as a beautiful, friendly and safe destination. A system for granting visas to visitors from China was established through a number of approved tour agencies. (The CNMI prior to November 28, 2009, had complete control of immigration and issued its own visas.) In 2003, the CNMI hosted about 2,500 visitors from China every month.

While talks on ADS were ongoing, it was a matter of general policy to consult with, and seek approval of, the U.S. Department of State. With the assistance of the CNMI Office of the Resident Representative, I was informed that the State department had "no objection" to the CNMI seeking ADS designation from the People's Republic of China. On April 16, 2004, I traveled to Beijing to conclude negotiations on the ADS for the CNMI. Except for additional provisions being included by the government of China, the ADS designation was already approved by the NTA chairman. In a ceremony hosted by the government and arranged by Mr. He Guangwei himself, the agreement was signed by the two parties. At the time of the signing, only 25 other countries had the ADS designation, including Australia.

In the two years before the signing, travel from China to the CNMI had steadily improved, and with the advent of ADS, the number of Chinese visitors to the CNMI would surely increase.

Tinian High School

Completion of the construction of Tinian High School was a campaign promise Diego Benavente and I had made. We made good on our promise in May 2004. The original construction was stopped due to various disputes between the contractor and the CNMI government, leaving unfinished a new six-classroom building, a gymnasium, a running track, a science laboratory, a library and a baseball field. The project was funded by Compact Impact funds that I had reprogrammed, sacrificing Saipan's and Rota's share of the funds in order to assure completion of the high school. I took some political heat from Saipan and Rota for this action.

Unfinished Tinian High School. Governor Babauta in February 2002 committed $2.5 million in Compact Impact funding to complete the stalled construction of the school.

Paseo de Marianas Pedestrian Mall

Long before it got the official name, Paseo de Marianas, the Strategic Economic Development Council's December 2000 economic plan referred to it as the Garapan Pedestrian Mall. The Strategic Economic Development Council still exists today, an initiative of the private sector that is supported and backed by the CNMI Government. In December 2000 during the Tenorio-Sablan Administration, the council adopted a forward-looking economic plan that included a long-term vision for tourism enhancement and economic development in the CNMI that would improve the quality of life for all its citizens. A major component of the council's plan was the Garapan Revitalization Project, which would transform the main tourist district in Garapan into an attractive focal point for visitors and residents alike. Other components of the plan included installation of medians on Beach Road from the Galleria shopping mall to the entrance of the American Memorial Park, and the extension of the pedestrian sidewalk from the Carolinian Utt to the already-existing Saipan Beach Pathway.

When the Babauta-Benavente Administration took over, I approved all three phases of the Garapan project. In November 2003, I approved the construction of the Pedestrian Mall, and construction was begun. The disruption of business activity on that strip caused by the yearlong construction of the mall resulted in temporary revenue losses and much criticism from businessowners who were directly affected by the street's shutdown. My Administration endured the criticism in support of the council's plan.

With the surface improvements made to the area, what the public did not see was the improved drainage system under the old street; the area no longer floods during heavy rains. Area businesses all have Americans with Disabilities Act (ADA) accessible storefronts, and access to a pleasant open-air space complete with benches, shade structures, water fountains and decorative landscaping. The mall area also was made safer – equipped with closed-circuit TV monitors throughout, and a renovated police koban.

During the final phase of construction, a decision was made to give the mall a different name. Thus, a CNMI-wide name contest was conducted. Several public and private high schools participated in the contest, which ended with one of the students walking away with a $500 reward for the winning name, "Paseo de Marianas." The unveiling of the Paseo de Marianas took place in November 2004, nearly a year after construction began. The opening of the mall marked the completion of the first phase of the Garapan Revitalization Project.

Japan Airlines Ceases Flights to Saipan

Rumors had been circulating for a while in the CNMI that Japan Airlines planned to end its daily flights from Narita and Kansai (Osaka) to Saipan by October 2005. Concerned that this action would adversely affect the CNMI economically, I traveled to Japan for face-to-face meetings with JAL President Toshiyuki Shinmachi to confirm the company's intention. I learned that while a decision had not yet been formally ratified by JAL's governing board, the plan to suspend the flights was already in progress.

JAL's pullout meant that we would lose 48% of the airlift from Japan to the CNMI immediately if it was not offset by a corresponding increase in flights from other airlines. The CNMI government would effectively lose approximately 15% of its revenue. Japanese tour operators, agents, hotels, golf courses, diving operators, retail shopping, and other businesses that relied on Japanese tourists would see a big drop in the number of visitors, resulting in layoffs and the closing of some facilities.

What did the CNMI do to try to convince JAL not to pull out?

a. I met with President Shinmachi and other senior executives in Japan when word first came out that JAL was considering pulling out.

b. The CNMI, through my Office and the Marianas Visitors Authority (MVA), made clear to JAL the negative impact the pullout would have on our economy, and asked the company to give the Commonwealth another six months to find alternative airlift before pulling out.

c. JAL had been a key partner of the CNMI for more than 28 years, and we valued this long and important relationship.

d. Because of the short notice given of the pullout, the CNMI asked JAL to postpone any decision for six months and up to one year, to give the Northern Marianas time to recover from such a sudden dramatic change.

e. The CNMI put together two incentive programs to try to convince JAL to stay longer. The MVA was given a $1 million emergency fund to put together a package of incentives and to work with travel agents and airlines in support of new flights, including encouraging JAL to maintain its service to the CNMI. Secondly, the CNMI government allocated $2 million in emergency funding for the Commonwealth Ports Authority in order to provide airport incentives to encourage new flights.

f. I brought up the matter in discussions with their Imperial Highnesses during their Saipan visit.

g. A petition was circulated and signed by several thousand people on Saipan, Tinian and Rota, asking that JAL not leave the CNMI.

h. I made JAL's pullout plans the main theme at the June 16, 2005 Marianas Tourism Summit held on Saipan. The message was that the CNMI has a huge, loyal Japanese client base that attracts between 350,000 and 400,000 visitors annually, and we are confident that market demand will encourage more airlifts from Japan in the near future.

On July 29, 2005, I received a letter from the Managing Director and Senior Vice President of JAL's International Passenger Division, informing me that the airlines did, indeed, intend to cancel its Saipan flights. The letter stated that airline officials had reached their decision after extensive discussions with their CEO, and after taking into due consideration the various requests for continuation of the flights to Saipan that they had received from me and others in the CNMI, and also from Japan's Ministry of Land, Infrastructure, Transport and Tourism, as well as the U.S. Department of the Interior. The Managing Director's letter also stated in part,

> "Considering the passionate support of the local community and our customers expressed in the many names listed on the petition, it is with heartbreaking anguish that I must deliver this news to you. I ask for your understanding of the critical financial condition that our company presently faces, and that at this present moment, we have no other viable alternative."

We were shocked by JAL's decision, mainly because the load factors on the flights to Saipan were extremely high. In the previous six months, the load factor on the Narita flights had been 84%, up from 68% over the same period in 2004. The load factor on the Osaka flights had been 83%. These were extraordinarily high, and the Marianas remained as popular a destination as ever for Japanese tourists. Before the airlines' announcement, the CNMI had been looking forward to another excellent year for tourism, because travel from Japan to the CNMI in 2004 was at the highest level seen in seven years.

The airlines listed these reasons for canceling their Saipan flights:
a. The Marianas is a leisure holiday destination, and so this means little business class and cargo traffic.
b. JAL is selling seats to the Marianas at very low prices, and apparently this has been the reason for the lack of profits on these routes.
c. With fuel prices already high, every $1 increase results in a $50 million loss in profits, according to JAL. Fuel costs are unfortunately beyond control, and have a bigger impact on relatively less expensive flights like those to the CNMI.
d. JAL also told us they wanted to retire older aircraft, like the DC-10s they were flying to the CNMI.
e. JAL also told us that they were not only pulling out of the CNMI, but also other beach destinations such as Guam and Honolulu. In the case of Honolulu, this represented only 15% of airlift from Japan, while in our case, JAL was pulling out 48% of our airlift from Japan with just four months' advanced notice, representing a huge blow to our visitor industry and economy, and deeply affecting the people and the islands.

Finally, with an October 26, 2005, letter to me from Mr. Shinmachi, JAL Corp. President and JAL Group CEO, the pullout of Japan Airlines from the CNMI became official. (See Addendum I., Letter.)

American Memorial Park Visitor Center

The funding and development of the American Memorial Park was part of the Covenant negotiated between the U.S. Government and the Northern Mariana Islands Political Status Commission. U.S. Public Law 95-348 authorized appropriations for the park's development, construction and administration. The primary purpose of the park, located in Garapan on Saipan, is to honor those American servicemen who lost their lives in the Northern Mariana Islands campaign in World War II. The first phase of the development was the park itself; the director of the National Park Service (NPS) is responsible for its administration. Included in the authorization as part of the park were a visitor/cultural center, a Marianas memorial garden, and an amphitheater. The NPS, with local input from the Commonwealth's American Memorial Park Development Advisory Board, developed a master plan of the park's facilities to include the Visitor Center, a Marianas Memorial, and improvement of the existing amphitheater.

For accountability purposes, the federal appropriations were received by the CNMI Government as Capital Improvement Project funds, which by federal and CNMI laws required CNMI legislative approval. Thus, the Twelfth Northern Mariana Islands Commonwealth Legislature, in approving Public Law 12-58, authorized construction of the planned facilities, along with the design of the Visitor Center's exhibit rooms.

Construction of the Visitor Center broke ground on January 17, 2004. Secretary of the Interior Gale Norton honored us by participating in the groundbreaking ceremony during her brief visit. She had been a strong advocate of the park to memorialize the war dead. By December 2004, the facilities were complete. The Visitor Center comprises historical exhibits, a 120-seat conference room and audiovisual theater, a World War II library, a bookstore and sales area, and office space for the park's interpretive staff. The Visitor Center was intended to have interactive capability to tell the stories of the War in the Pacific and the fighting in the Northern Marianas, in particular. Federal law dictates that all interpretive activities be conducted in English, Chamorro, Carolinian and Japanese.

In addition to the improvements and construction at the park location, there were the design, preparation and construction of World War II wayside interpretive signs regarding the Battle of Saipan. Seventeen signs were constructed at seven locations throughout the island, including one at Mt. Tapochau. These signs enhance the mission of interpreting and memorializing the events of World War II in the Northern Marianas.

The CNMI Government had committed $5.2 million to build the structures at the American Memorial Park, while the National Park Service committed significant development oversight and supervision. The CNMI Government partnered with the Strategic Economic Development Council and the Marianas Visitors Authority in leveraging its own funds to promote the CNMI as a premiere tourist destination. It was a major motivating factor, in addition to the much-anticipated 60th Anniversary of World War II in the Northern Marianas in June 2004, to complete the construction of the Visitor Center before the end of the year.

A ribbon-cutting ceremony for the Visitor Center was held prematurely on June 14, 2004, so that visiting World War II veterans got to appreciate the efforts being made to honor their comrades killed in action, and to offer the veterans a sense of being part of the process.

Tournament of Roses Parade

Tourism is the No. 1 industry in the CNMI. The garment industry was No. 2, but was facing the effects of the end of apparel import quotas for the U.S. under the World Trade Organization agreements.

Japan Airlines was ending its flights to, and from, Saipan. Northwest Airlines was switching its 747 jumbo jets to smaller aircraft, due to financial constraints. MVA statistics on visitor arrivals were showing a steady decline, especially from Japan and Korea. The only country showing a modest increase was China, but the numbers of tourists from China were still very low.

Our private sector partners were very concerned and urged the government to do something to promote the CNMI. The MVA promotions budget and attendance at trade shows were simply not enough. The idea of advertising on major TV networks was discussed, and the possibility of the CNMI participating in the annual Tournament of Roses Parade in Pasadena, California, was brought up. It came highly recommended.

I was willing to do something "outside of the box" to promote the CNMI. What better way to get exposure than to appear on national and international TV? At the recommendation of MVA and our private sector partners, I assembled a team to explore the idea of the CNMI participating in the Tournament of Roses Parade. As with everything else, money was a big factor. I turned to our federal partner, the Interior department's Office of Insular Affairs, for a $200,000 grant to fund the CNMI float. The Interior Department gladly awarded it for the construction of our float, and some money for travel expenses.

"Harmony of the Pacific" was the CNMI's float entry in the 115th annual Tournament of Roses Parade on January 1, 2004. It was the first time a Pacific Islands entity had ever entered the world-famous event. We won the prize for best international float, given to the most beautiful entry from outside the continental U.S., beating out China and other countries. The honor was announced two hours before the parade began, which gave the float extra air time for millions of viewers nationally and internationally. TV commentators explained the design of the float, told the audience where the CNMI is located, and even told the viewers the meaning of a commonwealth.

The parade began at eight in the morning and lasted close to two hours. Hundreds of thousands of people watched it from viewing stands or along the five-mile parade route. The CNMI float detailed a depiction of our islands' history and culture. The music from the float thrilled the crowd, and had people clapping in rhythm with the six dancers performing on the float. After the parade, tens of thousands of people flocked to the float viewing area, where I and the rest of the CNMI delegation handed out brochures from MVA, and from the Committee for the Commemoration of the 60th Anniversary of the Battles of Saipan and Tinian, an event that was to be held on Saipan later that year. The award-winning float remained on display for two days after the parade to give the public a chance to view it up close.

Tanapag Cemetery

I pushed for, and facilitated, the expansion of the Tanapag Cemetery in the Lower Base area on Saipan. I envisioned a cemetery that was organized, well-kept, and had trees throughout to provide shade for a comfortable place to visit. For the expanded cemetery, and before it authorized its first burial, I encouraged people who had expressed some interest in organizing a community group to regulate and provide supervision over the use of the cemetery.

I feel that the cemetery should not be set apart from life, for death is part of life itself. It should be a place of frequent resort for the living, who might commune with Nature as a way of finding life in death. I wanted to see the cemetery receive visitors wandering about under the "would-be" trees and benches where they could meditate and reflect. This cemetery is the horizon where Heaven touches Earth, the interplay of the ideal with the real. It is where the meeting of the sky and the earth takes place. It is the land (place) that borders between life and death. The border of two worlds is where we stand today.

Puerto Rico Dump and DEQ Award

One of many lessons I learned as a public servant was that in managing the disposal of our community's solid waste, the government is expected to provide reliable service that does not harm the environment, and at the same time protects the public's health. Managing solid waste is a tremendous challenge for communities everywhere, but especially in small islands like the CNMI, with limited land mass and a sensitive environmental and geological make-up. The Puerto Rico solid waste dump was an excellent example of such a challenge. The Puerto Rico Dump had been a target for closure since the CNMI inaugurated its first elected governor and legislators in 1978.

The CNMI Government is not the only responsible party in the management of solid waste in the CNMI; the federal government is, and will continue to be, an integral partner in managing solid waste, especially in regards to the Puerto Rico Dump. In April 1999, the U.S. Army Corps of Engineers listed the dump as a Formerly Used Defense Site (FUDS). The U.S. military's naval administration had started the dumping at the Puerto Rico site, and the U.S. Government never claimed responsibility for this until 1999.

For decades, the Puerto Rico Dump was the dumping ground for all of Saipan. It was an open dump for all solid waste imaginable, located along the western shoreline of Saipan between the commercial seaport to the north, and the Hyatt Regency, a premier hotel, to the south. Waste dumping at the Puerto Rico Dump was uncontrolled and unmonitored. Fires at the dump sparked by methane gas sent clouds of awful odors to nearby hotels and surrounding areas. According to the February 3, 1997 issue of *The Marianas Variety*, Garapan Elementary School had to be closed and the students, sent home for four days.

Visitors in Garapan were advised to stay inside their hotels, because of the noxious smoke blanketing the whole area. Of greater concern was the unknown level of dioxin in the air due to the burning of dangerous chemical substances and other, unknown hazardous materials.

The degradation of the environment along the shoreline and the area surrounding the dump presented a deplorable situation. With the recurring incidents of fires at the dump, Gov. Froilan C. Tenorio proposed the use of incinerators to alleviate the Commonwealth's solid waste problems. Three incinerators were to be strategically located throughout the island as part of the CNMI solid waste disposal system envisioned by the governor, who also designated land near the Kalabera Cave in Marpi for a new dump site. The planned construction of the incinerators, however, was met with strict environmental issues raised by the U.S. Environmental Protection Agency (EPA), and by the time those issues were resolved, a new administration had taken over and plans for the construction of the incinerators were permanently put on hold. The designation of the Kalabera Cave site for a new dump was never approved by any of the CNMI's permitting agencies, or by the EPA. In the meantime, the problems at the Puerto Rico Dump persisted.

In February 1998, one month after their inauguration, Gov. Pedro P. Tenorio and Lt. Gov. Jesus R. Sablan made it a priority of their Administration to address the issue. Gov. Tenorio achieved that goal by creating the Solid Waste Task Force and assigning it the responsibility of implementing plans to construct a new sanitary landfill and related facilities in Marpi, and to permanently close the Puerto Rico Dump. In addition, Gov. Tenorio on December 16, 1998, established the Division of Solid Waste Management within the Department of Public Works to oversee and manage the Commonwealth's solid waste issues. On July 20, 1998, a Request for Proposals was issued for the design of the landfill and related facilities. Meanwhile, Gov. Pedro P. Tenorio had started the construction of the $4.192 million refuse transfer station and recycling facility at the Lower Base area. The construction contract for the Marpi Sanitary Landfill, however, was still pending when the Babauta-Benavente Administration took office in January 2002.

A month into my governorship, I appointed Lt. Gov. Diego T. Benavente to head the new Solid Waste Task Force and to immediately issue the notice to proceed for the construction of the landfill. The construction of the $10 million Marpi Sanitary Landfill was awarded to Dick Pacific Construction, which collaborated on a joint venture with Pacific Drilling. The expected completion date was December 2002. But just as the CNMI Government thought construction was to begin, there was an unexpected delay due to requirements that the Division of Fish and Wildlife had imposed. The December 2002 completion date for the landfill suddenly vanished.

Despite the obstacles that had arisen, Task Force chair Lt. Gov. Benavente proclaimed that resolution of issues which might delay or stop construction of the landfill was a top priority, and that those issues would be resolved. He forged a working partnership for the CNMI Government with the EPA and the Interior department, not only to help accelerate construction of the landfill, but to complete it in advance of its scheduled completion date. The urgency to complete the construction of the sanitary landfill was twofold. First, the EPA had declared that the Puerto Rico Dump would reach its maximum capacity by the end of 2002, and after that, dumping at the site would be prohibited. Second, the EPA in February 2002 had notified the CNMI Government that administrative fines of $125,000 per day would be imposed under the existing Administrative Order for violations of the Clean Water Act. Adversarial as it may have seemed, the assistance and active participation of the EPA and the Interior department were crucial to the completion of the landfill in February 2003, two months after the original completion date. Through their assistance, major accomplishments were made and the official closure of the Puerto Rico Dump and the opening of the new Marpi Sanitary Landfill were finally realized.

Two formal ceremonies were held to mark an historic end and an historic beginning for the CNMI. In the early morning hours on February 20, 2003, at the main entrance of the Puerto Rico Dump site, the first ceremony marked its closure. An hour later, and after a 20-minute drive north to the Marpi area, the second ceremony marked the official opening of the new landfill. Both ceremonies were attended by students from at least three high schools, several members of the Legislature, me and Lt. Gov. Benavente, the bishop of the Diocese of Chalan Kanoa, and several representatives from the EPA, the Department of the Interior and the U.S. Army Corps of Engineers. The director of the Division of Environmental Quality (DEQ), Juan I. Castro, Jr., led the closing ceremony. He shared his thoughts on the occasion being personally and professionally significant, because he had been the director of DEQ when EPA issued its order against the CNMI Government in 1994 for Clean Water Act violations. The student representatives who were present were given the opportunity to padlock the entrance gate to the dumpsite. According to the February 20, 2003 issue of *The Saipan Tribune*, Aileen Alcala, a 9th-grader at Mt. Carmel School, remarked, "I'm so glad that they finally closed it [the dump]. It's such an ugly view, especially for tourists." I described the event as "A new era of respect for our natural environment."

The Marpi Sanitary landfill on March 27, 2003.

The opening of the Marpi Landfill brought the CNMI into compliance with CNMI and federal laws and regulations. A day prior to these two ceremonies, I was notified by the EPA's Regional Office in San Francisco that they, too, were having their own celebration. Lt. Gov. Benavente and Department of Public Works Secretary Juan S. Reyes lauded the efforts of the Solid Waste Task Force for the completion of the Marpi facility, considered at the time to be the Pacific region's first fully compliant sanitary landfill.

Long before closing the Puerto Rico Dump, many from the community had envisioned turning the dump site into a park with lighted walkways, rest areas and playgrounds. As Resident Representative and as governor, I shared that vision and worked closely with the EPA, the Army Corps of Engineers and the Interior department to initiate plans to develop the dump site into a public park. But first, an assessment of the condition of the Puerto Rico Dump would be required. The EPA's Pacific Islands Office manager, John McCarrol, pledged his assistance in funding the study in collaboration with the Honolulu-based Army Corps of Engineers. Because of the need for this assessment, a revised compliance schedule for the dump's final closure had to be issued by the EPA. Funding for a use assessment for the dumpsite came, in part, from the federal Brownfields grant and from the CNMI's Capital Improvement Projects funding. A private contractor, Earthtech, Inc., conducted the assessment study under a contract from the CNMI Department of Public Works.

After the opening of the Marpi Sanitary Landfill, the community's focus turned to the recycling program at the Lower Base site. In 2003, when the recycling program was established, the CNMI reduced its total waste stream by at least 25% by sending garment waste to off-island facilities for recycling. When the amount of garment waste declined about a year later due to the declining quantity of garment waste that was recoverable, the Division of Solid Waste Management continued the program and was able to increase the percentage of diverted waste in excess of 33% to off-island recycling facilities through much of 2004. With such an accomplishment, the DEQ, headed by Juan I. Castro, Jr., was honored with the Silver Award for Integrated Solid Waste Management Systems in 2004 by the U.S. EPA and by the Solid Waste Association of North America, the leading trade organization in the field. The other program in which DEQ did particularly well, together with the Coastal Resources Management Office and the Division of Fish and Wildlife, was keeping watch over the coral reefs surrounding the CNMI. In 2004, the CNMI was awarded more than a half-million dollars in federal grants to protect the coral reefs of Rota, Tinian and Saipan.

Hemodialysis Unit at CHC

The CNMI Government broke ground on February 2, 2003, for the construction of the Commonwealth Health Center Outpatient Clinic and the Hemodialysis Unit. It was a long-awaited expansion project that many viewed as the beginning of a new chapter in the development of health care infrastructure on Saipan. It had been envisioned since the early 1990s that this was needed when the CNMI first recognized that there was a rapidly growing population of hemodialysis patients. This also led to the realization of just how inadequate and inefficient the existing infrastructure was in serving our growing hemodialysis patient population.

In early 2003, following the groundbreaking, the Commonwealth Health Center (CHC) began construction of a new hemodialysis unit that would accommodate the growing demand for hemodialysis treatment and services. Dr. James U. Hofschneider, the Secretary of Public Health, envisioned the hemodialysis unit having at least 27 stations, at which patients could be dialyzed at decent hours of the day, rather than having to come in to be dialyzed late at night. Dr. Hofschneider said that there would be no more crowding and unreasonable waiting time for these patients to get medical services. He said that the new facility would have more clinic examination rooms and larger waiting areas so that patients could be seen on a timely basis.

The CHC Outpatient Clinic and Hemodialysis Unit expansion project began modestly at a funding level of $6 million, but with the recommendations for expansion of the facility, change orders, and faulty construction design for the new water treatment system, the cost nearly tripled. When construction of the facility was completed in early 2008, the total cost topped $18 million. It was the largest Capital Improvement Project of that year in the CNMI.

Today, CHC is providing dialysis treatment for patients in a state-of-the art hemodialysis facility. It is equipped with a seclusion room for critically ill patients, private treatment rooms, 26 hemodialysis stations, a peritoneal dialysis station, and large areas for visitors and family members. Hemodialysis is a specialty service CHC has been able to provide for its growing number of hemodialysis patients, which is attributed largely to the high incidence of diabetes in the CNMI, and end-stage renal disease and kidney failure.

As of June 2012, the number of patients receiving dialysis treatment in the CNMI reached 163. At the CHC dialysis facility alone, 108 patients were receiving hemodialysis treatment, and there were at least four active peritoneal dialysis patients. At the privately owned and operated St. Jude Dialysis Center, the number of dialysis patients was 51.

Land Compensation

During my first year as governor, I learned that there were at least 400 families whose lands were taken by the CNMI Government and who for years had not received compensation for the assessed value of their properties. To address this outstanding obligation of the government, I signed into law P.L. 13-17 on July 23, 2002. Public Law 13-17 authorized the Marianas Public Land Authority (MPLA) and the Commonwealth Development Authority (CDA) to incur public debt in the form of General Obligation Bonds, not to exceed $40 million, to be used in part for the purpose of settling land acquisition claims. In addition, P.L. 13-17 set aside a portion of the $40 million to complete a 324-bed prison facility in Susupe on Saipan. A total of $28 million was to be used to compensate landowners.

The remaining portion of the bond proceeds was used to repay the internal financing incurred by the CDA at $1,895,306, the prison project at $9,104,694, and for the costs of issuing the bond, such as legal, trustee, and other fees and expenses, $999,309. In addition, a Land Compensation Fund was created by P.L. 13-17, which also authorized the collection of the liquid fuel tax and certain aviation taxes to pay debt service on the Public School System bonds in the amount of $15,685,000, which had been authorized by a Joint Resolution adopted by the Legislature in May 1999. Public Law 13-39, which amended P.L. 13-17, requires the CNMI Department of Finance to deposit annually both the liquid fuel and aviation taxes, up to $2 million, into the Public School System Fund. The balance of the liquid fuel tax revenues, and up to the entire amount of the aviation tax revenues, were to be deposited into the Land Compensation Fund for payment of the debt service on the bonds issued pursuant to P.L. 13-17.

The balance of $28 million for land compensation for the nearly 400 families was just a start in addressing the outstanding obligations of the CNMI Government to the private landowners whose property was acquired for public use. P.L. 13-17 did not intend to provide funding for the entire obligation on the part of the CNMI Government. It is, therefore, the obligation of the CNMI Government to find ways to settle this matter for those whose property was taken and who have been waiting patiently for years.

A Marianas Volcano Observatory

Volcanic eruptions in the Northern Islands of the Marianas since the 1980s, and on Anatahan in 2003, got the attention of the U.S. Geological Survey (USGS), as evidenced by the increased monitoring and studying of volcanic activities on the islands of Pagan and Anatahan.

Anatahan volcano erupting on May 10, 2003.

The nine Northern Islands extend southward from Farallon de Pajaros to Anatahan. Six volcanoes (Farallon de Pajaros, Asuncion, Agrigan, Mt. Pagan, Guguan, and Anatahan) in those islands have erupted within the last 100 years or so, according to a study conducted by the USGS. The sudden and violent eruption of Mt. Pagan on Pagan on May 15, 1981, resulted in the issuance of a disaster declaration for that island by then-Acting Gov. Francisco C. Ada the same day. Residents were evacuated and relocated to Saipan. "The volcano continued to erupt intermittently and was relatively quiet until 1996," according to a USGS report. In the report entitled "Preliminary Geologic Map of Mt. Pagan Volcano, Pagan Island, Commonwealth of the Northern Mariana Islands, May-June 2005," the USGS also stated that, "During the past century, more than 40 earthquakes of magnitude 6.5 to 8.1 have occurred beneath the Marianas Trench."

Due to safety concerns, Gov. Lorenzo I. Deleon Guerrero on March 15, 1993, declared a state of emergency in the Commonwealth and declared Pagan "Generally Off-limits," except for authorized CNMI Government personnel or individuals on approved scientific missions. The CNMI Disaster Control Office was charged with conducting an early and thorough scientific study of Pagan, and with obtaining and installing all necessary sensor devices designed to give warning of dangerous volcanic activity.

The Anatahan volcano erupted on May 10, 2003, and continued to blow for two years. The spectacular nature of the eruption caught national and international attention. According to the USGS, airline companies, the public, and government regulatory and emergency response agencies, in particular, suddenly had to deal with natural hazards in an area where such potential problems had been known to only a few scientists and the CNMI's Emergency Management Office. A group of researchers from the USGS conducted geologic studies on Anatahan for the whole two years.

The eruptions of the Pagan and Anatahan volcanoes within the last 25 years have forced resettlement of the inhabitants of Agrihan, Pagan, Alamagan and Anatahan. The USGS conducted a preliminary numerical analysis of the tsunami run-up potential for Saipan, Tinian, Rota and Guam. The daily monitoring of plume heights by the USGS indicated that the Anatahan eruption sent plumes into the skies as high as 50,000 feet. At that elevation, the ash cloud could easily reach Saipan and Guam, with the potential of affecting aircraft routes in the region. The USGS also reported that Anatahan was capable of large, explosive eruptions, which could occur with very little warning. This scenario led to my decision that real-time monitoring was required. We were concerned that while a major explosive event had not yet occurred despite the Anatahan eruption, the volcano must still be watched closely because of the continued threat of ash-forming explosions and the volcano's proximity to busy air corridors, concerns also pointed out by the USGS. Thus, my Administration urged the Interior department to expand USGS monitoring of all the volcanoes in the Northern Islands in the interest of public safety on land, air and sea.

In the final year of my Administration, the CNMI Government and the USGS agreed to develop a major Hazards Initiative for FY2006. The envisioned Initiative included monitoring and assessment plans, and the establishment of a Marianas Volcano Observatory. The Marianas Volcano Observatory was to be established through a memorandum of understanding between the CNMI Government and the USGS. The memorandum would include estimates of the expected staffing level required and the equipment needs for the observatory. In FY2006, the Volcanic Hazards Program invested approximately $500,000 toward the implementation of the plan. The Hazards Initiative was incorporated into, and became part of, the Homeland Security Strategy for the Commonwealth of the Northern Mariana Islands, which was approved by the Office of Domestic Preparedness of the U.S. Department of Homeland Security.

Chapter 6: Activities after Serving as Governor

CEO, Commonwealth Healthcare Corporation

I took the job as Chief Executive Officer of the Commonwealth Healthcare Corporation (CHCC) in October 2011 at the behest of Governor Benigno R. Fitial. The governor asked me numerous times over a year to consider taking the job to facilitate the transition of the newly established Healthcare Corporation. I did so reluctantly for five reasons.

First, there had been no transition of the former Department of Public Health to the Healthcare Corporation. A two-year transition was established by law, but was never implemented up to the day the government finally decided to make the transfer, nearly three years after the law, P.L. 16-51, was signed by Gov. Fitial.

Second, the annual budget for the hospital was drastically reduced to an unrealistic level, placing the survival of the hospital in jeopardy. The CHCC was staring down at very severe financial challenges. At the time the corporation came into being, there was absolutely no money in the bank, not even the "seed money" of $5 million appropriated by the CNMI Legislature for the hospital, which was far short of the $39 million budget given to the hospital by the Legislature the year before. The CNMI Government simply did not have the funds to provide the seed money and ultimately, settled on payments that would be made on a monthly basis over a year. The bank account was only established a few weeks earlier, and there were no plans and procedures in place for payers and the accounting team to deposit funds into the account. From a purely business standpoint, bankruptcy filing would have been appropriate.

The Commonwealth Health Center in August 2008.

Third, the revenue cycle management component of the hospital was basically non-existent. It was public knowledge that the hospital was recovering only between 10 and 15 cents for every dollar it spent. There was no financial statement or financial plan, and no report of payables, receivables and/or capital assets. Furthermore, the CHCC was more than a full year behind in billings and there was the threat that bills would lapse, owing to the rules of the U.S. Centers for Medicare and Medicaid Services requirement that billings be submitted within one year.

Fourth, the CHCC was not even registered as a "provider" of services with the Centers for Medicare and Medicaid Services, or with the Medicaid program of the CNMI. This meant that neither the Centers for Medicare and Medicaid Services and the CNMI Government could make payments to the newly established CHCC, because it was not even an approved healthcare provider.

Fifth, even after the CHCC had been reinstated as a provider for Medicare, the hospital was in jeopardy of losing its accreditation because of a long history of violations of Medicare's Conditions of Participation. If accreditation were lost, a total shutdown of the hospital would follow.

Ultimately, the governor and a number of members of the Legislature assured me that financial support for the hospital would be made available for at least two years to prevent its closure. With that assurance, I took the job. It took me six months to figure out that I'd been had. The financial support was an empty promise, and the hospital's struggle for survival ensued.

The CHCC has a broad mission under a complex organization encompassing the Commonwealth Health Center Hospital, a wide range of preventive services through its public/community health programs and behavioral/mental health services, and several types of specialty care clinics (internal medicine, nephrology, general surgery, anesthesiology, orthopedic, pediatrics, obstetrics-gynecology, hemodialysis and peritoneal dialysis). The Commonwealth Health Center is the sole community hospital in the CNMI, with a mission to provide quality health care services to all residents of the Commonwealth, regardless of ability to pay. Without taxpayer support, the hospital suffers a severe disadvantage, financially. By U.S. law, the hospital is required to provide care for everyone. By comparison, the hospital, like the Public School System, should be tax-supported, because they are both compulsory. The argument against the hospital is that it can charge higher fees for patients who can pay to make up for the non-paying patients. This, however, drives up the cost of services, while the patient mix remains disproportionately disadvantaged.

Prior to the establishment of the CHCC, the hospital had been generously subsidized by taxpayer money through general fund appropriations. Since the establishment of the corporation, however, there has not been any comparable financial support provided to satisfactorily provide the health care services expected by the community. As such, the financial shortfalls during the first year of the CHCC made it nearly impossible for the hospital to maintain a level of care acceptable to the community. As painful as it was, we prepared for an immediate, partial shutdown should it have become absolutely necessary. P.L. 16-51 had established the CHCC as a successor to the Department of Public Health. While it is part of the CNMI Government, it is semi-autonomous. The law grants the corporation a level of autonomy needed "to operate as independently as possible." The hospital is removed from government personnel and procurement requirements, and handles its own finances and bank accounts. The advisory board recommends to the governor the hiring of the corporation's Chief Executive Officer.

The CHCC is now the operator of the Commonwealth's health care system and the primary provider of health care and related public health services in the CNMI, including the health centers on Rota and Tinian. The transition to CHCC as operator of the Commonwealth's health care system, however, proceeded with no transition planning or capital, resulting in near-collapse and noncompliance with Medicare Conditions of Participation. The hospital was at risk of losing its certification from Medicare, a major source of funding. This was totally opposite of what P.L. 16-51 envisioned – a well-planned and well-financed transition from a line department to an independent public corporation.

By the end of the first year as a corporation, CHCC had made substantial progress, the most important of which was the turnaround in the trajectory of the finances and operations of the hospital. The turnaround was the result of assistance provided by the State Medicaid Agency, the Marianas Public Land Trust, the Centers for Medicare and Medicaid Services (CMS), Region IX of the U.S. Department of Health and Human Services, and the dedicated and committed personnel of CHCC. The public corporation also made substantial progress in Revenue Cycle Management. There were five major actions undertaken to improve revenue management. First, the hospital was reinstated as a provider of Medicare. Second, the hospital hired additional billers and coders who received training and certification from a federally funded program. Third, the hospital established an electronic fund transfer account with CMS, and established an electronic billing interface with CMS and Aetna Insurance. The fourth major reason for the turnaround was the development and application of the Certified Public Expenditure (CPE) methodology for calculating Medicaid payments. The State Medicaid Agency and CMS worked hard to finalize the application of the CPE to the Commonwealth; the CPE approach has increased Medicaid assistance to the CHCC. Fifth, the hospital implemented the full Billing and Accounts Receivable package in the Resource and Patient Management System. This had never been implemented in the past, in large part because the CNMI Government received all of the revenues and had a central finance and accounting operation. An example of the progress made by CHCC was that the Hemodialysis Center for payment year 2013 was given a Quality Incentive Program (QIP) perfect score of 30. In 2010, the Hemodialysis Center had scored only 18 of 30 points, and the CMS assessed a penalty of 2% on the reimbursements for hemodialysis services for Medicare patients. The QIP score for 2013 was a significant, quality improvement. As described by the CMS, "the purpose of the End-Stage Renal Disease (ESRD) Quality Incentive Program (QIP) is to improve patient care by setting performance standards for quality of care that provide the following information to the hospital: Hemodialysis Unit performance on the quality measures during the Performance Period; information regarding the quality measures; the ESRD QIP Total Performance Score, and how the score was calculated; and information regarding how Medicare payments to the hospital will be affected as a result of the Total Performance Score. The ESRD QIP was established by Congress under the Medicare Improvements for Patients and Providers Act of 2008; it measures Anemia Management and Dialysis Adequacy. The CHCC Hemodialysis Unit reflects the level of healthcare service performance that the CHCC strives to attain. For a more detailed guide on how these scores were calculated, you can view the *Guide to the PY 2013 ESRD QIP Performance Score Report,* found at http://www.DialysisReports.org, under the Methodology section.

In short, the CHCC turned the corner after that first year. The assistance from the U.S. Department of the Interior and the Department of Health and Human Services greatly assisted the CHCC in the progress made. The transition of an operation from a government department to a public corporation is always full of challenges. The CHCC survived the worst.

The main challenge now and in the future for the CHCC, is financial. In the mainland U.S., a major component of health care reform is the expansion of insurance coverage. The CNMI is in the same situation. It is estimated, based on the 2010 Census, that about one-third of the CNMI population is uninsured. It is also estimated that a majority of this uninsured population is not eligible for Medicaid. When the CNMI Government, in Public Law 17-92, ceased mandatory health insurance coverage for all nonresident workers, this adversely impacted the hospital. The nonresident workers were ineligible for Medicaid and became "self-pay" to the hospital and private clinics. The problem is, they pay only an estimated 20% of the cost of care to the hospital. (Source: CHCC Grant Application by Dr. Norman Okamura)

The net result is that public revenue and private insurance revenue paid to the hospital end up subsidizing the uninsured, mostly nonresident, workers and Freely Associated States citizens, which impacts overall health care resources. Therefore, it would be in the best interest of the CNMI Government and the CHCC to develop a health plan for only low-income foreign workers to address this issue. The CHCC cannot depend on the Affordable Care Act (Obamacare), which has largely excluded the CNMI and other U.S. territories. The individual mandate in this law does not apply to the territories, and the territories have elected not to implement a Health Insurance Exchange program. Thus, health insurance coverage for the uninsured remains a major challenge.

The Patient Protection and Affordable Care Act (U.S. P.L. 111-148) and the Health Care Reconciliation Act of 2010 (U.S. P.L. 111-152) collectively, are known as the Affordable Care Act, or Obamacare. It was the Affordable Care Act that required the establishment of the Health Insurance Exchange and was to be operational in the CNMI by January 1, 2014. The Health Insurance Exchange was intended to be a marketplace for individuals and small business employers to choose from available private health insurance options on the basis of price, quality and other factors that qualified health plans, on the Exchange, would specify. The Affordable Care Act required that the Health

Insurance Exchange be established and approved by the CNMI Legislature, which would have created, in effect, a quasi-public agency or, if the CNMI Government chose, a non-profit organization wherein individuals and small businesses would have purchased their health plans.

On a positive note, the U.S. Government's percentage match rate of federal Medical Assistance Program funding for the Medicaid program has increased to 58% under the Affordable Care Act. The CNMI and other territories had been capped by law at 50%. It is now 58% federal and 42% CNMI. This should be a note of encouragement for the Legislature to provide increased appropriations so that the CHCC can take maximum advantage of federal dollars, and for use as Certified Public Expenditures for the hospital.

Publisher of *Homeland Magazine*

One year into her retirement, my wife, Charlene Tudela Babauta, wanted to publish a magazine that captured the essence of the CNMI – the people, history, culture, traditions, arts, education, health care, politics, the economy, and recognition of individuals who had contributed, in a positive way, to the community through private or public service. As a retiree myself, I was drawn into the project. We became co-publishers of the periodical that we named *Homeland Magazine*. We knew from the outset that it was going to be a major undertaking, but Charlene was fearless and wanted to start right away. We did.

In January 2007, we announced, and introduced to the public, *Homeland Magazine*. It was an objective, bimonthly publication filled with enlightening information on government, businesses, social activities, sports, health and fitness, and history and culture in the Northern Marianas. Our first issue featured two inspiring individuals: Vicky Borja Concepcion, the banker who started out as a teller and rose to be Assistant Vice President of First Hawaiian Bank, and the late former Gov. Lorenzo I. Deleon Guerrero. The other articles discussed the minimum wage, the CNMI Museum, Living Healthy in the CNMI, and included an interview with Frank "The Crank" Camacho, Jr., who at 17 years old was already making waves in the world of Mixed Martial Arts.

Homeland Magazine had a circulation of 3,500, which made it one of the best and most effective advertising venues in the CNMI. Copies of the magazine were located in waiting rooms, in lounges, and in seat pockets in one of the major airlines servicing Saipan. The magazine also was widely read by students who were studying abroad. Requests for additional copies came from students who used the magazine as a reference in studies related to the CNMI.

After two years of doing research and writing and in part, subsidizing the cost of publishing the magazine, I decided that it was not financially feasible to continue. *Homeland Magazine* ceased publication in August 2009.

My Participation in the 2009 Saipan Marathon

Running the Saipan Marathon in January 2009 was a dream come true. I finished 29th in my age group, and 65th overall, in the men's division. (*The*

Marianas Variety, Jan. 17, 2009). In completing the full marathon in that Winter Festival of Runs, I achieved a lifetime goal. More than a hundred men and women from Saipan, Guam and Japan had participated.

It was my first time to ever run a marathon. "My goal was to finish the run, not to compete with anyone." (*The Marianas Variety*, Jan. 17, 2009). I had been preparing for the event for at least seven years. The preparation, however, got serious only two years before the marathon. My training regimen was running a minimum of five days a week, between eight and ten miles each time. My training all took place in Marpi, at the northern end of the island. I had never felt more physically fit at any other time in my life.

Juan N. Babauta after running the 2009 Saipan Marathon.

I learned that good coaching from an experienced marathon runner was critically important. I received excellent coaching from my personal trainer, Mr. Jang-Chang Whan. I referred to him simply as "Coach." When I was governor, we used to run together on the Beach Road pathway for five miles each run.

I had been running pretty much all my life, much like my political life. I ran the marathon in part to put emphasis on achieving a goal, along with physical fitness and health. I endured a lot of pain, but it is something that helped me focus on what I wanted to gain in life.

Chapter 7: Reflections

Lieutenant Governor Diego Tenorio Benavente

Diego and I ran as a team and served as a team. We ran an effective campaign that garnered us 45 percent of the total votes cast in a four-way race for governor in 2001.

We both had solid experience in government, name recognition, and strong family ties. Diego's experience as a member of the House of Representatives is unparalleled, having served three consecutive terms as Speaker of the House of Representatives, the longest in NMI history. His leadership style won him the honor and distinction of serving in that position for so long. I made my mark having served for twelve years representing the people of the NMI in our nation's capital.

Our campaign strategy was multi-pronged. We walked the streets and knocked on every house door we laid our eyes on, and made education the centerpiece of our campaign as a way to build a strong economy for the CNMI, with hope for a bright future. We stayed on message and never wavered.

When we got into office, the role Diego played as part of the Governor's Office was significant. We continued to work closely as a team, just as we did during the campaign. Even our physical proximity was close. Our offices were ten steps apart, connected by a private door that either one of us could access at any time.

The lieutenant governor's staff was considered an extension of the Governor's Office and vice versa. Diego played a significant role in our Administration's agenda, and often was given major items to manage, such as the role of head of the Water Task Force, and as the Governor's Special Representative to the Section 702 Negotiations.

Covenant Section 702 provides for guaranteed, annual direct grants from the U.S. Government to the CNMI Government, especially for Capital Improvement Projects (CIPs). When Diego returned from Washington, he was happy to report having had successful negotiations with our federal partners; the CNMI would soon be notified that it had been awarded more than $1.4 million of extra funding for CIPs, in addition to the $11 million per year it was already receiving under the six-year Section 702 Funding Agreement. Diego had negotiated that agreement, as well. It was signed on June 21, 2004.

To address the chronic water supply problems on Saipan, I had established the Water Task Force in early 2003 and appointed Diego as its chairman. He conducted the first task force meeting on April 2 to review the water master plan prepared by the U.S. Army Corps of Engineers. Diego took his role as head of the newly established Water Task Force very seriously and wanted to use much of the Section 702 funding he had just negotiated for water improvements. He wanted to address the critical water supply and distribution system, additional pipeline projects, to upgrade wells, do test drillings, water conservation leak detection programs, and public education on water issues. He also wanted to address the significant problems related to the lack of sanitary sewer systems and the over-dependence on individual septic tanks, not just on Rota and Tinian, but many still on Saipan. Through his own initiative, Diego saw to it that the Administration allocated all the funding the Water Task Force needed for the water infrastructure projects he had planned. The goal of the task force was a complete, sustainable pressurization of the water system on Saipan, and to ensure that the entire system would be fully maintained in the future.

Working with the Legislature was an important task for both of us. From past experience, Diego as former Speaker of the House of Representatives, and me as a senator, we knew that the budget and its presentation to the Legislature would greatly influence our policy initiatives and the resolution of issues as they arose. Failure to consider the budgetary impact during the development of policy can result in discord between the Administration and the Legislature. The budget is "a spending plan and a policy tool." We tried to make it more than just a "tool." We initiated the Integrated Fiscal Plan to enhance revenue generation for the government.

Diego was, in effect, the Legislative Liaison Officer for the Governor's Office. He ensured effective communication with legislators by coordinating the lobbying activities of the Administration, and negotiating many issues with the Legislature. It helped, as well, when I had Bob Schwalbach and Adam Turner working closely with the Legislature; they made our work easier.

Diego loved being lieutenant governor. I believe he enjoyed it more than he did all his years as a member of the House of Representatives. He was relaxed, cool, calm and collected. Rolled out on the floor in his office was an artificial putting green on which he could sharpen his already great putting skills. I would sneak in there every once in a while, not to sharpen my skills, but to see who he was showing off to. Diego influenced my plans for travel to Washington, where the CNMI-federal political battles are fought, while he got to travel to the Philippines, all over Micronesia, Korea and Japan, all considered non-battlegrounds, politically. On these trips, he played hard, but he also worked hard. More than anything, the trips were inducements to come back home to the rigor of the hard work to which he was so devoted.

Diego knew how passionate I was about education. He believed, just as I did, that education, above everything else, is the one thing that could help everyone in the CNMI build a better future for themselves and their families. Diego believed strongly that education doesn't just create jobs, education creates good jobs. We bet the economic future of the CNMI on our becoming the most educated population in the Pacific, and we set out to achieve that by striving for excellence in our schools, and providing everyone the opportunity to learn.

Our aim was to have every illiterate person in the CNMI become literate. Even those with college degrees find that the shelf life of their degrees is shortening. Even I, who went to college in the 1970s, must continue to upgrade my skills and knowledge, or my education will become obsolete. Pursuing an education to advance and foster that college degree is to recognize that lifelong learning is a necessity.

With the average per-student spending going down, we made funding for education the first priority in our budget submission to the Legislature every year. We also made the construction of classrooms our No. 1 priority for Capital Improvement Project funding. We completed Tinian High School.

Our friends and foes alike have told us that our handling of the Commonwealth Utilities Corporation (CUC) power rates and charges may have contributed to our losing our re-election bid in 2005. The cost of fuel forced government subsidies off the table, and CUC had to increase power rates in the form of a "surcharge." Increasing power rates in an election year is not a good move. Diego took the position that a surcharge must be imposed, over recommendations from our more politically-minded advisors, who wanted more subsidies to hold us over until after the election. Diego said no, and I agreed with his position.

When Diego and I were candidates for office, people often asked us why we were running. Our response was always the same. "This is what our parents have taught us: to help our community and our people, as public servants." And that, "we are sons of a poor family, and we know how so many of you feel. This is what our lives have been." Diego and I share some core beliefs and values. We believe in the fundamental values of respecting all people; listening to, and sharing ideas with, others; caring for the disadvantaged; trusting in people; showing fairness to all; and most importantly, helping others.

Diego and I worked hard to get our message out, based on a single theme. We wanted our platform to be a plan for all the people of the CNMI, sharing in a Commonwealth, as it should be. But it also was a plan in which we shared in the sacrifice, and in the sweat, working together. When it was time to reap the benefits, everybody would have a piece of the pie. In Chamorro, we said, "Este na planu guiya este i Patin Ti'ao. Maulegña dididi' ya guaha, ki bula ya taya'."

Governor Lorenzo I. Deleon Guerrero and the UN on Termination of the Trusteeship

At the eleventh hour of the termination of the Trusteeship by the United Nations Security Council in December 1990, CNMI Gov. Lorenzo I. Deleon Guerrero made an impassioned plea to the Council to delay termination because of serious concerns between the CNMI and the United States over the issues of self-government and sovereignty.

In his December 20, 1990, letter to the president of the Security Council, Gov. Deleon Guerrero said:

> "Failure to maintain the Trusteeship Agreement may cause the United States to absorb further the Commonwealth of the Northern Mariana Islands into the Federal Government. It is the official position of this government that the United States has

failed the United Nations and the people of the Northern Mariana Islands in not delivering on its trusteeship commitment. As of this date, the United States of America and the Commonwealth of the Northern Mariana Islands continue to disagree sharply on key sovereignty questions. These questions directly affect our right to internal self-government. The United States has taken the position that the Northern Mariana Islands is a possession of the United States and that the Federal Government may legislate for the people of the Commonwealth. The United States stoutly rejects our claim to local control of the marine resources that surround the islands within our exclusive economic zone. The United States asserts that the territorial sea of the Northern Mariana Islands is limited to three miles; that the Commonwealth has no submerged lands jurisdiction; and the United States owns the ocean resources in the exclusive economic zone surrounding the Northern Mariana Islands."

The governor's plea to delay termination of the Trusteeship was supported by the UN Ambassador from Cuba, who presented the governor's letter to the Security Council. It also was supported by then-Delegate Eni F. H. Faleomavaega of American Samoa, with a letter to the U.S. State department concurring "wholeheartedly" with Gov. Deleon Guerrero and asking that the department support the position that the proposed resolution to terminate the Trusteeship be "rescinded" until the CNMI's concerns were addressed and resolved. In response to Del. Faleomavaega's letter, the State department, in part, stated:

> "Subject to the commonwealth agreement, the Commonwealth of the Northern Mariana Islands and the United States Government carry on an internal dialogue on problems the CNMI has with the commonwealth agreement. We firmly believe that the Commonwealth's concerns can be solved through our direct discussions with them and that it is highly inappropriate for the Commonwealth to use fora such as the United Nations Security Council to air their grievances."

The issues raised by Gov. Deleon Guerrero 25 years ago still stand to this day. He reasoned that a delay in the termination of the Trusteeship would serve as leverage against the federal government that, in his view, had gotten what it wanted and was in no hurry to address the lingering concerns of the CNMI. Gov. Deleon Guerrero left behind a legacy of foresight and political will at the expense of infuriating the federal government. He passed away believing that Washington had failed to live up to its commitments since the Northern Mariana Islands became a Commonwealth. In the hearts and minds of the people of the CNMI, Gov. Deleon Guerrero's legacy lives on.

The U.S. Ambassador to the UN, Thomas Pickering, played down the concerns raised by Gov. Deleon Guerrero as internal, saying they would be solved through bilateral negotiations under Covenant Section 902. He added that it was important that the Section 902 process continue as the way to resolve problems between the federal government and the Commonwealth. This is precisely what Gov. Deleon Guerrero considered pandering to the United Nations, and giving lip service to the CNMI.

When the resolution to terminate the Trusteeship was voted on two days after the governor's plea, only Cuba voted against it. Russia voted in favor of termination, concurring with the U.S. and others that the Northern Marianas had freely exercised its right of self-determination through a plebiscite, but claimed that the U.S. had bullied the NMI in exchange for rights to military bases (*The New York Times*, December 24, 1990). However, Russia felt that with the Cold War over, the strategic value of the islands, militarily, was marginal. In the same article, Moscow accused the U.S. of violating the Trusteeship Agreement by using the islands as "military bases and rocket-testing ranges." Moscow, therefore, preferred that the administration of the Trusteeship continue under the UN mandate and supervision. However, this view held by Moscow changed when the U.S. "privately" assured Moscow it would not be "deploying any additional military bases" on the islands, although it retained responsibility for their defense. This assurance made by the U.S. was disturbing; at the very least, it should be disclosed to the people of the Northern Marianas. There was no full disclosure made by the U.S. before, during, or after the Covenant negotiations. This would have been an important piece of information for the NMI when it gave away 2/3 of Tinian. It's a question of deception that continues to cast a dark shadow over the U.S. legacy in the Northern Marianas.

According to Ambassador Pickering, the Trusteeship Agreement was terminated by the Trusteeship Council in 1986. If such were the case, then why was action from the Security Council being sought? Another interpretation, primarily from the federal government, was that the Trusteeship was terminated by Pres. Reagan in his 1986 Proclamation 5564. Logically, therefore, if both Pres. Reagan and the Trusteeship Council lacked the authority to unilaterally terminate the Trusteeship, then the status of the NMI would have continued to be under the Trust Territory of the Pacific Islands up to December 1990, when it was terminated by the Security Council. On further examination, according to the December 1990 *New York Times* article, the NMI was one of three island groups that were originally designated as a "strategic" trusteeship, which meant that the Trusteeship Agreement had to be approved by the Security Council. If true, then the CNMI's official status as a U.S. Commonwealth did not begin until December 22, 1990.

The Chipping Away of the Covenant

There was something unique and special about the CNMI's negotiated status as a member of the American political family. Negotiating as equals, in and of itself, separated the CNMI from all other U.S. insular entities. The birth of the Covenant and certain of its provisions clearly defined the distinction between the CNMI and the rest of the non-state entities, with the exception of the District of Columbia.

However, no sooner than the ink was dry on the printed Covenant did the debates begin over the legal and political interpretations of the new political status. The debate continues to this day in the Halls of Congress, the CNMI Legislature, the Courts, and political fora. Not-so-friendly members of Congress would say, "The Mariana Islands can't be any more special than the state I represent." Legislative efforts to amend the Covenant came nearly as quickly as its passage. Recommendations put forth by the Commission on Federal Laws created by the Covenant on the applicability of U.S. laws to the CNMI were ignored by the federal government. This Commission was required by Section 504 of the Covenant; it requires the president to appoint this Commission, and requires this Commission to submit its reports to the U.S. Congress. Section 504 went into effect on March 24, 1976, the day Pres. Gerald R. Ford signed the Covenant into law as P.L. 94-241.

The pattern that has unfolded over the last 30 years is Congress choosing to ignore recommendations from the CNMI, such as the reports from the Commission on Federal Laws, and taking unilateral action to amend the Covenant.

The following are changes made to the CNMI Covenant that I have documented. There may be more that I am not aware of. All, except for the first one, deal with Title VII of P.L. 110-229, the Consolidated Natural Resources Act of 2008. Each item listed begins with the identifying section of the Covenant that was changed.

1. Section 606(b). Section 606(b) deals with applicability of the U.S. Social Security System upon termination of the Trusteeship Agreement. P.L. 98-213, which became law on December 8, 1983, made two technical amendments to Section 606(b). According to the CNMI Law Revision Commission website, these were the only amendments to the Covenant as of December 1996.
2. Section 6. The Consolidated Natural Resources Act of 2008 was signed into law by Pres. George W. Bush on May 8, 2008. Subtitle A – "Immigration, Security, and Labor" – of the Act added this section to the Covenant, which provides for the federal takeover of immigration control in the CNMI. This Section 6, entitled "Immigration and Transition," is included in the U.S. Code as 48 U.S.C. 1806.
3. Section 503(a). Section 503(a) was specifically eliminated by the Natural Resources Act. It states, "The following laws of the United States … will not apply to the Northern Mariana Islands except in the manner and to the extent made applicable to them by the Congress by law after termination of the Trusteeship Agreement." The first of these laws was listed in Subsection (a) as: "except as otherwise provided in

section 506, the immigration and naturalization laws of the United States." Subsection 503(a) was superseded by Subsection 6(a) in the Act, which states, "the provisions of the immigration laws, as defined in section 101(a)(17) of the Immigration and Nationality Act [8 U.S.C. 1101(a)(17)], shall apply to the Commonwealth of the Northern Mariana Islands, except as otherwise provided in this section."

4. Section 506. Section 506 also was specifically eliminated by the Act. Section 506 stated how, and to what extent, the Immigration and Nationality Act of the United States would apply to the Northern Mariana Islands upon the termination of the Trusteeship Agreement and establishment of the Commonwealth, "notwithstanding the provisions of Subsection 503(a)." Section 506 was superseded by Subsection 6(a) of the Act, as explained above, in no. 3.

5. Section 703(b). The Act specifically eliminated the words "immigration and naturalization" in Section 703(b). The relevant part of Section 703(b) stated, "There will be paid into the Treasury of the Government of the Northern Mariana Islands, to be expended to the benefit of the people thereof as that Government may by law prescribe, … all quarantine, passport, immigration and naturalization fees collected in the Northern Mariana Islands…"

6. Section 901. Section 901 stated, "The Constitution or laws of the Northern Mariana Islands may provide for the appointment or election of a Resident Representative to the United States, whose term of office will be two years, unless otherwise determined by local law…" Section 901 was amended and superseded by Subtitle B – "Northern Mariana Islands Delegate" – of the Act. Subtitle B is included in the U.S. Code as 48 USC 1751-1757. Section 711 of Subtitle B states, "the Resident Representative to the United States authorized by Section 901 of the Covenant … shall be a nonvoting Delegate to the House of Representatives, elected as provided in this subtitle." Section 712 of Subtitle B states how this Delegate will be elected.

7. Subsection 6(a)(2). Section 10 of P.L. 113-235, the Consolidated and Further Continuing Appropriations Act, 2015, changed the date December 31, 2014, in Subsection 6(a)(2) to December 31, 2019. This change extended for five years the "transition period" for the immigration "transition program" in the CNMI. Subsection 6(a)(2) stated, "There shall be a transition period beginning on the transition program effective date and ending on December 31, 2014, … during which the Secretary of Homeland Security … shall establish, administer, and enforce a transition program to regulate immigration to the Commonwealth."

8. Section 6(d), paragraph (5). Section 10 of P.L. 113-235 also eliminated paragraph (5) of Subsection 6(d), as included in the Appropriations Act, which gave the Secretary of Labor the authority to extend, for

up to five years, the immigration transition period in the CNMI. The Labor secretary made an initial, five-year extension official when this decision was published in the Federal Register in June 2014. The elimination of paragraph (5) means that the Labor secretary cannot make any more extensions of the transition period.

9. Section 6(d), paragraph (2). Section 10 of P.L. 113-235 also amended paragraph (2) of Subsection 6(d) by eliminating the language "not to extend beyond December 31, 2014, unless extended pursuant to paragraph (5) of this subsection," and replacing it with the phrase, "ending on December 31, 2019." This amendment achieved the two changes concerning the transition period, as explained above, in nos. 7 and 8. Eliminating the language "unless extended pursuant to paragraph (5) of this subsection" is one of the two changes in Section 6(d) that took away from the Labor secretary the authority to extend the transition period any longer.

Consultations under Section 902 of the Covenant

Section 902 is a provision of the Covenant (U.S. Public Law 94-241). It provides opportunities for the Government of the United States and the Government of the Northern Mariana Islands to "consult regularly on all matters affecting the relationship between them." At the request of either side, each designating its own representatives, the parties can arrange "to meet and to consider in good faith such issues affecting the relationship" between the two parties and to "make a report and recommendations with respect thereto." Among the insular areas, only the CNMI has the ability, by law, to meet, consult, and make recommendations to resolve matters affecting either party.

The United States has used the 902 Consultation Process as an excuse to get what it wants. A case in point was when U.S. Ambassador to the United Nations Thomas Pickering objected to Gov. DeLeon Guerrero's request to delay termination of the Trusteeship. Ambassador Pickering reasoned before the Security Council that just because there were differences in views between the United States and the CNMI on some issues, did not mean that the Security Council had to go so far as to delay the termination of the Trusteeship. Those differences, the Ambassador said, were internal and were being "worked on and, indeed, resolved under the terms of the Compact" (sic) (he meant Covenant). He stated that, "Section 902 of the Covenant provides for a series of negotiations, which have been carried forward", and that "at this stage we think it is important for the negotiations to continue." The United Nations, he said, "is not the place to carry on those negotiations."

Similarly, the U.S. State Department, in objecting to Gov. DeLeon Guerrero's request to delay the termination of the Trusteeship, said in a letter to Delegate Faleomavaega of American Samoa that, "The Commonwealth of the Northern Mariana Islands and the United States Government carry on an internal dialogue on problems the CNMI has with the Commonwealth agreement." The letter added, "We firmly believe that the Commonwealth's concerns can be solved through our direct discussions with them in the 902 talks."

According to the U.S. Government, the 902 Consultation Process is alive and well. Structurally, the mechanism is there. Both parties have gone to the consultation table. But what has it gotten the CNMI? The CNMI's concerns on internal self-government and sovereignty issues remain unresolved.

The 902 Consultation Process is an option for the CNMI. For as long as the CNMI is unwilling or unable to utilize the 902 process to its advantage, the "chipping away" of the Covenant will continue. Timing has its rewards and consequences. The 902 process is not as effective as it could be. If strengthened, the 902 process could better achieve the results we want. Otherwise, the CNMI will render itself just another territory and possession of the United States.

The 902 Consultation "team" during the Administration of Governor Lorenzo I. Deleon Guerrero when Lt. Governor Benjamin T. Manglona served as Chairman of the 902 Consultations. L to R: Senator Herman R. Deleon Guerrero; Robert Schwalbach, Staff; Juan N. Babauta, Co-Chairman; Eric Smith, Legal Counsel; Chairman Manglona; Donald Woodworth, Legal Counsel; House Speaker Pedro R. Deleon Guerrero; and Mike Malone, Advisor.

It is not in the CNMI's best interest to keep 902 issues dormant for long periods of time and to have inconsistencies in momentum from one administration to the next. Often 902 issues are left lying around for long periods of time without the benefit of further study and scrutiny. It is also not in the CNMI's best interest for any CNMI government administration or governor to disavow as useless the 902 Consultation Process. A case in point was when Governor Froilan C. Tenorio in June 1997 terminated the Section 902 consultation talks with the federal government on the proposal by Pres. Bill Clinton to impose federal control over immigration in the CNMI.

The next big 902 agenda issue for the CNMI is likely to involve the U.S. military's proposal to use the island of Pagan for military exercises. There is a growing voice of opposition from certain quarters of the community to the use of Pagan by the military. If the CNMI government, because of community opposition, said no to the use of Pagan by the military, concerns are being raised whether the U.S. military would recommend to the U.S. Congress the exercise of eminent domain over the island of Pagan for military use. If so, what options will the CNMI have? The 902 consultation talks would likely be the CNMI's last option to stop the military. The CNMI leadership must begin aligning its support in Congress in order to be successful. The people of the CNMI must also demonstrate overwhelming opposition to the exercise of eminent domain by the U.S. Government. As it stands, if a deal is not struck between the CNMI and the U.S. military, the future of Pagan is in the hands of the U.S. Congress.

Another likely 902 agenda issue for the CNMI is the training of local U.S. citizens and U.S. permanent legal residents to replace the CW nonresident workers by December 31, 2019. How can the CNMI utilize the new comprehensive workforce training law, the "Workforce Innovation and Opportunity Act" of 2014 (P.L. 113-128). This Act replaced the Workforce Investment Act of 1998.

A third likely 902 agenda issue for the CNMI is expansion of CNMI control of Submerged Lands beyond the three-mile limit. To do this, Congress would have to amend two U.S. laws on Submerged Lands: the Submerged Lands Act of 1953 and the Territorial Submerged Lands Act of 1974 (48 U.S.C. Sections 1705-1706) (P.L. 93-435).

The 902 Consultations are a political forum, not a legal forum. The CNMI has a better chance achieving a positive outcome by way of the 902 Consultations rather than going to the Courts. That is why the 902 Consultation Process is provided for in the Covenant. But inside the Commonwealth, the 902 process is sometimes misunderstood. And misunderstanding can lead to disappointment. We need to understand that 902 is a process of consultation, not negotiation. The Special Representatives only recommend solutions to the governor and the president.

For that reason, we need to strengthen the link between the governor and the president and their Special Representatives. The Commonwealth can take the initiative by asking the U.S. Congress to raise the standing of the President's Special Representative. Designation by law of a position within the Executive branch, close to the President, with duties of 902 Consultation would help. Senate confirmation of the person in this position would help. Raising the status of the present "interim" Special Representative to "permanent" Special Representative would help.

The CNMI too should look at reform of the Section 902 Consultation Process. I respect the governor's desire to have a group of Special Representatives who reflect a broad spectrum of community opinion. But this diversity can result in the Commonwealth not always speaking with one voice in the 902 Consultations, and lack of unity weakens the CNMI.

I suggest restructuring the existing 902 advisory group. The advisory group would draft the Commonwealth's positions on Section 902 issues and submit them to the governor for his approval. A single Special Representative of the Governor would then present the approved positions to the Special Representative of the President.

The Legislature must be a part of this process, through representation in the advisory group, the opportunity for commenting on CNMI positions on Section 902 issues or periodic oversight hearings with the Special Representative. A priority for the advisory group must be to agree on a definition of self-government. The meaning of self-government underlies so many of the 902 issues. We must acknowledge, however, that there are limits in the Covenant on our ability to govern ourselves. The Commonwealth might also consider Legislative confirmation of the appointment of the Special Representative of the Governor.

Labor, Immigration, and the Minimum Wage

The Covenant gave the CNMI control over immigration. During the negotiations, there was concern that the indigenous people would be overwhelmed by immigrants, especially from Southeast Asia, if federal immigration law were to apply to the CNMI. Ironically, we have been overwhelmed by a population of foreign immigrants under our own control of immigration.

I maintained that CNMI control of immigration was an important hallmark of our self-government and that we should retain that power. I made this statement before the U.S. Senate Energy and Natural Resources Committee on September 22, 1994 and in numerous other Congressional hearings thereafter. Local control of immigration was conceived as a tool of economic development and for protecting the indigenous people. Federal control of CNMI borders was an unwarranted reduction in local responsibility despite the many immigration and labor problems the CNMI was facing. For these reasons, I did not support any of the several efforts by the U.S. Congress to take that away from the CNMI.

The Covenant also exempted the CNMI from the federal minimum wage. Our local economy could not support a high minimum wage at the time the Covenant was negotiated. Some would argue that this exemption was intended to be temporary because the people of the NMI wanted to have a U.S. standard of living eventually. Others would say that it was never intended to be temporary. With the economic growth in the 1980's and 1990's it was reasonable to increase the minimum wage, but the CNMI did not. In fact, it was common practice to keep the minimum wage low while at the same time giving nonresident workers housing, health insurance, and other benefits in addition to their wages. This made the job market unattractive and reduced job opportunities for our own local U.S. citizen work force.

I felt then that local officials who best understood local conditions and who were answerable to local voters, had crafted local policies to deal with guest worker abuse and the criticisms that were being made against the CNMI. The goal of the CNMI was to create an economy that is less dependent on foreign labor and a society in which every individual is treated with dignity and fairness. I was disappointed at the time that the CNMI did not act quickly to address those concerns about guest worker abuse.

My vision for the Northern Marianas' economy was to move away from low-skill labor intensive industry toward activities that require a smaller but well-educated workforce. Education is such an economic activity and has the additional benefit of putting us in a position of being able continually to upgrade our human resources using local capacity.

For more than 30 years, the CNMI had control of immigration until it was taken over by the federal government on May 8, 2008. The U.S. Congress amended the Covenant and made applicable to the CNMI the U.S. Immigration Laws by enacting into law U.S. Public Law 110-229, the Consolidated Natural Resources Act of 2008. According to this Act, Congress decided to federalize immigration in the CNMI

> "...to ensure that effective border control procedures are implemented and observed, and that national security and homeland security issues are promptly addressed, extending the immigration laws of the Immigration and Nationality Act to apply to the Commonwealth of the Northern Mariana Islands."

Interestingly, in this statement of purpose, Congress made no mention of the alleged violations of U.S. labor laws on non-payment of wages, substandard working and living conditions, and the mistreatment of workers as the basis for the federalization. The federal government didn't need to, because it is hard for anyone to argue against national security and the safety of the islands. This action by the federal government, however, was viewed by the CNMI as an attack on its right of self-government.

Public Law 110-229 outlines the orderly phasing out of the nonresident contract worker program of the Commonwealth and the orderly phasing in of federal responsibilities over immigration in the Commonwealth. The U.S. Congress, however, was concerned that implementation of the transition concerning the nonresident workers not adversely impact the future economic growth of the CNMI. Thus, the following provisions in Public Law 110-229 provided for an orderly transition of the nonresident workers.

a. A transition period was set for all nonresident workers to end on December 31, 2014.

b. The Secretary of Labor, based on factors set out in P.L. 110-229, is authorized to extend the transition period for the CW-1 non-immigrant worker program for up to 5 years to ensure that an adequate number of workers will be available for legitimate businesses in the CNMI. The Secretary of Labor, based on these factors, in June 2015 extended the CW-1 non-immigrant worker program for an additional 5 years ending on December 31, 2019. P.L. 110-229 requires that the authorized number of CW-1 non-immigrant workers be reduced every year. In U.S. P.L. 113-235, the Consolidated and Further Continuing Appropriations Act, 2015 the transition period was extended for five years and will end on December 31, 2019. This law removed the authority of the Secretary of Labor to make any further extensions of the CW-1 worker program. Thus, any further extension beyond December 31, 2019 would have to be authorized by Congress.)

c. The Secretary of Homeland Security is put in charge of the transition program but must consult with the Secretary of State, the Attorney General, the Secretary of Labor, and the Secretary of the Interior. They are charged with the responsibility to ensure that the employers in the CNMI have access to adequate labor, and that the tourists, students, retirees, and other visitors have access to the CNMI without unnecessary delay or impediment.

d. In addition to fees charged through the Immigration and Nationality Act to recover the full costs of its services, the Secretary of Homeland Security shall charge an annual supplemental fee of $150 to each prospective employer for each of the employer's non-immigrant workers who is issued a CW-1 work permit, and the money received for this fee shall be paid to the CNMI government for purposes of funding vocational education curricula and program development by educational institutions in the CNMI.

e. Asylum (Section 208 of the Immigration and Nationality Act) shall not apply to the CNMI during the transition period. The CNMI is an easy target of destination for dissidents seeking asylum, as was the case in the early 1990's here in the CNMI. In U.S. P.L. 113-235, the Consolidated and Further Continuing Appropriations Act, 2015, signed by the President on December 16, 2014, the prohibition on seeking political asylum in the CNMI was extended for five years. This was necessary to prevent a negative impact on the economy and social welfare of the CNMI. For example, political asylum seekers might seek to land anywhere in the CNMI, including in the remote Northern Islands, and this could be a major national security concern.

f. Nonimmigrant Investor Visas for the CNMI only would expire on December 31, 2014. In U.S. P.L. 113-235, the Consolidated and Further Continuing Appropriations Act, 2015, the E-2C CNMI-only foreign investor visa status was extended for five years, which was necessary because otherwise the CNMI would lose a lot of the smaller businesses along with the many employees hired by them. This would have had a negative impact on the tourism industry also.

g. The Secretary of Homeland Security is authorized to establish a visa waiver program for tourists to visit Guam and the CNMI. In exercising this authority, the Secretary extended this waiver only to the CNMI. Guam was viewed as a high risk.

h. The Secretary of Homeland Security set a ceiling of 13,999 CW-1 worker permits that can be issued for the CNMI in fiscal year 2015 and a ceiling of 12,999 CW-1 worker permits for fiscal year 2016. The ceiling for fiscal year 2014 was 14,000.

If the CNMI wants to have a viable economy, we need to invest in the local U.S. citizens now. The CNMI Government should assess our current workforce, identify current and future labor needs, and institute an aggressive, detailed program to train local people to meet those needs. Development of the local workforce should be our focus.

The CNMI Department of Labor should work closely with the business community to identify the needs and problems associated with the employment of local workers and find ways to address those problems. The department should also work closely with the Northern Marianas College, the Public School System, the Northern Marianas Trades Institute, and the institution selected to train local workers under U.S. Public Law 113-128, the Workforce Innovation and Opportunity Act signed by President Obama on July 22, 2014. This law replaces the Workforce Investment Act. Public Law 113-128 consolidates the various federal laws on workforce training. The CNMI, as well as other territories, is included in this law.

Extension of the Federal Minimum Wage

U.S. Public Law 110-28, the U.S. Troop Readiness, Veterans' Care, Katrina Recovery, and Iraq Accountability Appropriations Act of 2007, included the extension of the federal minimum wage provisions of the Fair Labor Standards Act of 1938 (as amended) to the CNMI and American Samoa. Thus, the CNMI and American Samoa are now subject to Section 6, the minimum wage provisions of the Fair Labor Standards Act (FLSA).

The minimum wage increases began, incrementally, on July 26, 2007. The increases were based on the transition provisions of the law beginning sixty days after the date of enactment of the law. At the end of the sixty-day period, the CNMI minimum wage increased by $.50 to $3.55 per hour. This amount was scheduled to increase by $.50 until it reached the new federal minimum wage of $7.25 per hour established by P.L. 110-28. Even prior to the extension of the federal minimum wage, the FLSA was already applicable to the CNMI with respect to overtime pay, recordkeeping, and other labor standards.

CNMI Wage Levels per Hour, 1979 to 2007
Public Law 1-20, 01/12/79 through 06/22/82 ...$1.35
Public Law 3-16 06/23/82 through 09/30/83 ....$1.75
10/01/83 through 09/30/84..............................$1.95
10/01/84 through 12/31/92..............................$2.15
Public Law 8-21 01/01/93 through 12/31/93 ....$2.45
01/01/94 through 12/31/94..............................$2.75
01/01/95 through 12/31/95..............................$3.05
Public Law 9-73 postponed the 01/01/96 increase up to $3.35 to 07/01/96.
Public Law 10-13 on 06/15/96 P.L. 10-13 repealed the increases for 07/01/96 and for 1997 through 1999 as mandated under P.L. 8-21.
01/01/96 through 07/25/07 ....$3.05
(Source: *Homeland Magazine*, "History of the Minimum Wage in the CNMI," March-April 2007)

Extension of the Federal Minimum Wage in the CNMI
U.S. P.L. 110-28 07/25/07 through 05/25/08....$3.55
U.S. P.L. 110-28 05/26/08 through 05/25/09....$4.05
U.S. P.L. 110-28 05/26/09 through 09/29/10....$4.55
U.S. P.L. 111-244 09/30/10 through 09/29/12..$5.05
U.S. P.L. 113-34 09/30/12 through 09/29/14....$5.55

U.S. P.L. 113-34 09/30/14 through 09/29/16....$6.05
U.S. P.L. 113-34 09/30/16 through 09/29/17....$6.55
U.S. P.L. 113-34 09/30/17 through 09/29/18....$7.05
U.S. P.L. 113-34 09/30/18 ....$7.25

The following job categories are exempted under the Fair Minimum Wage Act of 2007, which is a part of Public Law 110-28.
1. Employees engaged in fishing. Such employees continue to be paid under the CNMI Minimum Wage Law.
2. Farmers. Farmers are exempt from the minimum wage if they are employed by an employer. The number of farmer employees permitted per employer is six. Such employees continue to be paid under the CNMI Minimum Wage Law. By definition, gardeners are not farmers, and therefore are not included in this exemption.
3. Domestic workers. These are workers who "provide companionship services for individuals who are unable to care for themselves because of age, infirmity, or special disabilities. Such employees continue to be paid under the CNMI Minimum Wage Law.
4. There are other exemptions such as babysitting and other similar jobs.

(Source: U.S. Public Law 110-28, Fair Minimum Wage Act of 2007)

Compact Impact Funding

The term "Compact Impact" is derived from a provision in U.S. Public Law 99-239, "The Compact of Free Association Act of 1985," which approved the Compacts of Free Association between the United States Government and the Federated States of Micronesia (FSM) and the Republic of the Marshall Islands (RMI). The compacts allow citizens of these two nations to enter, live, and work in the United States and its territories and commonwealths. Later on October 1, 1994, the Republic of Palau's Compact of Free Association with the United States was also approved, allowing citizens of Palau to enter, live, and work in the United States and its territories and commonwealths.

Under the terms of these three compacts, the United States is said to be committed to address any adverse consequences due to migration of Freely Associated States citizens to the U.S. mainland, its territories and commonwealths, and Hawaii. Public Law 99-239 stated that the U.S. Congress is committed to "act sympathetically and expeditiously to redress those adverse consequences." In the case of the impact from immigration, Congress authorized for funds to be appropriated to cover "impact" costs incurred by the State of Hawaii, the territories of Guam and American Samoa, and the Commonwealth of the Northern Mariana Islands.

Public Law 99-239 required the president of the U.S. to report to Congress annually on the impact of the compacts, and these annual reports "shall pay particular attention to matters relating to trade, taxation, immigration, labor laws, minimum wages, social systems and infrastructure, and environmental regulations." The Office of Territorial and International Affairs in the Department of the Interior was designated as the office responsible for preparing and providing the annual report to Congress describing and quantifying the adverse consequences of this immigration. The reports would serve as the basis for Congress to act in appropriating funds necessary to cover the "impact" costs borne by the CNMI, Guam, American Samoa, and Hawaii.

In 1994, eight years after the compacts with the FSM and RMI went into effect, the Department of the Interior still did not have a report to send to Congress. Thus, Congress would not appropriate any money without any cost information to base it on. This inaction on the part of the Administration frustrated the CNMI and Guam, forcing them to press the issue in Congress as well as by legal action taken by Guam.

Through a coordinated effort between the Office of the Resident Representative and key members of the CNMI Legislature, the CNMI was able to receive Compact Impact Aid of $400,000 in fiscal year 1993, and an equal amount in fiscal year 1994. These funds were taken out of the Department of the Interior's Technical Assistance Funding, which clearly did not come from Congress in the form of direct appropriations for this purpose.

In fiscal year 1995, the CNMI received $1.6 million in Compact Impact Aid, which Congress took from the Covenant Section 702 funding that already belonged to the CNMI. This action greatly upset the CNMI Resident Representative and the Legislature and prompted a letter from the Resident Representative to Department of the Interior officials calling the move "unfair for the Congress to 'charge' Compact Aid compensation from the already assured Covenant section 702 CIP annual funding grant because they should be treated separately."

The $1.6 million appropriation in Compact Impact Aid for the CNMI was arbitrary and based on a report the Administration was to prepare for Congress. The cost/benefit study, supposedly conducted by the Department of the Interior, was never officially submitted to Congress. This was tantamount to Congress making decisions in an information vacuum.

The CNMI, through the Resident Representative, the governor, and a number of legislators, took the matter up with the White House Inter-Agency Group on Insular Areas, the House Appropriations Subcommittee on Interior, and the Secretary of the Interior. Despite these efforts made by CNMI officials, neither the Administration nor Congress bothered to address the Compact Impact matter until 2001. Frustrated by the inaction of the federal government, the CNMI's neighbor island of Guam filed a lawsuit in 1996 seeking a Judicial Order that a report on the impact of the Compacts be prepared by the Administration. In 1997, the U.S. District Court for Guam ordered the Department of the Interior to provide such a report. Guam reportedly was impacted to the tune of $70 million for fiscal year 1996 alone. In fiscal year 1999, the CNMI was impacted by nearly $34 million in capital expenditures and $16 million in operating expenditures. The operating expenditures are public services such as public safety (police and fire), public works, roads, water, wastewater, solid waste, public health, public education, and others.

Amounts in Compact Impact Aid for the CNMI from 1986 to 2018

Fiscal Year	Amount
1986	$0
1987	$0
1988	$0
1989	$0
1990	$0
1991	$0
1992	$0
1993	$400,000
1994	$400,000
1995	$1,600,000
1996	$0
1997	$0
1998	$0
1999	$0
2000	$0
2001	$1,000,000
2002	$2,000,000
2003	$ 840,000
2004	$5,100,000
2005	$5,100,000
2006	$5,100,000
2007	$5,100,000
2008	$5,100,000
2009	$5,100,000
2010	$5,100,000
2011	$5,100,000
2012	$5,100,000
2013	$5,100,000
2014	$5,100,000
2015	$5,100,000
2016	$5,100,000
2017	$5,100,000
2018	$5,100,000

(Source: CNMI Department of Commerce)

In December 2003, under legislation signed by President George W. Bush, the first annual installment in Compact Impact Aid started to flow to the CNMI, Guam, and Hawaii. Secretary of the Interior Gale Norton and I, as CNMI governor, signed the Compact Impact Grant Agreement on January

15, 2004 on Saipan, during the Secretary's visit that provided $5.1 million to the CNMI annually for the next twenty years. The funding source was a $30 million appropriation by Congress that it decided to proportionately divide among the CNMI, Guam, and Hawaii based on their non-immigrant population from the Freely Associated States.

Although this is a much needed infusion of money to offset the impact of migration from the Freely Associated States (FSM, RMI, and Palau), there is no logical explanation as to how the Congress arrived at the figures in the absence of a cost/benefit study mandated by law.

Regardless of the cost under the Compact Impact, the people from Micronesia are our brethren. The United States policy, such as the Compact Impact, intended or unintended, is resulting in divisiveness rather than comradeship.

Submerged Lands and the EEZ

The most significant economic sources for the CNMI are its submerged lands and the Exclusive Economic Zone (EEZ), including the outer continental shelf. The extent of the riches there is largely unknown, but it is vast and at this time incalculable. The economic future of the CNMI may very well be right in its ocean floor.

Submerged lands are all lands that are permanently or periodically covered by tidal waters up to, but not above the ordinary high water mark. The EEZ is the body of water that lies seaward of the territorial sea and extends 200 nautical miles from the coastlines of every island of the NMI island chain, except for the distance between the CNMI and Guam, where the EEZ is shared equally. The outer continental shelf refers to the seabed and subsoil of the submerged lands areas that lie beyond the coastline.

After the approval of the Covenant in 1976, ownership and control of the submerged lands and the EEZ were largely assumed by the CNMI. The CNMI Government assumed that the conveyance to it of all public lands that were once under the Trust Territory government, pursuant to Section 801 of the Covenant, included the submerged lands and the EEZ. The CNMI's presumption of ownership led to the passage of the Commonwealth's Submerged Lands Act of 1979 (P.L. 1-23) asserting management and control of the submerged lands owned by the CNMI, and the passage of the Marine Sovereignty Act of 1980 (P.L. 2-7) that claimed extension of CNMI sovereignty over the territorial sea for 12 miles from the shoreline and over the EEZ beyond the 12-mile limit.

However, the U.S. Government takes the position that as a result of the CNMI agreeing to United States sovereignty pursuant to Sections 101 and 104 of the Covenant, the Commonwealth's Submerged Lands Act of 1979 and the Marine Sovereignty Act of 1980 both are contrary to federal law after Sections 101 and 104 went into effect on November 4, 1986. Not only was this made clear in the Covenant, but the U.S. District Court for the NMI and the U.S.

Court of Appeals for the Ninth Circuit ruled in 2003 and 2005, respectively, that the Commonwealth's Submerged Lands Act of 1979 and the Marine Sovereignty Act of 1980 are both preempted by federal law.

The CNMI position is further weakened through its own account on page 144 in its *Section-by-Section Analysis of the NMI Constitution* issued on December 6, 1976, acknowledging that the United States "has a claim to the submerged lands off the coast of the Commonwealth" based on the paramountcy doctrine because of the sovereign authority of the United States Government over foreign affairs and national defense. The Analysis further states on page 144 that Article XI Section 1 of the CNMI Constitution "recognizes this claim and also recognizes that the Commonwealth is entitled to the same interest in the submerged lands off its coasts as the United States grants to the states with respect to the submerged lands off their coasts."

Article XI of the NMI Constitution recognizes that the ownership of the submerged lands is determined by U.S. law. Article XI Section 1 states in part that

> "…the submerged lands off the coast of the Commonwealth to which the Commonwealth now or hereafter may have a claim of ownership under United States law are public lands and belong collectively to the people of the Commonwealth who are of Northern Marianas descent."

The supremacy of the U.S. law in this matter is also recognized in Article XIV of the NMI Constitution. Article XIV Section 1 states that "The marine resources in waters off the coast of the Commonwealth over which the Commonwealth now or hereafter may have any jurisdiction under United States law shall be managed, controlled, protected and preserved by the legislature for the benefit of the people." The paramountcy doctrine clears away any doubt, as the CNMI's interest is subservient to the federal government's rights and authority. (See Addendum J., Presidential Proclamation 8335.)

However, prior to the 1947 U.S. Supreme Court decision in United States v. California, it was generally believed and accepted that the states were the sovereign owners of the submerged lands beneath the navigable waters within their boundaries and the waters within three miles of their coastlines, and of the natural resources within such lands and waters. For example, California had leased to oil companies the right to explore, drill, and extract oil and other petroleum products from submerged lands within three nautical miles off the coast of California. That was the case until the U.S. Government took California to court and California lost the case. So from 1947 to 1953, before Congress passed the Submerged Lands Act of 1953, the U.S. Government owned the submerged lands, once claimed by the coastal states that were within three miles of their coastlines. The passage of the Submerged Lands Act of 1953 returned to the states ownership of the submerged lands that were within three miles of their coastlines.

In disregard to the CNMI's claim of ownership of all of the submerged lands, President Barack Obama on January 16, 2014 by Presidential Proclamation conveyed to the Government of the Commonwealth of the Northern Mariana Islands certain of the submerged lands located up to three miles from the coastlines of the CNMI, pursuant to section (a) of the Territorial Submerged Lands Act of 1974 (Public Law 93-435), as amended by Section 1 of Public Law 113-34, unless the president designates otherwise pursuant to Section 1(b) (vii) of Public Law 93-435.

U.S. Public Law 93-435, the Territorial Submerged Lands Act of 1974, was amended by Section 1 of Public Law 113-34, which was signed into law by Pres. Obama on September 18, 2013. To implement Section 1 of Public Law 113-34, President Obama on January 16, 2014, issued a Presidential Proclamation that declared that the Government of the Commonwealth of the Northern Mariana Islands does not own or control the submerged lands adjacent to the islands of Farallon de Pajaros (Uracas), Maug, and Asuncion – which are included in the Marianas Trench Marine National Monument – that are permanently or periodically covered by tidal waters up to the mean high tide line extending three geographical miles seaward from the mean low water mark along the coastlines of these islands. The 2014 proclamation also applies to the submerged lands adjacent to the islands of Tinian and Farallon de Medinilla that are permanently or periodically covered by tidal waters up to the mean high tide line and extending seaward to a line three geographical miles distant from those areas of the coastline that are adjacent to the U.S. military's leased lands on Tinian and Farallon de Medinilla.

The Controversy over Tax Issues

One of the most contentious issues in the context of CNMI-Federal Relations during my term as governor was disagreement over tax policies between the CNMI and the Internal Revenue Service. It was an issue that had significant impact on the local economy simply because it can either encourage or discourage investment in the CNMI.

The Covenant is the primary source of taxing authority the CNMI draws from. The following are pertinent sections of the Covenant that established the coordination of the taxing authority of the U.S. and the CNMI. Under Section 601 of Covenant, the income tax laws of the United States are enforced in the CNMI in "mirror form" as a local territorial income tax. In addition to the mirrored income tax, the Covenant authorizes the CNMI to impose other taxes, which is the focus of this discussion concerning Section 703 (b) of the Covenant.

Section 601 of the Covenant provides that the provisions of the U.S. Internal Revenue Code are mirrored as the CNMI's own tax system. Section 601 of the Covenant also provides that U.S. tax laws are to apply in the CNMI as they do in Guam where the U.S. income tax code is also mirrored. Under Section 602 of the Covenant the CNMI is allowed to impose local taxes and rebate taxes collected by application of the Mirrored Internal Revenue Code. The CNMI created a system of local taxes that applies to wages, gross receipts and earnings and profits that when paid would be a non-refundable credit toward the mirrored Internal Revenue Code. With regards to the application of the mirrored Internal Revenue Code, the CNMI created a graduated rebate system.

In general, the income tax laws of the U.S. Internal Revenue Code were adopted as a local territorial income tax entitled "The Northern Marianas Territorial Income Tax" (NMTIT). The NMTIT mirrors the Internal Revenue Code in most respects, except where inapplicable or incompatible with the intent of the Covenant or U.S. income tax laws. The Covenant agreement between the CNMI and the federal government was good up to that point, but was unclear as to the dispute between the U.S. Treasury and the CNMI Treasury over taxes generated by application of the mirrored Internal Revenue Code and who would keep these funds. The only guidance on this issue was Section 703(b) of the Covenant.

Section 703(b) states in part that the U.S. Government will transfer to

"...the Treasury of the Government of the Northern Mariana Islands ... the proceeds of all customs duties and federal income taxes derived from the Northern Mariana Islands, ...the proceeds of any other taxes which may be levied by the Congress on the inhabitants of the Northern Mariana Islands."

Despite the longstanding disagreements between the U.S. and the CNMI on the application of the Mirrored Internal Revenue Code, neither party had implemented a program under this section. Section 703 (b) is perhaps the best example of the ongoing disagreement between the CNMI and the federal government on tax matters pertaining to the coordination of collection of withholding taxes, especially estate taxes. In question was who had authority over taxes imposed federally on residents and businesses in the CNMI – the CNMI or the federal government. In this particular case, the center of dispute was on the definition of residency. Once an individual firmly established residency, the CNMI had authority to retain all tax revenues associated with that individual.

To the CNMI, Section 703 (b) was critical, not only for establishing the fundamental tax relationship between the CNMI and the federal government, but also for clarification when there was overlap of tax authority as outlined in Section 703 (b) of the Covenant. The authority to tax under Section 703 (b) often depends on who was making the interpretation of the terms of the agreement. On the issue of estate taxes, the federal government had used the argument that the language used in Section 703 (b) was imprecise and the interpretation of the terms of the agreement was subjective.

For clarity on this issue, the tax policy of my Administration in regards to relations with the federal government, and the IRS in particular, had three major elements: (1) The specific language of the Covenant controlled the tax authority of the CNMI; (2) The tax policy language of the Covenant established the standards to be used for residency, the tax authority of the CNMI, and tax revenues that were to be covered over (transferred) to the CNMI; (3) Changes in tax policy language of the Covenant cannot be done unilaterally by the federal government.

The position I took as governor on the U.S. tax policy reflected my belief that the establishment of a strong tax authority was critical to self-governance and economic development. A government's ability to control and collect tax revenue is essential for long-term development and stability, and a fundamental prerequisite of self-governance. Through the use of this authority, the government can determine who bears the burden of taxation and the amount of revenues to be generated. Thus, this authority was a critical component of a government's authority to regulate its own internal affairs and to be able to exercise self-governance. I further believed that if a government concedes this authority to another government, it directly undermines its control over these critical components of governance. The framers of the Covenant recognized this and thus, this unique control over taxation was included as a critical element to ensure self-governance.

Having outlined the tax policy of the CNMI in 2005 as governor, I requested the Secretary of the Interior to settle any claim of the CNMI arising pursuant to the Covenant. An issue that remained outstanding was tax cover-over as addressed in Section 703(b) of the Covenant. Congress requested the Secretary of the Interior in 2004 to submit a report on progress in determining the cover-over amount due the CNMI. Section 703(b) of the Covenant provides for the cover-over (transfer) from the Federal Government to the CNMI of federal income and estate taxes and taxes on articles produced in the NMI. Congress at the time supported a resolution that clarified that the cover-over (transfer) of federal collections to the treasuries of certain territories included all taxes and fees, including taxes on estates and gifts.

The U.S. Treasury Department and the IRS took the position that estate taxes were not part of the CNMI revenue base and that estate taxes were to be retained by the U.S. Treasury because they were not considered a direct tax. A direct tax is a tax imposed on a taxpayer himself or herself or on his or her property.

The CNMI took the position that there was a legal relationship between the CNMI and the Federal Government as defined in Section 703 (b) of the Covenant that granted tax authority to the CNMI which the CNMI interpreted as including estate taxes. The source of disagreement between the CNMI and the Federal Government was over the interpretation of this relationship.

On further examination, the center of the dispute in the case of the cover-over (transfer) of taxes was the residency requirements. The CNMI asserted that expressed Congressional intent on estate tax vis-a-vis excise tax was that the estate tax was not a tax on property, but excise tax on the right of the decedent to transmit property at death, the amount of tax to be measured by the value of the property transmitted. (Note: The IRS would like to bring in the "source of revenue" as a way to limit the cover-over, but that is not the law. All tax revenues attributable to residents of the CNMI are the CNMI's, regardless of source.)

Clearly, the CNMI had authority to enact its local estate tax. The Covenant Section 703(b) stated that federal excise tax was eligible for transfer in the cover-over program. The question that neither side seemed able to answer with direct clarity was: Did the Congress explicitly or implicitly authorize the levying of taxes on estates to go to either the CNMI or to the U.S. Treasury? The CNMI's answer to that question is in Section 703(b) of the Covenant which states, "the proceeds of any other taxes which may be levied by the Congress on the inhabitants of the CNMI." The back-and-forth argument between the CNMI and the U.S. Treasury Department had turned into an argument of legislative intent.

The failure of the Internal Revenue Service to account for and remit payments to the CNMI covering the income tax collections on military and federal civilian personnel, including estate and gift taxes identified as cover-over by the Department of the Interior in 1993, placed unnecessary additional burdens on the CNMI budget and increased pressures on the limited discretionary funds available from the federal government for the needs of the CNMI. It is my belief that the continued refusal of the U.S. Treasury Department and the IRS to acknowledge that the plain language of Section 703(b) of the Covenant is counterproductive for the U.S.-CNMI relationship.

The CNMI continues to hold its position that the use of the phrases "all taxes" and "any other taxes" in Section 703(b) means just that – "all" means all – including estate taxes. As governor, I felt that it was time to make this a 902 Consultation talks issue and if not successful, to file a complaint seeking relief against the U.S. Treasury Department for the estate taxes that were wrongfully being withheld by the U.S. Treasury and the IRS.

However, much to the dismay of the CNMI and the other insular jurisdictions, President Bush on October 22, 2004, signed into law the American Jobs Creation Act of 2004 that had tax implications for the CNMI and the other insular jurisdictions. In this new law, Congress made significant changes to the bona fide residency requirements to apply to all the insular jurisdictions, including the CNMI. U.S. citizens in all the insular jurisdictions must meet requirements to be considered bona fide residents of these jurisdictions. The new residency rules issued by the Treasury Department and the Internal Revenue Service, which set out to implement the American Jobs Creation Act of 2004, permitted the IRS, in the context of U.S. citizens and permanent residents – rather than the local governments – to determine residency requirements for the CNMI and the other insular jurisdictions for tax purposes. The new law placed significant restrictions on who may file income tax returns in the CNMI, and these restrictions reduced the tax base of the Commonwealth. The new law in effect diminished the CNMI's ability to determine its own residents for tax purposes and gave the IRS significant power to retain jurisdiction over U.S. citizens and permanent residents. (Note: The Source Rule does not apply to the CNMI, only the Virgin Islands and Puerto Rico.)

It became abundantly clear, based on the American Jobs Creation Act of 2004, that U.S. tax policy towards the CNMI and the other insular areas was not adequately explained, nor were the insular areas consulted. Such unilateral imposition of tax policies undermined the Covenant and gave even greater power to the Internal Revenue Service in establishing tax policies for the insular areas and indirectly impact the insular areas government budgets. It could be argued therefore, that there is currently no overall tax policy towards the insular areas, including the CNMI, other than a general approach being pushed by the Internal Revenue Service to limit island revenues and expand U.S. Treasury income.

In light of these concerns, in December 2004, I requested the assistance of the Secretary of the Interior in the following areas.

1. Sponsorship of a joint meeting of representatives of all five insular areas affected by Section 908 of P.L. 108-357, the American Jobs Creation Act of 2004 (Northern Mariana Islands, American Samoa, Guam, Puerto Rico, and the Virgin Islands) to identify problems associated with this law.
2. Establishment of a permanent committee comprised of representatives of the U.S. Departments of the Interior and the Treasury and the insular areas to foster self-sufficiency through the coordination and implementation of federal and insular tax policies. This group could perhaps be a subcommittee of the President's Interagency Group on Insular Areas.
3. Amendment of U.S. P.L. 108-357, and in the interim participation by the Department of the Interior and the affected insular areas in the drafting of implementing regulations by the IRS.

On the issue of whether the U.S Government can unilaterally amend Article VI (Taxation and Revenue) of the Covenant the U.S. takes the position that although Congress voluntarily relinquished its authority to unilaterally amend Articles I, II, III, and Sections 501 and 805 of the Covenant, the tax provisions in Article VI of the Covenant are not designated by Section 105 as "fundamental provisions" of the Covenant that cannot be amended except by mutual consent. Therefore, unilateral action on the part of the Congress is permissible and the CNMI has no more prerogative to determine its own tax code than do the 50 states or the U.S. territories of Guam and the Virgin Islands. Obviously, this position of the U.S. Treasury severely undermines the authority given in Covenant Section 105.

In short, the effect of the changes contained in Section 980 of U.S. P.L. 108-357 is to reverse the long-standing supportive benevolence (nature) characterizing the United States' relationship to the Northern Mariana Islands and instead to convert the islands and their residents into a source of revenue for the Federal Government, a relationship that could be characterized as colonial, in nature. Enactment of Section 980 of U.S P.L. 108-357 only underscores that more needs to be done to ensure that federal tax policy works to support the self-sufficiency of the insular areas rather than a policy of continued dependency.

Saipan tax attorney Alexis A. Fallon in her February 14, 2005 article on the new tax law (The American Jobs Creation Act of 2004) correctly stated: "The Taxman Cometh to U.S. Possessions."

The Controversy over the Territorial Clause

The nature of the political relationship between the U.S. Government and the CNMI cannot be more pronounced than their disagreement on the applicability to the CNMI of the Territorial Clause, which is Article IV, Section 3, Clause 2 of the U.S. Constitution. According to a May 13, 1992, Congressional Research Service report for Congress, "The U.S. Government maintains that the Territorial Clause of the U.S. Constitution governs its relationship with the Northern Marianas." The Commonwealth takes the position that it is not a U.S. territory and therefore, is not subject to the Territorial Clause, because the clause is not enumerated in Section 501(a) of the Covenant, which lists those parts of the U.S. Constitution that do apply to the CNMI, and that only the actual language of the Covenant governs the Commonwealth's relationship with the U.S.

The authority of the U.S. in the areas of foreign affairs and defense is met with no disagreement. This authority is clearly established in Section 104 of the Covenant. Where it becomes unclear is the applicability of the Territorial Clause, which states, "The Congress shall have the Power to dispose of and make all needful Rules and Regulations respecting the Territory or other Property belonging to the United States." This authority, according to the U.S., extends to all matters in the Covenant relationship as applying of their own force, and the absence of mention of this Clause in the Covenant does not constitute omission or deliberate inapplicability. Furthermore, if the Territorial Clause does not apply to the CNMI, then the Covenant (U.S. P.L. 94-241) is unconstitutional and void, because the only source of power in the U.S. Constitution for Congress to execute the Covenant is the Territorial Clause.

There are several categories of territories, including:
a. Incorporated– A territory on a path to statehood. The U.S. Constitution is fully applicable to the territory.
b. Unincorporated – The U.S. Constitution is less than fully applicable. Guaranteed protection only of the "fundamental provisions" of the U.S. Constitution.
c. Organized Territory – Has an Organic Act, as in Guam and the Virgin Islands.

    d. Unorganized Territory – Has no Organic Act for its government.

    e. Unorganized, Unincorporated – American Samoa likely fit.

Guam and the Virgin Islands are both organized, but unincorporated. This means that there is, at least, the potential for modified applicability of the U.S. Constitution. They each have an Organic Act, but neither is on a path to statehood.

The Commonwealths of the Northern Mariana Islands and Puerto Rico are perceived as having more autonomy or self-government than Guam, the Virgin Islands, and American Samoa. Structurally, the primary difference between a commonwealth and a territory is that instead of having an Organic Act, the commonwealth government is chartered by a "covenant" or a "compact" between the people of each commonwealth and the U.S., and by a constitution written and ratified by commonwealth citizens under the authority granted by the compact and subject to requirements stated in that compact. But there is a point to be made: Organic Acts are acts of Congress, as is the Covenant, in the case of the CNMI. Is the Covenant set up to be the equivalent of an Organic Act? If the Covenant is a treaty, it would have required approval only of the Senate. The Covenant, however, was an act of Congress – as a joint resolution – approved by both the House and the Senate. The same goes for the Compacts of Free Association for Palau, the FSM, and the Republic of the Marshall Islands.

American Samoa has the least autonomy among all the territorial governments. Structurally, it is not a self-governing entity for the following reasons.

    a. In 1929, Congress passed legislation pertaining to governance in American Samoa. It was not considered an Organic Act, but a cession of a territory involving delegation of all government power in the territory to the president of the U.S.

    b. The president has the Secretary of the Interior as his representative. The president's representative authorized the people of American Samoa to adopt a constitution which provided for an elected legislature, which they did. The president's representative approved an amendment to the territory's constitution to provide for an elected governor. The president clearly can change the structure of the American Samoan government, unilaterally.

    c. In 1983, the U.S. Congress passed a law prohibiting American Samoa from altering its constitution without the consent of Congress. Because of this, the American Samoan Constitution takes on some attributes of an Organic Act, but it has no formal Organic Act. In American Samoa, the U.S. Constitution is less than fully applicable. Before 1983, American Samoa could amend its constitution with the permission of the president alone. Now, it requires the permission of the president and Congress. This is absolutely not self-government. (Note: The CNMI can amend its constitution so long as it is consistent with the Covenant, which is an act of Congress.)

The Insular Cases Doctrine is based on the Territorial Clause of the U.S. Constitution and judicial precedence on issues involving the application of the Constitution to the territories, and the appropriate application of doctrines developed by the Supreme Court and lower federal courts. The Insular Cases Doctrine is an interpretation of the Constitution which guarantees all citizens in the territories fundamental rights, while fulfilling the American promise to territorial residents that they can affiliate with the U.S. and still preserve their lands and culture. Four cases decided by the Supreme Court in 1901, and four other cases decided by the same court in 1903-05 and 1922, together compose the Insular Cases. (See footnote 9 in Rayphand and Torres v. Sablan, C.N.M.I. 1999). The Insular Cases would come to stand for two propositions:

1. The constitution fully applies ex proprio vigore (of its own force) throughout an incorporated territory. The most important of the Insular Cases was Downes v. Bidwell (1901).
2. In unincorporated territories, the Constitution does not "follow the flag" with full ex proprio vigore. In the Insular Cases, the Constitution guarantees to the residents of unincorporated territories only those rights that are fundamental in the international sense. In Downes v. Bidwell, the Supreme Court ruled that Puerto Rico is an unincorporated U.S. territory and therefore belongs to the U.S., but is not a part of the U.S. and thus, is not a part of the U.S. customs zone and the tariff duties imposed by the Foraker Act of April 12, 1990, on goods imported into the U.S from Puerto Rico are constitutional. Furthermore, residents of Puerto Rico have natural rights, such as freedom of speech, press, and religion; the right to life, liberty and ownership and use of property; due process of law and equal protection of the laws; freedom from unreasonable searches and seizures; and immunity from cruel and unusual punishment. However, residents of unincorporated territories such as Puerto Rico are not entitled to remedial rights in the Constitution, such as citizenship, the right to vote, and the right to trial by jury.

The Territorial Clause, which is Article IV, Section 3, Clause 2 of the U.S. Constitution, is not included on the list, in Section 501(a) of the Covenant, of those parts of the Constitution that "will be applicable within the Northern Mariana Islands as if the Northern Mariana Islands were one of the several States." If the Territorial Clause had been included on that list, then it would not apply to the CNMI. The Territorial Clause applies to U.S. territories, not its states.

The fact that the Territorial Clause does apply to the CNMI was recognized by the U.S. Court of Appeals for the Ninth Circuit in Wabol v. Villacrusis (1990), and by a three-judge panel of the U.S. District Court for the NMI in Rayphand and Torres v. Sablan (1999).

Without the Territorial Clause, the U.S. Congress would not have the authority (1) to approve the Covenant as a U.S. Public Law, (2) to grant to

Rota and Tinian equal representation in one house of the CNMI Legislature, and (3) to restrict the ownership and long-term interests in land in the CNMI to persons of NMI descent, as stated in Section 805 of the Covenant and as implemented in Article XII of the NMI Constitution.

According to the Congressional Research Service, there is sufficient legislative history to reveal that the understanding at the time Congress was considering the Covenant was that the CNMI would be subject to the plenary power of the Territorial Clause when the Trusteeship was terminated *(Welcoming America's Newest Commonwealth*, August 1985). The fact that the Territorial Clause is not listed in Section 501(a) of the Covenant as one of the constitutional provisions that apply to the Commonwealth appears inconsequential. Because such a provision would apply of its own right after the Trusteeship was terminated, there was no legal need for it to be listed.

The view that a territory was destined to become a state changed in the last hundred years. The fear of annexing distant ocean communities led to the theory of "territorial incorporation," which makes the distinction between territories that were, and territories that were not, destined for eventual admission as states. Territorial status is no longer looked at as transitional to independence or statehood. The Territorial Clause has become the vehicle for holding property in perpetuity.

The Controversy over Equal Representation in the Senate

Section 203(c) of the Covenant requires equal representation for Saipan, Rota and Tinian in one house of the CNMI Legislature. Debates on equal representation for Rota, Tinian and Saipan in the CNMI Senate have the tendency to surface, notoriously, in battles over the CNMI budget. It is one issue that brings out either the best or worst in people. When Rota and Tinian cannot get what they want from the House of Representatives, they will likely get it from the Senate. The history over budget battles goes back to the first Legislature. It was not uncommon to see tempers flare and walk-outs happen in budget meetings involving the three Rota and the three Tinian senators versus the three senators from Saipan. When Saipan loses out in the division of funds, it cries foul, arguing for fairness and reminding all that more than 90% of the CNMI population is on that island.

On occasion, the same occurs in the selection of officers of the Senate, especially in picking the next president. When the makeup of the Senate majority is a coalition of senators from Tinian and Rota, the three from Saipan become a minority with no power other than floor privilege, and at times, not even that. Often, the floor debates end up in bitter arguments and discord.

The history of the Senate in selecting its president reveals that the majority coalition can be a combination of the three senatorial districts being split up in different factions. A case in point was the selection of Juan S. Demapan as the Senate president on May 13, 1994, when he and his newly formed coalition unseated Jesus R. Sablan, the president duly elected on January 10,

1994, at the organizational session of the Senate of the Ninth Northern Marianas Commonwealth Legislature. Both were Saipan senators, but Demapan teamed up with senators from Rota and Tinian to unseat Sablan. The incident involved Gov. Froilan C. Tenorio when he called a special session of the Senate, which resulted in Demapan's election. This upset Sablan, and he filed a lawsuit challenging the apportionment of the Senate seats as unconstitutional, as a violation of equal protection of the law. The lawsuit filed by Sen. Sablan was the first court case challenging the Senate's composition. The case was Jesus R. Sablan v. Governor Froilan C. Tenorio, Senators Juan S. Demapan, Paul A. Manglona, David M. Cing, Eusebio A. Hocog, Ricardo S. Atalig, and the Ninth Commonwealth Legislature. The case was filed in the CNMI Superior Court on June 9, 1994, and designated as Civil Action No. 94-500. According to court records, Sen. Sablan sought a:

> "...declaratory judgment that the composition of the Senate of the Ninth Legislature of the Commonwealth of the Northern Mariana Islands, which gives each of the islands of Saipan, Tinian, and Rota three senators, violated the right of every citizen of Saipan to the equal protection of the laws under the Fourteenth Amendment of the United States Constitution because of the great disparity in the population of those islands."

Sen. Sablan asked the court to compel Gov. Tenorio and the Legislature to establish nine election districts based on population for the election of the nine senators, and in so doing, to declare the Ninth Commonwealth Senate to be illegally constituted and to order a special election after the Senate seats were reapportioned. Sablan reasoned that the malapportionment of the Senate gave the senators representing 10% of the population the power to control virtually all legislation and to control absolutely all gubernatorial appointments requiring Senate confirmation. On the disproportionality of representation, Sablan argued that based on the 1990 Census, the Saipan senatorial district was about 90% of the total population of the Commonwealth, Tinian was about 5%, and Rota also was about 5%. He argued that based on this information, the voting power of the people of Saipan was diluted to a ratio of 18 to 1. In other words, a U.S. citizen residing on Tinian or Rota, in elections for the CNMI Senate, had about 18 times the voting power of a U.S. citizen residing on Saipan, which according to Sablan, was grossly unfair. Furthermore, Sablan asserted that the CNMI Senate, as constituted, violated the NMI Constitution because the composition of the Senate denied the people of Saipan the equal protection of Commonwealth election laws. Article I, Section 6 of the NMI Constitution guarantees to every person residing in the Commonwealth the equal protection of the law. It is worth noting the glaring contradiction between Article I, Section 6 and Article II, Section 2 of the NMI Constitution, which requires equal representation for Saipan, Tinian and Rota in the CNMI Senate by giving each of these islands three senators. The CNMI Senate, as constituted by virtue of the Covenant and the CNMI Constitution, also violates the equal protection of the law, as guaranteed by the Fourteenth Amendment of the U.S. Constitution. Both the CNMI Superior Court and the CNMI Supreme Court ruled against Sablan in this lawsuit.

The second case involving the equal representation for the three islands in the CNMI Senate was Jeanne H. Rayphand and Stanley T. Torres versus the members of the Board of Elections, along with several Intervenors, all of whom opposed the plaintiffs in this case. This case involved an equal protection challenge, under the Fifth and Fourteenth Amendments of the U.S. Constitution, to the composition of the CNMI Senate. This lawsuit was brought in the U.S. District Court for the Northern Mariana Islands and was designated as Civil Action no. 97-0029. Rayphand and Torres sought a court declaration that the CNMI Senate's composition violated the Fourteenth Amendment's Equal Protection Clause and that the "one man, one vote" principle that the U.S. Supreme Court first applied to the apportionment of the seats in state legislatures in Reynolds v. Sims (1964) and Lucas v. 44th General Assembly of Colorado (1964) is a fundamental right in the CNMI guaranteed under the U.S. Constitution. Rayphand and Torres asked the court to order a special election to be held to elect CNMI senators based on population.

A three-judge panel of the U.S. District Court for the NMI ruled that the composition of the CNMI Senate does not fall within the "one-man, one-vote," population-based apportionment rule applicable to state legislatures in Reynolds v. Sims and other cases. In addition, the court upheld the constitutionality of Section 203(c) of the Covenant, which provides for the equal representation composition of the CNMI Senate. Rayphand and Torres argued that the Insular Cases Doctrine does not allow the U.S. Congress to deny the residents of Saipan the right to "one-man, one-vote." The attorneys for the Board of Elections argued that the U.S. Congress does have that right, under the Insular Cases Doctrine, because the CNMI's form of government provides and protects fundamental rights that are the basis of all free governments. In addition, the compromise reached between Rota and Tinian and the representatives from Saipan resulting in the approval of the Covenant "was necessary for political union within the NMI, and Congress properly accommodated the unique social and cultural conditions and values of the particular territory." (*The Marianas Variety*, December 16, 1999.) Without this compromise, there would have been no Covenant and no Commonwealth for all of the islands in the Northern Marianas. A summary judgment was handed down in favor of the Board of Elections and the Intervenors.

Not satisfied with the court's decision, Rayphand and Torres appealed the case to the U.S. Supreme Court. The Supreme Court declined to hear the appeal and remanded the case back to the District Court without the benefit of review. This action meant that the decision of the District Court stands. Based on the decision of the District Court, the provisions in the NMI Constitution and in the Covenant for equal representation for Saipan, Rota and Tinian in the CNMI Senate constitutes no violation of the Equal Protection Clause of the U.S. Constitution.

The Controversy over Asylum

Extension of the prohibition on seeking political asylum in the CNMI that is included in Public Law 110-229, the Consolidated Natural Resources Act of 2008, was important for the CNMI. Had the U.S. Congress not extended the prohibition on seeking political asylum in the CNMI, it would have negatively impacted the Commonwealth's economy and social welfare.

Political asylum seekers could seek to land anywhere in the CNMI, including in the Northern Islands, and this would have been a major national security concern. Our geographic configuration would make the CNMI one of the most challenging jurisdictions for the U.S. Department of Homeland Security to monitor. Moreover, the seeking of political asylum by Chinese who enter the CNMI as tourists with visa waivers could lead to action by the U.S. government that would jeopardize, or even end, the visa waiver program for the Chinese visitors to enter the CNMI. Furthermore, many former nonresident contract workers employed by the garment industry or in other industries, such as security, are primed to file political asylum applications. While the actual number of such aliens present in the CNMI, legally or illegally, is an elusive number, estimates were as high as three thousand. Based on the track record of the U.S. Citizenship and Immigration Services of the Department of Homeland Security, and other studies including the reports of investigators from the Government Accountability Office, U.S. Citizenship and Immigration Services does not have the resources needed to address the magnitude of potential applications from the potential asylum seekers in the CNMI. Extension of the exemption for the CNMI from claims for asylum under Section 208 of the Immigration and Nationality Act was included in S. 1237, the Omnibus Territories Act which the Senate passed on June 18, 2014, and in the Senate version of H.R. 83, which was included in U.S. Public Law 113-235.

Before the federalization of immigration in the CNMI under U.S. Public Law 110-229, the CNMI had no procedures for processing asylum claims. Even though the CNMI is part of the United States, and is subject to treaty obligations by the United States, there were no procedures for handling an asylum claim to determine if a person can be deported. The absence of a procedure was particularly serious because of the many foreign contract workers from China who had signed shadow contracts that severely limited their religious and political rights.

As Resident Representative and later as governor, I supported a related issue on a refugee protection program designed to meet U.S. treaty obligations that was negotiated between the CNMI and the U.S. Departments of State, Homeland Security, Justice and Interior, with the blessing and approval of the United Nations Human Rights Commission. New anti-trafficking and anti-smuggling laws were enacted by the CNMI government and prosecution under these laws was implemented.

In 2002, Acting Attorney General of the CNMI Robert T. Torres said that the United Nations Convention on Refugees is an international treaty to which the United States is a signatory and which is binding on the CNMI under Article I of the Covenant. Attorney General Torres also stated that an application for asylum filed in the CNMI does not guarantee that an applicant will be granted asylum. To qualify for asylum, Torres said, it should be well established that an applicant has a well-founded fear of persecution on account of political opinion, status, race, or gender.

On April 3, 2003, the CNMI Task Force on Refugee-Asylum and the U.S. Department of Justice agreed on acceptable terms for a Memorandum of Agreement that would provide procedures for aliens in the CNMI to request protection pursuant to the United Nations Protocol Relating to the Status of Refugees and the Convention Against Torture. On September 12, 2003 the Memorandum of Agreement was officially signed by Governor Juan N. Babauta and David Cohen the U.S. Deputy Assistant Secretary of the Department of the Interior, Office of Insular Affairs. The CNMI, as a self-governing Commonwealth under the sovereignty of the United States, is covered by certain treaty obligations of the United States, including obligations under the 1967 United Nations Protocol Relating to the Status of Refugees and under the Convention Against Torture and Other Cruel, Inhuman or Degrading Treatment or Punishment. The Task Force on Refugee-Asylum headed by Attorney General Ramona V. Manglona, who succeeded Robert Torres as the Attorney General, and the governor's legal counsel, Pamela Brown, negotiated the agreement for several months before it was completely ready for signing by the CNMI and the Department of the Interior.

On August 30, 2005, Attorney General Pamela Brown, who succeeded Ramona Manglona, signed a Letter of Understanding between herself as Attorney General and Joseph E. Langlois, Director of the Asylum Division, U.S. Citizenship and Immigration Services (USCIS) of the Department of Homeland Security. The purpose of the letter of understanding was to provide procedures for USCIS, as Protection Consultant to the Commonwealth, to conduct quality assurance reviews and to present comments and concurrence on protection decisions made by the Commonwealth Administrative Protection Judges.

Honoring our Men and Women in the Armed Services

"Military service is the highest form of commitment that one could give to our country. This means Honor, Duty, and Country. If they can give of themselves, government and every individual must also." (Juan N. Babauta)

In all my years in public service, it was always especially rewarding to be able to honor our men and women who wear the uniform as well as those who served, our veterans. I spoke at numerous ceremonies and commemorations in their honor and I was always moved with emotions in appreciation of their many sacrifices.

One of the most difficult tasks I had to perform as governor was to see off our soldiers to war. The emotion that ran through my body and in my head could not be described. After the war against Iraq began on March 20, 2003, I took to the podium three times before families and friends to say a few words to our soldiers preparing for deployment. I spoke twice at the Cathedral in Chalan Kanoa and once at the Kristo Rai Church in Garapan.

The following are the three statements I made to our men and women in uniform, and to families and friends, concerning the Iraq war.

March 20, 2003
Mount Carmel Cathedral, Chalan Kanoa, 6:30 p.m.
War announced against Iraq

Many of us watched and listened to the President of the United States as he addressed the nation and the world on the conflict in Iraq.

One line summarized it all when the President said: "The United States is acting because the risk of inaction is greater." The President's statement, short as it was, had far-reaching implications. It triggered engagement in war for our men and women in uniform that are already there in harm's way.

Bishop Camacho, we thank you for bringing our community together to pray for peace and for our soldiers.

We as a people understand the meaning of war. We understand it because we have experienced war. And we know the suffering that it causes both immediately and over time. While those of us here at home are safe, we have family members and friends that are in harm's way. Here at home we will continue to provide what is needed to keep our home safe, but let us not forget those that are not as safe as we are.

We are here tonight to pray for the safety of our brave and courageous men and women engaged in this conflict. We are here tonight to support the families of our sons and daughters in uniform. We feel the anxiety of war and that is why tonight we are pulling together as one.

We are proud of our troops.

We support our troops.

We commend them for their courage and for their commitment to God and Country.

We pray for their safety and for their safe return home after the conflict.

Thank you, yan si Yu'us Ma'ase'.

March 15, 2004
Mount Carmel Cathedral, Chalan Kanoa
Departing Soldiers Ceremony

Thank you, Bishop Tomas Camacho and Father Isaac Ayuyu, for tonight's special mass to ask God's blessing and protection for our sons and daughters who go to battle in Iraq, in Afghanistan, and Haiti and for their families, who wait for their safe return home.

Last month, I met with one of those young soldiers at Walter Reed Army Hospital in Washington, D.C. She is recovering from injuries she received from a roadside bomb as her unit drove through the streets of Baghdad. I admire her courage for going into battle, her bravery as she faces the pain of recovery, her willingness to risk death for the good of all of us.

For her and all those who have already been to Iraq, we thank God for your safe return home. And we thank you for taking action to rid the world of tyranny and make our world a better place.

For those now serving in Iraq, we ask for God's blessing in protecting you from harm. Your duty requires you to work in constant danger. Mentally, as well as physically, this places a great burden on you. We pray that you return to us safely.

Finally, for those who may be called to duty in the future, we ask God to guide you, as you train for service, so you may learn skills to keep you safe. If you are called, we ask God to give you courage. And we pray your courage will be rewarded with greater security and peace for our nation and for the people of all the world.

We pray this evening as a grateful people, so proud of each of our soldiers' decision to serve. As President Lincoln said many years ago, "Your service to our nation speaks for itself. You have put yourself in harm's way for the good of your families and your fellow citizens." We pray for God's blessing on you, and look forward to your safe return home. Thank you and may God bless us all.

July 11, 2004
Kristo Rai Church, Garapan
Troop Deployment

Soldiers of the 100th Battalion, 442nd Infantry Division, families and friends.

I do not know how other US communities send their soldiers off to face danger and uncertainty.

But in our community and in an event like this, we come together to show our respect for your courage, our concern for your safety, our pride in your service to country, our commitment to watch over your loved ones while you are far from home, and our prayers for your safe return home after your duty is complete.

That is why we have come here today.

I will not pretend to know the depth of your feelings. But I can imagine the uncertainty you feel about the danger you may face.

We all know our country is at war. We know the risks of injury and death are real. Yet, we know, too, that you have been well-trained. You have practiced your skills. You have prepared in your minds for the possibility you could be deployed.

And I must believe that preparation gives you confidence, and helps you find the courage to do what your country asks. I hope, too, that your families will take comfort knowing that you are prepared.

They have seen you train here on the weekends and off island for extended training. They know how hard you have worked. That knowledge should give them a sense of security and confidence you will be well.

But no matter how well prepared, your leaving will have an impact. Please, look around you today, and in the weeks to come remember this scene: Remember there is a community of family and friends who admire you for the service you give our country and for the bravery you show. Remember there is a community here who knows the hardship and worry your family feels. You know your family will be in good hands. Most especially, remember there is a community here who prays for your safe return home.

Return to us safely and soon and Godspeed.

Si Yu'us Ma'ase'.

Tinian's Military Land Lease

Tinian and Farallon de Medinilla: The military leases on Tinian and on the entire island of Farallon de Medinilla are authorized and required by Sections 802 and 803 of the Covenant. Section 802(a)(1) and (a)(3) state that the leased areas on Tinian and the entire island of Farallon de Medinilla include "the waters immediately adjacent thereto." Section 803(a) states that this lease is for 50 years, and that "the Government of the United States will have the option of renewing this lease for all or part of such property for an additional term of fifty years if it so desires at the end of the first [50-year] term." The lease agreement grants to the U.S. leasehold interest to 17,779 acres on Tinian, the equivalent of 7,203 hectares of land.

Tinian Lease Agreement: The Tinian Lease Agreement was signed on January 6, 1983, by three officials of the U.S. Government and by five officials of the CNMI Government. The Commonwealth officials were: Gov. Pedro P. Tenorio, Senate President Olympio T. Borja, House Speaker Benigno R. Fitial, and the board chairmen of the Marianas Public Land Corporation (MPLC) and the Commonwealth Ports Authority. Article 1(c) of this agreement states, in part, that the leased areas include:

> "...waters of the commonwealth immediately adjacent to the leased surface lands on Tinian and Farallon de Medinilla islands ... The United States shall have the right within the waters to facilitate access and egress to the leased surface lands and to construct reasonable port facilities ... The Commonwealth retains the right, without undue interference to the rights of the United States under this Lease Agreement, to exploit the living and non-living resources of the waters immediately adjacent to the leased surface lands."

This provision refers to a right to use, not ownership or a right of ownership.

Land Acquisition and Deferred Payment Agreement: On the same day that the Tinian Lease Agreement was signed, the "Land Acquisition and Deferred Payment Agreement" also was signed by the same three U.S. officials and five CNMI officials. By the terms of this agreement, the parties "also entered into a Technical Agreement setting forth additional terms and conditions of the lease to the United States for defense purposes." The Technical Agreement required the CNMI "to execute a lease for the lands described in Section 802 of the Covenant and to acquire title to certain homestead parcels located within the lands on Tinian Island to be made available to the United States for defense purposes." The homestead areas are all located within the leased premises designated as Zones 1, 2 and 3. The total adjusted sum to be paid to the CNMI by the U.S. under the agreement was $33 million. However, because the areas designated as Zones 1, 2 and 3 were not yet acquired by the CNMI Government and the MPLC, and thus unusable by the U.S., a deferred payment schedule was agreed upon pursuant to a timeframe in which the homesteads were acquired and cleared of leasehold interest by the CNMI Government. The CNMI Government, MPLC and the U.S. Government set up an escrow fund pending the securing of all the private land holdings within the leased area on Tinian. Subsequently, the fund was terminated when it was agreed that the monies could be used by the CNMI Government to acquire the private lands through direct acquisition or through the exercise of eminent domain.

Leaseback and Disposal Agreement: Twelve years after the Tinian Lease Agreement was executed, the CNMI and the U.S. entered into a "Leaseback and Disposal Agreement," signed August 8, 1994, by an official of the U.S. Government and an official of the CNMI government, Lt. Gov. Jesus C. Borja, who also was Acting Governor at the time. Under this leaseback agreement, the U.S. agreed to release to the Commonwealth its leasehold interest in approximately 1,245 acres of the leased premises on the condition that the Commonwealth purchased this interest from the U.S. This agreement was entered into pursuant to the Covenant, the original lease agreement, and a separate, Technical Agreement that said that until such time as required for military purposes, the U.S. shall lease back to the Commonwealth approximately 5,955 acres of land for 10 years and for successive, additional periods of 10 years.

The leaseback of 1,245 acres under this agreement may be used by the Commonwealth only for agriculture, grazing, and other uses permitted by the U.S. However, the U.S. has the right to terminate the leaseback agreement and to require removal of any temporary improvements that may be installed by the Commonwealth in the event of urgent military requirement, upon a one-year notice to the Commonwealth, or in the event of default by the CNMI.

Partial Release of Leasehold Interest Agreement: Five years after the Leaseback and Disposal Agreement was executed, the CNMI entered into yet another agreement with the U.S., a "Partial Release of Leasehold Interest Agreement." It was signed September 23, 1999, by one U.S. and one CNMI official,

Lt. Gov. Jesus R. Sablan, and acknowledged by three other CNMI officials: Roman S. Palacios, board chairman of the Commonwealth Ports Authority; Manuel P. Villagomez, board chair of Public Lands, and Mayor Francisco M. Borja, of Tinian and Aguigan. This partial release agreement amended the original 1983 lease agreement and the 1994 leaseback agreement, and terminated the 1988 leaseback by the U.S. to the Commonwealth Ports Authority. The purpose of this last agreement was to accommodate the proposed expansion of the Tinian airport, and for other public purposes.

Reevaluation of U.S. Defense Requirements: As Resident Representative to the United States, I asked the U.S. military whether it still needed the whole leased area on Tinian. I wrote to Rear Admiral Edward Kristensen, the Commander of U.S. Naval Forces in the Marianas, on February 14, 1993, and asked him whether part of it could be used by the people of Tinian for economic activities. I indicated that while the CNMI Government fully respected all the provisions of its lease agreement with the U.S. Government, we recognized that dramatic changes were occurring throughout the world which compelled a comprehensive reevaluation of U.S. defense requirements, especially in our region. I felt, at the time, that the island of Tinian was suffering from the effects of a reduced level of economic activity and had not yet achieved a level of prosperity envisioned with the military presence on the island.

Lack of Economic Opportunity: Many of the people of Tinian had left the island because of the lack of economic opportunity there. I believed then that the lack of available land was a contributing factor to Tinian's stagnation, and if more land could be developed, the result would help the people of Tinian bring their incomes up to a level where they would not have to leave for employment elsewhere. Two-thirds of the island, or about 7,203 hectares, were leased to the U.S. Government.

Planned Military Base Closures: That was not the only reason I wrote to Rear Adm. Kristensen. My letter was written in anticipation of an announcement by the Department of Defense recommending that 31 major military installations be closed, and that 12 others be realigned, to support a smaller, less costly force structure. This announcement was made by Secretary of Defense Les Aspin on March 12, 1993. In addition, Secretary Aspin announced recommendations for closure, realignment, and disestablishment of 122 smaller bases and activities. He said that the Defense department was reducing its forces overseas much more than it was in the U.S., but under a different process; the plan was to downsize the overseas base structure by 35 to 40 percent. In Hawaii alone, three installations, all on the island of Oahu, were recommended for closure: Naval Air Station at Barbers Point, as a Major Base; the Naval Computer and Telecommunications Area Master Station near Wahiawa, and the Naval Supply Center at Pearl Harbor, each categorized as a Smaller Base or Activity. Not far from Hawaii, Midway Island's Naval Air Facility also was recommended for closure, which was classified as a Major Base Realignment.

Rethinking the Use of Leased Lands: I was not the only elected official to call for the return of the military leased properties on Tinian. Gov. Lorenzo I. Deleon Guerrero had written to Rear Adm. Kristensen in December 1992, pointing out that the people of Tinian had already prepared a public land use plan for commercial or agricultural development, consistent with the lease agreement under the Covenant. Gov. Deleon Guerrero also noted the desire of the CNMI for the military to return the land in Marpi on Saipan, following the announcement to deactivate the Marpi Tracking Station.

Since the announcement by the Department of Defense on planned military base closures in 1993, leaders in the CNMI Government, including Tinian Mayor James M. Mendiola and past mayors, had been rethinking the use of the leased lands there. To encourage economic growth on the island of Tinian, the CNMI Government asked that nonessential public lands leased to the military be opened for uses which do not conflict with security requirements. That was not much to ask for, considering that in 1982, just prior to the signing of the Tinian Lease Agreement in January 1983, the U.S. Government Accountability Office had reported to the House Appropriations Committee that the Defense Department had not demonstrated a need for most of the land proposed to be leased. The Government Accountability Office was concerned that the length of the lease would preclude commercial development on Tinian and recommended future leaseback of properties not being utilized. This is exactly what Senator David M. Cing had pointed out to Gov. Deleon Guerrero in his February 11, 1993 letter. Sen. Cing wrote, "The arrangement was made with U.S. national defense in mind and lately it has become apparent that the military retention land will not be needed for this purpose."

"Gift Back" Proposed: During the time I was the Resident Representative, I believed that the return of the entire Military Leased Lands on Tinian would be ideal. I coined the phrase "Gift back," a concept that would enable the people of Tinian to use the leased lands without conditions, unlike a leaseback, in which the military can reclaim use of the property. A "gift back" would mean that ownership of the leased lands reverts to the CNMI. This idea was not just a dream; I actually discussed it in meetings with Congressman Ronald Dellums, chairman of the House Armed Services Committee, in February 1993. Chairman Dellums was receptive to the idea, but wanted the CNMI to develop plans on how the land would be used. Separately, the military had shown no desire at all to return ownership of the leased property to the CNMI.

With the breakup of the Soviet Union, the strategic environment had changed. The U.S. lost its bases in the Philippines in 1991 and '92, but had indicated no plans for military construction on Tinian to replace them. The military buildup would be going to Guam. Thus, relaxing control on the leased lands in Tinian in a way that was consistent with U.S. defense requirements would have associated the military with economic growth. In the event that land on Tinian would have been needed for defense purposes, the military would have encountered there a reservoir of goodwill, not accumulated resentment.

Uncertain Future: At present, the CNMI Government and the people of the CNMI recognize the ongoing military and security concerns emanating from the disputed islands in the South China Sea. The U.S. is sending military aircraft and ships on patrols in the region. The U.S. and the governments of Australia, Japan and the Philippines, all allies of the U.S., are in meetings of preparedness over land disputes and conflicts in the South China Sea. This could potentially cast a new, Cold War era-like situation, and redefine the military posture and needs for its leased lands. What the U.S. military is lacking in its dialogue with the CNMI Government and its citizenry is an open and honest discussion about its immediate and future needs in the CNMI.

National Guard Unit for the Northern Marianas

As Resident Representative and later, as governor, I supported the establishment of a National Guard unit for the CNMI. The commonwealth is one of the few American jurisdictions without one. Since the terrorist attacks of September 11, 2001, the nation has become aware of its strengths, as well as its weaknesses, in homeland security, and it has become national policy to enhance the capability of first responders. Except for the CNMI, other U.S. governors have the ability to activate National Guard units immediately in the event of natural disaster, civil unrest, a health emergency, or in response to the demands of national security. Some 2,700 communities in the 50 states, as well as the District of Columbia, Guam, Puerto Rico and the U.S. Virgin Islands, have National Guard units. Although an Army Reserve unit exists in the CNMI, the governor has no jurisdiction to call up this force for emergency response. A CNMI National Guard unit would likely have a larger force than the Army Reserve unit that exists today.

The aftermath of September 11 demonstrated the detriment to a community minus a National Guard unit, such as the Northern Mariana Islands, when the Federal Aviation Administration raised its security requirements. National Guard units were stationed at 400 U.S. airports, but security at the three CNMI airports had to be provided initially by civilians. Arrangements were made weeks later to pay for the Guam Army National Guard to be deployed to the CNMI. The Northern Mariana Islands are, in effect, isolated from quick emergency assistance from other parts of the U.S. In the event of unexpected situations calling for rapid response at a scale exceeding the capability of local first responders, the Northern Mariana Islands are days, if not weeks, away from aid.

If a national emergency were to occur that required protection of all CNMI ports, it would be beyond the capacity of local resources to carry out. Furthermore, the Northern Marianas is a typhoon-prone area which, when struck by a storm, require a disaster declaration by the President of the United States and an extraordinary local response effort.

During my last three years as Resident Representative and my first two years as governor, I expressed the CNMI's interest to the Defense department in establishing a local militia and a National Guard component. In an April

14, 2000 letter from Lt. Gen. Russell C. Davis, Chief of the National Guard Bureau, I was provided guidance for the creation of an Army National Guard unit in the Northern Marianas. Lt. Gen. Davis indicated that the Secretary of the Army is the official responsible for approving creation of an Army National Guard unit in the Northern Marianas, and that such approval would be contingent upon (1) the Total Army Analysis process, which determines the number of units in the branch's force structure, and (2) analysis of the capability of the CNMI population base to support a unit at the required strength. Furthermore, Lt. Gen. Davis stated that prior to the Secretary of the Army's review of this question, the CNMI would have to enact a law to provide for a militia, and Congress would need to amend certain sections of the U.S. Code to authorize a National Guard unit in the CNMI.

In an act of solidarity, the Babauta-Benavente Administration and the Legislature met the first precondition by enacting CNMI Public Law 13-32 on November 25, 2002. The law authorized the establishment of a National Guard unit for the CNMI. In addition, I formed a five-member task force to assist my office in addressing various concerns while legislation in support of a National Guard unit made its way through Congress. I appointed former Presiding Judge of the Superior Court Edward Manibusan to chair the task force, along with three others to serve as members.

The second precondition was already under consideration; the U.S. Senate had approved an amendment to S. 1050, the National Defense Authorization Act for fiscal year 2004, which provided for the establishment of a National Guard unit for the Northern Marianas. The amendment would have authorized the Secretary of Defense to cooperate with the governor of the CNMI, and to integrate into the Army National Guard and the Air National Guard of the U.S. the members of the National Guard of the Northern Mariana Islands. The legislation went to a conference committee, but never made it out. The concerns raised by Congress were cost, which would have been more than anticipated, and the capability of the NMI population base to support a unit at the required strength.

The Retirement Fund Program

The Northern Mariana Islands Retirement Fund was established on October 1, 1980, by the First Northern Mariana Islands Legislature, in P.L. 1-43, as a defined benefit, cost-sharing pension plan for CNMI Government employees. The law was successively amended by P.L.s 2-18, 2-47, 3-99 and 4-20, and Constitutional Amendment No. 19 of the second constitutional convention, to provide pension benefits to all civil service employees, including those working for autonomous agencies. These amendments also extended benefits to elected officials and employees of the former Trust Territory of the Pacific Islands who were U.S. citizens pursuant to the CNMI Covenant.

Public Law 6-17, the Northern Mariana Islands Retirement Fund Act of 1988, passed in 1989, repealed the above-mentioned laws and re-established the Northern Mariana Islands Retirement Fund as an autonomous agency and a public corporation of the CNMI to provide retirement security and other benefits to government employees, their spouses and dependents, and former governors and lieutenant governors, and to provide for an actuarially sound, locally funded pension system pursuant to the Agreement of the Special Representative on Future United States Financial Assistance for the Northern Mariana Islands. This Act was later amended by lawmakers in the 8th, 9th, 10th, 11th, 12th, 13th, and 14th Legislatures. (Source: NMI Retirement Fund.)

The CNMI Government, by P.L. 15-13 in June 2006 and P.L. 15-70 a year later, switched the defined benefit plan to a 401(k)-style Defined Contribution plan. These laws sounded the wake-up call for every government employee and retiree; they put them on notice that the Retirement Fund was in peril. P.L. 15-13 established the CNMI Public Employees' Defined Contribution Plan, a portable individual retirement account for all new government employees hired to work on, or after, January 1, 2007. Under the Defined Contribution Plan, employees could take their contributions when they left government employment. The law also gave Class I members the option to transfer from the defined benefit plan to the Defined Contribution Plan. The rationale was that the latter met the conditions and provides the protection required in U.S. law, specifically 26 U.S. Code 401(a), 414(d), 414(k), and 457, and including Internal Revenue Service laws, as a qualified retirement plan for government employees.

The CNMI Government has a long history of unfunded mandates that create an unsustainable level of unfunded liability which it simply cannot afford. More than 52 amendments were made to the original Retirement Fund law that, one way or another, contributed to the unfunded liability that grew so big, it bankrupted the program. Attempts to reduce and thereby ease the burden on the government of its unfunded liabilities – by repealing the 3% bonus for elected officials, benefits for board and commission members, vested credits for college education and military service, compensatory time, and eliminating credit towards retirement on unused sick leave and annual leave – all came too little, too late.

Meanwhile, P.L. 15-15, also enacted June 2006, freed the government from paying its employer contributions to the Retirement Fund for the last seven months of FY2006 and all of FY2007. This law was challenged in the CNMI Superior Court, and was ruled unconstitutional in Northern Mariana Islands Retirement Fund v. CNMI Government. The CNMI Government defied the Court's order to pay its past due obligations to the Retirement Fund. This led to the filing in 2009 of the "Betty Johnson case" in the U.S. District Court for the NMI. The Settlement Agreement in this case mandates the government to make annual payments to the Settlement Fund as follows.

    2014 _____ $25 million
    2015 _____ $27 million
    2016 _____ $30 million

2017 _____	$33 million
2018 _____	$45 million
2019 _____	$44 million
2020 _____	$43 million
2021 _____	$42 million
2022 _____	$41 million
2023 _____	$40 million
2024 _____	$39 million

Although the government has been able to remit to the Settlement Fund its employer contributions and annual payments as required, NMI Retirement Settlement Fund Trustee Joyce Tang has stated that the Retirement Fund's investments will be depleted by 2019, because they were used for paying pension benefits. She also reported that, based on 2016 financial conditions and arrangements, pension payments from 2019 onward will have to come entirely from the government's employer contributions, minus its required annual payment.

The Fiscal Condition of the Government in 2002

The CNMI economy had already been showing signs of decline in the latter part of the 1990s. The decline was more pronounced as government revenues decreased from $248 million in 1997 to $225 million in 2001. (See *Economic Impact of Federal Laws on the Commonwealth of the Northern Mariana Islands*, October 2008.) The size of government, however, did not see a corresponding decrease, as it should have. When I and Lt. Gov. Benavente took office on January 12, 2002, the CNMI Government was faced with serious fiscal challenges. We were confronted with an extremely difficult economic situation, further complicated by the 9/11 attacks in New York and at the Pentagon, and the consequences of those attacks.

The government was spending more than it was generating. In fiscal year 2001, it was spending at an annual rate of $225 million, even though revenues were projected to be only $179 million, and was $20 million behind in tax rebates. By the end of that fiscal year, the government was facing a $28 million deficit. With this huge deficit looming, and after consulting with Lt. Gov. Benavente, I issued an expenditure control directive to reduce travel and eliminate overtime, except for essential services. Working with the lieutenant governor, I empaneled an expenditure control task force with specific targets – reduce utility costs, office space rentals and car leases, and enforce the overtime ban. We hired an experienced manager for Capital Improvement Projects, so that we could pump more federal dollars into the economy. After consulting with the leadership of the Legislature and the Judiciary, we cut their budgets by 12% for the last two quarters of FY2002. They were not happy about the cut, but we also cut the Executive Branch budget even more, at 16%.

With all the controls and cuts, we reduced government-wide spending by $1.5 million per month. Our expenditure control task force had cut travel by

27%, office rentals by 20%, car leases by 14%, professional services by 14%, and overtime by 33%. Aside from the reductions, the government was on track to spend $40 million on CIPs – more than we had projected, and $10 million more than at any other time. The economic recovery that the CNMI Government started in January 2002 used the oldest trick in the book to stimulate the economy: public works projects. By 2004, we had spent more than $111 million – surpassing $35 million per year – the most ever by the CNMI Government. That total included $10 million for water on Saipan, $17 million for the hospital expansion and hemodialysis center, $2 million for the new Tinian High School, $2 million for the Rota courthouse, $11 million for revitalizing Garapan, $7 million for the Tinian airport, and $22 million for a new prison facility. Much of the CIP money also went to cleaning up the environment. We closed the Puerto Rico Dump and opened the state-of-the-art landfill in Marpi. We began to recycle garment waste that made up half of our garbage. By 2004, the Marianas recycling rate was better than the national average. In addition, the CNMI received more than $20 million in federal grant funding due to the credible relationship our Administration had with the federal government.

The success of our strategy was due to the strong leadership provided by the Department of Public Works under the direction of its secretary, Juan S. Reyes. The result was, instead of the $28 million deficit, as the CNMI Finance Department figures had indicated in FY2002, the deficit was down to $17 million. We reduced it by $11 million. With a reduced budget of $210 million for FY2002, government operations amounted to $24,000 per hour. Compare this with other state governments: Hawaii was spending $600,000, and California was spending $12 million per hour. However, the cost of operating the CNMI Government per hour is essentially meaningless. What counts is the cost of government per person served, and what you get for that cost. The CNMI was spending a little less than the average state government, at about $8 per person per day, for which the public received round-the-clock police and fire protection, a school system for our youth, public health and the hospital, scholarships, roadways, ports (sea and air), medical referrals, sports, solid waste, electric power and water, to name a few.

The size of the government was an issue we kept our eye on. Of the 5,000 government employees, the Executive Branch comprised just 20% of that total. The Legislature, the Judiciary and the autonomous agencies of the government composed 80%. At the time the budget controls and cutbacks were in effect, I encouraged the autonomous agencies to be creative and to work with the Administration and the legislature.

From a broader perspective, the primary cause of the financial crisis in the CNMI, and in every insular government, is the continued decline of general revenues without sufficient corresponding reduction in government expenditures. In an October 2012 Financial Assessment Report conducted by the U.S. Department of Agriculture Graduate School and funded by the Office of Insular Affairs, it was noted that the accumulated General Fund Balance (Deficit) based on Audited Financial Statements of Revenues and Expenditures had consistently grown from $25 million in 1993 to $350 million in 2011. Furthermore, the report suggested that in order for the CNMI to reduce its out-of-control deficit, it must prioritize public services, base its budgeting process on reliable historical data and projections, institute a deficit reduction program that pays off outstanding debt by creating new revenue streams and increasing existing ones, and enforce reductions in expenditures when revenues fall short.

Highway Improvements

Roadways in the CNMI are constructed under the administration of the Department of Public Works. Most of the road projects are financed by the federal government, using Federal Highway Administration (FHA) funds. Most of these funds can be used only for primary, and in some cases secondary, roads. Roadways like Rota's Route 100 and Saipan's Talofofo Road, Route 36, are not included in the primary road system, because they do not traverse all the way around the islands and are, in effect, dead-ends. Improvements in these roadways would provide numerous benefits for residents, as well as open up areas for economic development.

Rota Route 100 is a narrow, two-lane, coral base road that provides access to agricultural lands and tourist attractions. This proposed expansion project involved construction of a coastal roadway that is approximately 10 miles in length, providing the only alternative route from the island's international airport to the main village. Due to cliffs and other spatial restrictions, it is composed of only two lanes. Drainage and safety features, such as guardrails, were all part of the proposal. Route 100 navigates through historic areas, wildlife habitats, cliff lines and other topographic features. It was anticipated that the completed Route 100 would serve doubly as a means to enhance access to the island's naturally astounding features and provide safety measures that would allow the area to be more inviting and thus, help to boost the island's economy.

The CNMI Government had long sought for a fully paved Route 100, but neither federal nor local funds were ever sufficient for such a massive project. Funds under the federal Emergency Relief project were authorized in November 1997, but the FHA determined that these monies were insufficient for the entire Route 100. The CNMI receives only $3.2 million in federal aid for highways under the Territorial Program. Competition for this money from Saipan, a more heavily populated and developed island, precludes completion of a fully paved Route 100. With a concerted effort, Commonwealth leaders could, however, pave that important roadway by dedicating all of this FHA funding to it for the next several years, until it is completed.

Saipan's Talofofo Road, Route 36, is a roadway on the east side of Saipan that, when completed, would provide circle-island connectivity and would relieve the traffic pressure on Chalan Pale' Arnold Road (Middle Road) and the San Roque area. This proposal involved construction of a two-lane roadway with lanes 12 feet wide and shoulders 8 feet wide on each side, a two-lane concrete bridge with a span of approximately 150 feet, drainage structures, and right-of-way acquisition. The Talofofo Road improvements would benefit commuters traveling to the northern end of the island, connecting the backside roadway with Marpi, from beyond the Kingfisher golf course. This project would link two of the island's most scenic areas, and visitors could access attractions such as the War Memorials, Banzai Cliff, the famous Grotto, and Bird Island from either this new road, or the Chalan Pale' Arnold Road.

This proposal had an advantage over the Rota plan, because there was a total of $12 million made available for it. It was the first time the CNMI had been included in the reauthorization of the Transportation Equity Act (TEA 21). Project funding under TEA 21 was usually given to each congressional district; the CNMI had traditionally been left out because we had no representation in Congress. However, during the 108th Congress, when I was governor, the CNMI mobilized early – submitting required documents, lobbying congressional and staff members – and I met with Rep. Don Young in 2003 regarding this issue. In early 2004, Lt. Gov. Benavente followed up, at which time the congressman, who chaired the House Committee on Transportation and Infrastructure, added our project to the Alaska listing. He literally made us part of his congressional district. Through this collaborative effort, the CNMI was made eligible for federal-aid highway funds under TEA 21. Construction planning began, but was suspended by the new Administration of Gov. Benigno Fitial. Other underway planning – for extensive bicycle and pedestrian facilities along this roadway that would provide excellent recreational opportunities for residents and tourists alike – also was put on hold.

Along with the Talofofo Road improvements, my TEA 21 funding request included the construction of ferry terminals on Saipan and Tinian, when the ferries were still operating. Unfortunately, that request did not get funded. The Tinian-Saipan ferry had been the main source of transportation between the two islands, providing service to Tinian commuters working on Saipan, and to visitors traveling between the two islands. The two ferries had been purchased and were operating privately, but there was no terminal or station to service them.

While Resident Representative to the U.S., I had worked with Tinian Sens. David M. Cing, Joaquin G. Adriano and Jose M. Dela Cruz to have the Tinian-Saipan ferry service added to a national database of ferry operations. We completed lengthy survey materials for the Tinian Shipping and Transportation Co., which my Office transmitted to the Volpe National Transportation Systems Center in Cambridge, Massachusetts. The national ferry inventory provides policymakers with a fully georeferenced database of routes, terminal locations, vessel types, passenger loads and other information to aid in setting transportation policy and making funding decisions.

ENMU Alumni Distinguished Service Award

On July 24, 2003, the Board of Directors of the Eastern New Mexico University Alumni Association selected me to receive their 2003 Distinguished Service Award. Several others received the same award, but the one, in particular, that I want to mention is Mr. Albert Smith, one of the original 29 Navajo Code Talkers. The recipients of the alumni awards were featured on October 11 of that year at the Friends of Eastern Homecoming Breakfast. I personally traveled to Portales, New Mexico, to receive my award. Gov. Bill Richardson of New Mexico, a former Secretary of Energy under Pres. Clinton, received the Honorary Lifetime Alumni Award for his contributions to the state of New Mexico. This special event attracted more than 300 donors and friends of ENMU.

Telecommunications and the Sale of Verizon

Telecommunications is a key component to economic development in the CNMI. When the CNMI and the other insular jurisdictions were added to the 1996 Telecommunications Act, we cut long-distance rates to the U.S. mainland from $3 per minute to 10 cents a minute. That was why I was so involved with the Verizon Micronesia (Verizon) sale.

In this transaction, Bell Atlantic New Zealand Holdings, Inc., a wholly owned subsidiary of Verizon Communications, Inc., had agreed to sell 100% of the stock of its wholly owned subsidiary, Micronesian Telecommunications Corporation (MTC), to a consortium of investors which had incorporated in the CNMI as Pacific Telecom, Inc. (PTI). The primary investor was Citadel Holdings, Inc., through its overseas telecommunications investment arm Prospector Investment Holdings Inc., a diversified transportation and logistics services company headquartered in Makati City, Philippines.

Concerned about the future of the CNMI, I insisted that any new owner of Verizon Micronesia in May 2004, at the very least, continue to invest in equipment and train human assets so that the CNMI would always have a state-of-the-art telecommunications system. I also insisted that toll charges throughout Saipan, Rota and Tinian be eliminated so that a call from Susupe, Saipan, to Songsong Village, Rota, was the same cost as a call from Susupe to Chalan Kanoa on Saipan. In order to create a competitive market for telecommunications between the CNMI and the rest of the world, I also insisted that we break the monopoly on the fiber-optic cable. These were just a few of my concerns.

Divestiture is Key to Competition in the Market: The sale of Verizon Micronesia in 2004 was historic for the Commonwealth. It was the first sale over which the Commonwealth Telecommunications Commission (CTC) had presided since it was established by Public Law 12-39. It was the first time the people of the Commonwealth had the opportunity to determine to whom the essential telecommunications assets on which we all depend should be entrusted, and under what terms those assets should be operated. As governor, my duty was to ensure that the sale of Verizon Micronesia was in the public's best interest.

The intent of P.L. 12-39 was to ensure the protection of the telecommunications rights of everyone in the Commonwealth, and to protect the public interest. I had, therefore, exercised extreme diligence to protect the interests of the people and the Commonwealth throughout the entire proceedings. My concern had been heightened because of the virtual monopoly held by the owner of the sole fiber-optic cable connecting our islands to the rest of the world. It was evident that this monopoly had led to pricing structures that were anti-competitive and anti-business and that had, in effect, stunted economic growth.

Petition Filed with the FCC: On June 17, 2002, my Office filed a petition before the Federal Communications Commission (FCC) to deny the application for the sale of Verizon to PTI, which had been filed April 11. Before the commission could consider my Administration's petition, however, it would first have to make a declaratory ruling based on the Communications Act of 1934 to permit indirect foreign ownership exceeding 25% in a Common Carrier Licensee, and to allow Verizon to transfer control of the license held by MTC and its wholly owned subsidiary, GTE Pacifica, from Bell Atlantic New Zealand Holdings, Inc. Our petition to deny the application was based on concern that foreign ownership could jeopardize U.S. national security, as well as public safety. PTI also failed to show that such transfer of ownership was in the best interest of the public, and to prove that it was technically and financially qualified to operate the Commonwealth's telecommunications network.

In a separate statement before the CTC on February 3, 2005, I stressed the importance of telecommunications to our islands' economic progress. By "telecommunications," I meant state-of-the-art quality of service at a globally competitive price. I impressed upon the commission that divestiture was key to competition in the marketplace. My reasoning follows.

Verizon is a monopoly. It dominates the CNMI's telecommunications industry. Verizon's monopoly is anti-business, and hurts the CNMI's security. Verizon's monopoly on the cable stunts the CNMI's economic growth more than any other aspect of a monopoly. All internet communications, long-distance calls and most cellular calls must travel over this cable, regardless of which company offers the service or whether the communication is within one island. E-mail from the Attorney General's office to the legislature must still travel to California. Cellular calls within Saipan are switched in Guam for some companies. All other providers must lease from Verizon. Verizon increases costs and limits capacity when Verizon charges more than $7,000 for a T1 line from Saipan to Guam. The same service from Guam to Los Angeles costs around $1,500. Verizon used this monopoly to limit competition in the CNMI for other services. This monopoly must be changed. The current situation is unsafe and anti-business.

There are few industries that impact our community and its economic growth as profoundly as telecommunications. Almost everyone makes or receives phone calls, e-mails, text messages or other communications sent through the telecommunications system. Moreover, this system is one of the first factors any businessman considers when deciding whether to invest in the Commonwealth. Without a state-of-the-art, reliable, reasonably-priced telecommunications system, individuals and businesses, and our economy, will suffer.

The CMI Administration's Conditions on the Sale: As governor, my goals throughout the negotiations and proceedings before the CTC were straightforward. First and foremost, I wanted to end the inter-island toll. I also wanted to ensure that the employees were protected, that the latest technology was brought to our islands, that phone rates were not increased, that the people of the Commonwealth benefited from increased competition, that the purchasers of Verizon Micronesia had adequate plans and support, that we knew how this transition was being funded, and the effects of any financing on future operations.

The following are some of the demands I made, which PTI agreed to fulfill, and which I then presented to the CTC for review and action.

1. End Inter-Island Long-Distance Charges: As noted above, a call from Susupe to Songsong Village on Rota should cost no more than a call from Susupe to Chalan Kanoa. PTI agreed to end long-distance charges between the islands, which had a profound and positive impact on the lives of our people.

2. PTI Will Make New Technology and Quality Commitments: I was very concerned that the new company might not continue the upgrades that Verizon Micronesia had made to its network over the years, because the financing of the transaction would encourage the new owners not to do so. Therefore, I insisted on and obtained a commitment to invest $20 million in capital improvements over the first five years of operations. PTI also agreed to implement quality standards for service and performance, and file quarterly reports to the CTC on whether those standards were being met. This would ensure that PTI lived up to the high standards that we all expected and have a right to demand.

3. Local Workers Will Be Protected: Verizon Micronesia (MTC) had historically been an employer that hired locally instead of bringing in workers from outside of the Commonwealth. I was very concerned that this policy would change with the transfer in ownership. PTI agreed to give a one-year guarantee of employment to existing employees, including benefits. PTI also agreed to maintain a workforce that consisted of a minimum of 85% resident workers for a minimum of five years, and to create a management training program so that they could rise through the ranks of the new company. This was very important, because it meant that as PTI expanded, more local workers would be hired. PTI had planned to add up to 300 jobs in the following three or four years.

4. PTI Will Not Raise Rates on Long-Distance Calls or Local Service: PTI agreed not to raise local phone rates for five years, which were

$19 per month for residences and $45 per month for businesses, and to justify all increases, which would have to be approved by CTC. PTI also promised not to raise long-distance rates above rate integration levels for five years.

5. New Competition Will Be Encouraged: Verizon Micronesia's (MTC) operations in the Commonwealth had a monopoly status and were anti-business, and this hurt the economy. My goal was to have a fully competitive telecommunications industry with all the resulting benefits of higher quality, lower prices, and more choices. PTI agreed to open up its network to allow competitors to lease access, like DSL, without having to replicate MTC's entire network.

6. Financial Protections Will Be Put In Place: PTI agreed that an independent auditor would make recommendations to the CTC to set working capital and capitalization requirements to ensure that PTI is run in a safe and sound manner. PTI agreed to comply with minimum requirements, which would be recommended by the auditor. Furthermore, PTI agreed to fund half of an audit to prove that, even in a worst-case scenario, it had sufficient funds for operations.

7. PTI agreed to an important ethical wall to separate the wholesale group, which can sell to competitors, from the retail group, which competes with those same competitors. PTI also agreed that the wholesale group would conduct all business at arm's length, and offer competitors the same deals as affiliates. Finally, PTI agreed to open its network to competitors on a wholesale basis, as had been done throughout the U.S. (Although PTI agreed to these demands, it offered no specific plans for actual implementation.)

8. New Technology: PTI agreed to install fiber-optic lines, upon request, to allow for greater data speeds for their customers. PTI also agreed to offer new services, such as ISDN Primary Rate Interface. (Although PTI agreed to these new technology demands, it offered no specific plans on how to implement the new offerings.)

9. Regulatory Support after Verizon: PTI agreed to a Transitional Services Agreement with Verizon Micronesia, which the CNMI Government and CTC would review. (The Transitional Services Agreement that PTI claimed it had with Verizon Micronesia was never produced.)

10. National Exchange Carrier Association: PTI agreed to join the National Exchange Carrier Association (NECA), which would provide additional support and funding to PTI.

11. CTC Funding: PTI agreed to support a bill that would increase funding of the CTC by four times. The bill also proposed to provide the Office of Consumer Counsel funds for telecommunications enforcement.

12. Information on Financing Arrangements: PTI agreed to provide the CNMI Government and CTC with all its financing documents prior to the sale of Verizon Micronesia being closed. (PTI offered only vague information about its financing.)
13. Board Membership: PTI agreed that it would provide the CNMI Government and CTC with written commitments regarding its board members and management.
14. Current Finances of PTI Applicants: PTI agreed that it would provide the CNMI Government and CTC with specific information about the finances of the PTI applicants, and audited financial and other reports from MTC for several years. In addition, PTI agreed that more information about Ricardo Delgado, the owner of PTI, would be provided if the auditor indicated it was necessary for the evaluation of the sale. (Only pro forma balance sheets for PTI applicants and one year's audited financial reports from MTC were offered.)

The CNMI Government could not force MTC to sell the cable, because MTC built it; but the CNMI could stop the transfer of the cable from MTC. All transfers are required to be in the public interest, and the transfer of the cable, as a monopoly, was not in anyone's interest, except PTI's.

In 1981, GTE Corporation, which became Verizon in 2000 upon its merger with Bell Atlantic Corporation, purchased all of MTC and was operating MTC continuously since that date. In June 2000, GTE and Bell Atlantic consummated a merger and formed Verizon. At that time, MTC became a wholly owned subsidiary of Verizon known as Verizon Micronesia. The purchase of MTC by GTE in 1981 required the approval of the CNMI Government, which at the time was granted in the form of legislation entitled "Franchise Agreement to the Micronesian Telecommunications Corporation for the Provision of Telecommunications Services." The CNMI Government recognized at the time that the reason that a government may grant a "franchise monopoly" would be in the case of the product or service being a natural monopoly, i.e., the market was too small to sustain more than one producer. Thus, a government may decide to simply give a producer a monopoly, so that the producer is convinced that there is an adequate market to achieve efficiency in sales.

In the case of the sale of Verizon Micronesia, Verizon Micronesia argued that it had a "franchise monopoly" by virtue of its franchise agreement which was authorized by the CNMI Government. However, in 2001, the Legislature in P.L. 12-39 dissolved, rescinded, and superseded the "franchise agreement," effective February 21, 2001. The Legislature clearly stated in its findings in P.L. 12-39,

> "...that the telecommunications industry has gone through phenomenal technological development in recent years. This industry

once considered a natural monopoly may not hold true anymore. The long distance telecommunications market has already been opened to some degree of competition. Under such circumstances, the Legislature finds an ever increasing need to ensure a smooth transition in the telecommunications market place in order to protect the interests of the consumer."

In 2004, the Micronesian Telecommunications Corporation had network facilities that were in excellent condition which included both satellite and fiber optic connectivity. MTC's outside plant was 100 percent buried cable and had approximately 24,000 access lines, with approximately 22,000 lines on the island of Saipan, 1,000 lines on the island of Rota, and 1,000 lines on the island of Tinian.

The 1996 installation of the deep-sea fiber optic cable connected the CNMI to the rest of the world. The deployment of the fiber optic cable required the complete upgrading of the transport network to digital interfaces with certain levels of capabilities. The fiber optic cable is a 12-strand single mode submarine cable that connects the islands of Guam, Saipan, Rota, and Tinian. It ensured that the islands had all the bandwidth required for the foreseeable future. MTC's internet service was officially launched in 1997. In addition to the fiber optic cable, MTC owned and operated two satellite earth stations, both located on Saipan, and a digital cellular network consisting of seven cell sites.

The 2004 book value of MTC's network and plant facilities was $104,175,217. In short, MTC was a complete, full-service telecommunications company that had been redesigned and rebuilt from the ground up.

Meeting with the Philippines President

My meeting with Philippines President Gloria Macapagal-Arroyo in Manila on July 31, 2002, was highly anticipated amid growing concerns by the Philippine Government involving working conditions in the CNMI, where 18,000 nonresident workers from the Philippines were living. The concerns included poor conditions, non-payment of wages, and the threat of federalization of immigration control. Because of local and federal concerns, the problems were already being addressed on a continuous basis by appropriate law enforcement agencies. Specific concerns discussed during our July meeting were the number of complaints and the lengthy processing time, and restrictions on employees' ability to move about freely. While the CNMI was challenged in that respect, I indicated to Pres. Arroyo that the laborers from the Philippines had made positive contributions to our community economically, socially and politically. My goal going into the meeting was to acknowledge occurrence of labor problems and to assure the Philippine Government that overseas workers were being treated well, that many of the problems had been addressed, and that the CNMI Government was continually working to address other problems and ultimately, to prevent them from happening again.

The improvements made involved putting in place a system within the CNMI Department of Labor that was fair, impartial and equitable. Dr. Jack A. Tenorio, the CNMI Secretary of Labor and one of several officials who accompanied me to the Philippines, explained in detail the efforts being made. He noted that the number of labor complaints was half that of 1999, and that processing time for complaints that used to span six months had been shortened to between 30 and 60 days. Pres. Arroyo was pleased to hear that conditions were changing for the better. She indicated that complaints from workers were the reason she visited Saipan when she was a senator, and that she was a strong critic of the CNMI on the reported poor labor conditions and practices taking place.

The meeting was historical, with practical underlying significance, involving a first-time meeting over controversial labor issues. These were issues of mutual concern whose time had come to be addressed at the highest levels of government. In effect, at least symbolically, we built a bridge between the CNMI and the people of the Philippines by way of this meeting. The hour-long visit was cordial and full of goodwill, with both sides looking forward to working together closely.

After meeting with the president, I met with Philippine Secretary of Labor and Employment Patricia Santo Tomas. We reached agreement on increasing the CNMI capacity to conduct National Council Licensure Exam (NCLEX) testing for would-be nurses who might otherwise travel to the U.S. Mainland for this. The arrangement is mutually beneficial, because the CNMI is closer, therefore costing less to undergo the examination; and because those who take the test in the CNMI will spend money while in the islands. Secretary Santo Tomas also noted that the Republic of the Philippines was interested in not only sending workers overseas, but that more Filipinos also might venture to invest in the Northern Marianas.

Governor Babauta meeting with the Prime Minister of Japan, Junichiro Koizumi, in Tokyo, Japan, on August 28, 2002, to promote tourism and opportunities for investment in the CNMI. The Japanese Ministry of Foreign Affairs in 2002 called the CNMI one of the "world's safest" destinations.

Meeting with Japan's Prime Minister

In September 2002, I traveled to Japan to meet with the prime minister, the Honorable Junichiro Koizumi. Tourism was the main focus of my meeting with the Prime Minister. Japan had long been the Northern Marianas' visitor industry mainstay. Close to 85% of our visitors at this time were coming from Japan. The challenge was that the CNMI was getting only 300,000 visitors per year out of 17 million Japanese who traveled abroad. We needed to go after them in marketing the CNMI, because they were not going to come on their own, given the competitiveness of tourism markets around the world.

The safety of Japanese tourists abroad was, and remains, a paramount concern of the Japan Government. The Ministry of Foreign Affairs, for example, monitors the relative safeness of different destinations. Our challenge was, and is still, to keep the CNMI on the list as one of the safest, if not the safest, destination for our visitors.

Meeting with Fiji's President

Fiji's President Josefa Iloilo and First Lady Adi Salaseini Kavu arrived in Saipan for their first visit ever, to attend a Leaders' Conference for the Third Annual National Day of Prayer held at Hopwood Junior High School in Chalan Piao. But their visit was anything but low-key. The president also met with me and Lt. Gov. Benavente, then with members of the Legislature, other community leaders, and representatives of the CNMI's Fijian community.

In our meeting, Pres. Iloilo shared his country's experience following the May 2000 attempted military coup. It affected Fiji's economy and the stability of the government, so the president worked to promote unity, cooperation and reconciliation between the various political factions to reestablish a stable government.

The president was 83 years old when he visited. He had served as a senator in the Fijian lawmaking body, and had been a longtime educator in Fiji's public school system. I hosted a dinner reception for the visiting dignitaries the day before they returned home.

Pacific Basin Development Council

The Pacific Basin Development Council (PBDC) was formally established on February 17, 1980, by a Memorandum of Understanding executed by the governors of the Northern Mariana Islands (Carlos S. Camacho), Guam (Paul M. Calvo), American Samoa (Peter Tali Coleman), and Hawaii (George R. Ariyoshi). The signing of the memorandum took place in Hawaii during a meeting of these governors, and representatives of federal agencies and the private sector. Their purpose was to identify and assess the development needs of the American Pacific Islands, and to examine various regional strategies that the governors could utilize in providing for the comprehensive economic and social development of their jurisdictions.

The council is a nonprofit corporation organized exclusively for purposes listed in Section 501(c) (3) of the Internal Revenue Code. The council serves as a joint agency of its member governments created, supported and directed by them. Its principal office is located in Hawaii, and all business matters are conducted by vote of its board of directors. In addition to the general statement of purpose, PBDC also exists to: (1) Identify and assess the economic and social development needs of the member jurisdictions, (2) Provide a research capability to address issues of importance within the jurisdictions, (3) Promote cooperation among members, the federal government, and the private sector in providing for the comprehensive development of these jurisdictions, (4) Collect and distribute beneficial information, and (5) Promote collective action to enhance the quality of life for all.

PBDC meets at least twice a year. The main, annual meeting is held somewhere in the region, at a time and location determined by members. Its Winter Meeting is generally held to coincide with the National Governors Association Winter Meeting in late February in Washington, D.C. A PBDC reception is traditionally held in conjunction with the governors' Winter Meeting.

While Resident Representative, I worked with PBDC on major issues that concerned the CNMI. The issues were not just about tapping into federal resources, they were also about goodwill involving the history of our islands, such as the unique role of the Navajo Code Talkers during World War II. (See section entitled Navajo Code Talkers.) As governor, I played a more direct role as a participating member of PBDC. I served as its president during my entire term. It was a pivotal time in the council's organizational life, a time when many felt it had outlived its usefulness. As president, I demonstrated that the council continued to be a critically important organization as a resource for its member jurisdictions. Under my leadership, PBDC pursued and accomplished three major initiatives:

1. The Midway Initiative of 2003. The Midway Initiative involved using the island of Midway as an alternate landing runway and a staging airfield in case of emergencies for the 500+ weekly flights between the West Coast/Hawaii and East Asia. However, this Initiative involved more than just dealing with emergencies, it illustrated the challenges of global competitiveness that involved technology, geography and demography.

    The availability of alternate route (diversionary) airports was an important consideration in the quantity and quality of air service in the Pacific, as well as the economic viability of mid-Pacific air routes. Without alternate landing sites, the weekly flights between the U.S. and Asia were under scrutiny. The operational option was the "Northern" route, using airports across Alaska and Siberia, but which that would likely reduce the number of flights through Hawaii and other insular areas.

    The PBDC was quick to point out that Midway Island also was a critical support facility for the U.S. Coast Guard missions, which include search and rescue, law enforcement and marine environmental protection. Midway was routinely being used as a staging airfield for evacuations of sick and injured seamen, particularly because of its proximity to trans-Pacific shipping routes. The council raised two key policy issues involving Midway: (1) Recognition of federal aid for the role of certain transoceanic airports, and (2) Expansion of the Airport Improvement component of the Military Airports Program to encompass transoceanic infrastructure, such as Midway's, as an alternate landing runway.

2. The Homeland Security Initiative of 2004. This initiative was important to the economic health of the island communities. It involved strategic preparedness that included a partnership with the Naval Postgraduate School, an annual senior executive seminar for review of homeland security policy priorities, and cabinet-level discussions with key officials. The initiative also involved plans for rapid regional response by identifying resources to fill gaps identified during the strategic planning process. And finally, identifying future needs in order to minimize risks. This involved the PBDC taking an active role in the Stevens Institute-led consortium and in the National Center for Secure and Resilient Maritime Commerce, a U.S. Department of Homeland Security designated Center of Excellence. PBDC's role provided direct access to island-relevant, direct economic benefits, such as the locating of a saltwater test bed in the region.

   The strategic preparedness process and PBDC's partnership with the various federal agencies yielded strong relationships among federal, state, military and territorial participants, which significantly furthered the safety and security of the Pacific region. Resulting from the annual reviews and technical seminars, PBDC developed and selected three priorities that directly benefit the Pacific region. One was the Chief Executive consultation system in which the objective was to connect a governor with a subject matter expert within 72 hours of a request. The second was to develop a Regional Public Health Alert Network in order to exchange, assess and address health threats using efficient and effective processes. The third was Risk Communication that increases the understanding of the Pacific and its role in national homeland security during an emergency.

3. Capacity-building of 2003. This was a mechanism to build capacity within the region to encompass several tracks with different outcomes, including on-site training for junior practitioners, specialty student internships at the Homeland Security Science and Technology Agency, an advanced course for senior homeland security/port security officials sponsored by the Center for Secure and Resilient Maritime Commerce, and staff support for the technical advisory committee members.

In total, these initiatives during my tenure as president of the council provided a 'Millennium Agenda' that was forward-looking, including mid- and long-term strategies, and was targeted, focused and proactive.

Chaba and a Trip to the Northern Islands

Tens of millions of dollars poured into the CNMI economy through the islands' recovery efforts in the aftermath of Super Typhoon Chaba. It had been one of the strongest to hit the Northern Marianas in recent years.

The devastation extended up and down the Marianas chain, including the northern islands of Alamagan, Pagan and Agrigan, where there were small numbers of people residing. The extent of destruction there could be determined only from reports received from residents, which triggered my wanting to see the damage firsthand. I flew on a chartered helicopter the very next day (August 22, 2004) for an aerial view of the three islands, and to meet the residents in person. In addition to emergency supplies already delivered to the islands – tents, cots, fuel, batteries, lanterns, etc. – I brought food, water and cigarettes. Due to time constraints for the return trip back to Saipan, I spent the night on Agrigan with the 12 people living there. It was a night to remember, camping on the beachside of the island next to a bonfire, eating fish and coconut crabs.

My request for a disaster declaration was granted only 96 hours after Chaba's visit, when President George W. Bush declared the CNMI a major disaster area. While recovery was still underway for residents and commercial establishments, they were aided by more than $36 million from the federal government. Of the $36 million total, more than $8.2 million went to assist 2,814 households with housing needs, and more than $4 million benefited 3,488 families with other needs. At the same time, the Small Business Administration (SBA) approved more than $4.68 million in low-interest loans to 136 individuals and several businesses. Public assistance programs received more than $9.3 million, with hazard mitigation programs getting more than $1.03 million.

The disaster declaration also paved the way for the CNMI to receive emergency food stamps under the Food and Nutrition Service program. This resulted in more than $2 million's worth, in one-time issuance, to 29,427 households on all three islands (24,510 for Saipan, 2,192 for Tinian, and 2,725 for Rota). In addition, other direct federal assistance administered by the Federal Emergency Management Agency (FEMA) provided hundreds of thousands of dollars in disaster relief supplies, such as tents, tarps, cots and camp kits, distributed immediately after the typhoon. In all, more than 110 representatives of FEMA, OSHA, SBA and other federal agencies were on the islands working with local officials on our recovery.

The CNMI Government, through its Workforce Investment Agency, applied for, and received $2 million in a National Emergency Grant from the U.S. Department of Labor to help residents displaced by the typhoon. The funding enabled the government to hire workers to fill temporary jobs cleaning up typhoon debris, assisting in flood prevention, mitigation, recovery efforts and repair work.

The Role of the Media

To have a free and open society, citizens must feel safe enough to express themselves. The First Amendment of the U.S. Constitution guarantees the protection of this freedom of expression. The first 10 Amendments of the constitution, the Bill of Rights, were ratified December 15, 1791. Our First Amendment right says, "Congress shall make no law respecting the establishment of religion, or prohibiting the free exercise thereof; or abridging the freedom of speech, or of the press, or the right of the people peaceably to assemble, and petition the Government for redress of grievances."

The media, therefore, plays the important role of facilitator in the dissemination of information to the general public. Throughout the many years I served as a public servant, and as a private citizen, I witnessed firsthand the role the media plays in the gathering of information and in conveying it to the public. Citizens expect the news to be reported in the most accurate, honest and impartial manner possible, and for newsgatherers to keep the integrity of the information, and the processing of the information for public consumption, intact. I could not have effectively communicated to the citizens of the Commonwealth the pertinent information on decisions I made, and actions I took as a public servant, without the media.

Resident Representative Babauta in an interview with an unidentified reporter in front of the White House in Washington, D.C., in December 1997.

Although the primary role of the media as a transmitter of information is of the highest priority, the media is also in the business of selling information in order to maintain its very existence. The financial survival of the news organizations, both print and electronic, creates a symbiotic business relationship between the news outlet and its advertisers that often results in the news organization walking a fine line while reporting information that may negatively impact a good, paying advertiser. The reporting of such news, therefore, is often done in a subdued manner in the interest of preserving that symbiotic business relationship. In the absence of such a business relationship, the news organization and the subject being reported find the intensity of coverage much more than subdued. This is especially true when the subject being reported is a public figure whose beliefs are fundamentally different from, or opposite to, those of the news organization. In many places, not just in the CNMI, it is difficult to discern reporting the news factually from editorializing the news. Objective reporting is difficult anywhere, and the CNMI is no exception. At the "micro" level, more often than not, there is a personal connection between a reporter and the subject about which he/she is writing. This is a situation that is simply unavoidable. News organizations have a difficult and challenging task if the goal is to report the news free of personal, professional, or even cultural, bias. In the CNMI, reporting the news free of personal, or political, or cultural bias, is nearly impossible. Inherently, the news is reported with varying levels of bias.

The late journalist, Frank S. Rosario, once told me that a picture could easily be interpreted five different ways by five different people looking at it at the same time. Similarly, even a car accident could be reported differently by five people witnessing the same accident from the same spot.

Reporting is no less an honorable profession than a doctor caring for the sick. However, there are good reporters just as there are good doctors, and ... this doesn't mean, however, that just because we live in an imperfect world, we shouldn't be striving for excellence. An elected public official is no more honorable than a reporter, for they serve the same master. We can do better by constantly reminding ourselves that in a free society, expressing our personal opinions is essential, and guaranteed by the First Amendment. We also must remember that this freedom bears responsibility, has boundaries. For example, is making false and malicious accusations against an individual or a group of people a protected expression? Scholars have argued that the First Amendment did not intend to protect all kinds of speech, particularly libelous speech or publications. Rather, it has been widely accepted that freedom of speech and press, exercised responsibly, promotes individual growth and human dignity.

Perspectives on the Covenant

In the chronicles of the history of the Covenant, I have found one person's perspective that mirrors mine. It was in July 1975, when the Covenant was approved by the House Committee on Interior and Insular Affairs and the U.S. House of Representatives, in House Joint Resolution 549. On the floor of the House, Congressman Don H. Clausen (R-CA), just before passage of the Joint Resolution on July 21, declared: "The political, legal, and social precedents to be established with approval of the Marianas Covenant are salient. Foremost, a new system of local government, unique in the annals of U.S. history, will be enacted."

Euphoria had filled the air over the Northern Mariana Islands about their new political relationship with the United States of America since NMI voters chose overwhelmingly to approve the Covenant. In the U.S. Congress, however, there were members who felt that the NMI was no different from any of the States in the Union, or any of the other insular area jurisdictions. Many saw the Covenant as an experiment with a shelf life to be arbitrarily determined by the Congress. Federal laws trump local laws, the NMI Constitution, and at times, even certain provisions of the Covenant. In my 12 years in Washington, D.C. as the Resident Representative, I never heard any member of Congress refer to the Covenant as "unique," other than Congressman Clausen. I had many meetings and dealings with officials from federal agencies, including the Department of the Interior and the White House, and the word "unique" was never used when referring to the Covenant. The word was muffled in Washington.

The Covenant is, in fact, unique, because Section 105 of the Covenant requires the consent of both the U.S. and CNMI governments to change its mutual consent provisions, namely Articles I, II and III, and Sections 501 and 805. The Covenant is also different in that it was freely negotiated by representatives of the people of the NMI and the U.S. Government, with both sides having equal status in the negotiations.

Another perspective on the Covenant was articulated by Ruth Harris in her testimony at the hearing of the U.S. Senate Committee on Interior and Insular Affairs in Washington, D.C., on July 24, 1975, regarding Commonwealth status for the Northern Mariana Islands and the political status of Micronesia. At the hearing, Ms. Harris asked rhetorically,

> "Should this committee and, subsequently, the Senate, approve the commonwealth covenant? Our answer is no, and certainly not without considering the matter. We are dismayed that very few Americans, including very few congresspersons, even know where Micronesia is and the Marianas are located, let alone what is involved in the commonwealth covenant. We are dismayed that the House of Representatives approved the covenant by voice vote, with only 25 members present and voting. Your committee has held one day of hearings, which we also believe to be inadequate."

She asked a second question: "Why do we feel commonwealth status should not be approved?" And proceeded to answer,

Resident Representative Babauta with Haydn Williams, the President's personal representative in the Covenant negotiations, in the Resident Representative's office in Washington, D.C.

> "It is our belief that the United States, looking after its own interests rather than those of the Micronesian people, has instead fostered economic and cultural dependence among the people of Micronesia and is now moving toward acquisition of their territory instead of fostering a new independent nation."

Ms. Harris concluded her statement before the Committee by saying that U.S. military strategists applied the "divide and conquer" technique by negotiating separately with one part of Micronesia, the Northern Marianas. America, she said, "turned its back on the United Nations' understanding that Micronesia was to be treated as a whole."

Ruth Harris was a staff member of the Board of Global Ministries of the United Methodist Church. At the Senate hearing, she spoke on behalf of the Women's Division of the board.

A similar view was presented by Jose A. Cabranes of Puerto Rico. He testified that,

> "The separation of the Northern Marianas from the rest of Micronesia runs counter to paragraph 6 of the United Nations Declaration on the Granting of Independence to Colonial Countries and Peoples [Resolution 1514 (XV) of the UN General Assembly]: Any attempt aimed at partial or total disruption of the national unity and the territorial integrity of a country is incompatible with the purposes and principles of the Charter of the United Nations."

Jose A. Cabranes was a member of the Bar of the State of New York, and the Bar of the District of Columbia. At the hearing, he represented The International League for the Rights of Man under the auspices of the United Nations Educational, Scientific and Cultural Organization (UNESCO). He is now a judge of the U.S. Court of Appeals for the Second Circuit.

The CNMI stumbled on local control of immigration. Immigration controlled the CNMI. We hit bumps along the way with the millions of dollars in financial assistance from the U.S. Government; we could have managed those funds better. We were preoccupied with the small projects, and lost sight of the bigger and more important ones. There have been challenges and disappointments, even to this day, in regards to the CNMI-U.S. relationship, but even with all the shortcomings and misgivings associated with this political union, those from the NMI who participated in the negotiations of the Covenant chose right. It is great to be a part of the U.S.A.

The Judiciary: Appointments, Pardons, and the Commemorative Celebration

The enactment of the Commonwealth Judiciary Act in 1978 created the Commonwealth Trial Court that served the CNMI until 1989. Appeals arising from the Trial Court were taken to the U.S. District Court for the Northern Mariana Islands. In 1989, eleven years after the Trial Court was created, the Legislature approved the Commonwealth Judicial Reorganization Act, which created the Commonwealth Supreme Court and renamed the Trial Court the Superior Court. Since May 2004, by virtue of Section 403(a) of the Covenant, decisions of the Commonwealth Supreme Court are no longer heard by the U.S. Court of Appeals for the Ninth Circuit; those decisions now are either final or are appealed directly to the U.S. Supreme Court.

One of the many responsibilities the governor has pursuant to the Constitution and laws of the CNMI is the appointment of judges to the Commonwealth courts, with the advice and consent of the Senate. The persons appointed as judges must meet the requirements set forth in the CNMI Constitution and laws. Appointment of judges is not an easy task if you are looking for someone you think would make a good judge. Beyond the legal requirements, I would be less than candid if I did not admit that my appointments of judges were greatly influenced by my own personal philosophy about the judicial system. A good judge is a person deeply committed to the rule of law, but at the same time, possesses compassion and humility. A good judge also is a person who understands fully that laws are made by human beings, just like you and me, who are inherently imperfect. A good judge is not arrogant and self-centered. These were my guiding principles when I appointed three judges to the CNMI bench.

My first appointment was Associate Judge Robert C. Naraja to be the Presiding Judge of the CNMI Superior Court, a position vacated by retiring Presiding Judge Edward D. Manibusan. My second appointment was Ramona

V. Manglona as Associate Judge of the Superior Court. Prior to her appointment, she had served as the CNMI's first female Attorney General. My third appointment, also for Associate Judge of the Superior Court, was Kenneth L. Govendo, a lawyer in private practice for as long as I could remember. In subsequent years, all three of my appointments were affirmed by the people; they have been retained in their respective retention elections. Presiding Judge Naraja and Judge Govendo are still with the Superior Court, while Judge Manglona is now Chief Judge of the U.S. District Court for the Northern Mariana Islands.

Resident Representative Juan Babauta and Presiding Judge of the Superior Court Alexandro C. Castro, who became Chief Justice of the CNMI Supreme Court on October 11, 2012.

In addition to the power to appoint judges, the CNMI Constitution, under Executive Functions in Article III, Section 9, also gives the governor "the power to grant reprieves, commutations and pardons after conviction for offenses and after consultation between the Governor and the board of parole." This is a very powerful grant of authority given to the governor. When exercised, it is a power that ostensibly nullifies the action by the court in a criminal case. As governor, I pardoned two individuals with misdemeanor convictions. Having exercised the power to pardon, I am not one to question the immense power that the governor has, but to simply raise the rationale and wisdom of such authority. While I understand fully that this is a grant of power given to the governor from the people, the power to adjudicate cases rests with the Judiciary in fair and impartial court proceedings. For one person, that person being a governor, to be armed with such an executive power, and by the stroke of a pen able to nullify a decision of the court, makes futile the decision of the judicial system. While I believe in giving criminals a second chance to assimilate back into the community, I also believe that such authority should be restrained.

On May 3, 2004, the Judicial Branch of the CNMI Government celebrated increased self-governance and autonomy with a Commemorative Celebration marking the day on which the CNMI Supreme Court became an appeals court of last resort, except for cases appealed to the U.S. Supreme Court. The CNMI Supreme Court now has the same standing as the supreme courts of the 50 states, in which appeals arising from it go directly to the U.S. Supreme Court. Prior to May 2004, appeals from the CNMI Supreme Court were heard by the U.S. Court of Appeals for the Ninth Circuit. The Ninth Circuit is the largest appellate circuit in the U.S., a circuit that includes Alaska, Arizona, California, Hawaii, Idaho, Montana, Nevada, Oregon, Washington,

Guam and the CNMI. There had been numerous cases in the past that were appealed to the Ninth Circuit; those cases will stand as adjudicated.

The keynote speaker at the Commemorative Celebration was Chief Judge Mary M. Schroeder of the U.S. Court of Appeals for the Ninth Circuit. She pointed out that the CNMI was celebrating judicial independence by ending an era of the current judicial system and starting another. The next era, she said, would bring greater responsibility by building a new tradition without review by a higher court, except by the U.S. Supreme Court. What that meant in practical terms, according to Judge Govendo, is that almost all ordinary legal matters will start in the CNMI Superior Court and, if appealed, will end in the CNMI Supreme Court. Section 403(a) of the Covenant states that for the first 15 years after the establishment of a Northern Marianas appeals court, the U.S. Court of Appeals for the Ninth Circuit will have jurisdiction to hear appeals from the NMI appeals court.

The district courts, as in the case of the U.S. District Court for the Northern Mariana Islands, are created by Congress. They serve as the trial courts in the federal judicial system. It is in these courts that most federal cases are first tried and decided. Often referred to as the circuit courts, the Courts of Appeals are divided geographically into 12 circuits. The jurisdiction of these courts covers appeals from the District Courts and appeals from actions of government agencies. There also is a Court of Appeals for the Federal Circuit, with a nationwide jurisdiction and which reviews lower court rulings in, among other things, patent, trademark and copyright cases. Also, there are several special courts of the U.S. that have jurisdiction over specialized subjects. The jurisdiction of each court is indicated by its title. For example, the U.S. Claims Court hears various kinds of claims against the U.S.; the Court of International Trade hears claims against the government arising from federal laws that govern imports and importation, and so forth.

Federal Territorial Policy

A federal policy is needed that defines the future of U.S.-territorial relations. There has not been a clear statement of policy for years, at least since I first went to Washington, D.C. as Resident Representative in January 1990. The Department of the Interior has been inconsistent at best about its role in territorial and insular area affairs. The perception that Interior serves as an advocate for the territories is incorrect. Rather, that department's role is to advocate for and implement the president's and his Administration's policies for the territories. The Interior department represents the president, not the territories or any particular insular jurisdiction. Interior's role in this may often work against the territories.

Similarly, according to Arnold H. Leibowitz in "The Applicability of Federal Law to Guam," published in the *Virginia Journal of International Law* in 1975,

"The term 'organic act' has a traditional reference point in American law, such that the standard relationship between an unincorporated territory governed by an organic act and the federal government typically works to the territory's disadvantage. It has been accepted over time, in the case of Guam and other unincorporated lands, that the U.S. Department of the Interior has the legal right and the practical duty (a) to represent the territory before the executive and legislative branches; (b) to review various expenditures in the territory; and (c) to play a direct administrative and supervisory role in certain specific areas."

The same could be argued in the case of the CNMI. Although the Covenant was negotiated between the Northern Mariana Islands and the United States, the Covenant was ultimately approved by the U.S. Congress and thus is an Organic Act, and the powers of the CNMI contained in it are a grant of power by the Congress. Therefore, this places the CNMI in the same predicament as Guam, American Samoa, the U.S. Virgin Islands and Puerto Rico.

The broad role of the Department of the Interior when it comes to territorial matters is muddied, which explains the lack of a uniform, coordinated federal policy for all the insular areas. Puerto Rico, for example, often is treated separately from the rest of the insular areas. In the case of the Northern Mariana Islands, the U.S. did not do a good job as the administering authority for the Trust Territory of the Pacific Islands under the Trusteeship Agreement. That is why the six districts of the Trust Territory all went their separate ways. The Greek root of the word "govern" means "to steer." This is a common theme in all the insular jurisdictions; each wants to steer its own political and economic future. Each territorial government aspires to be economically self-sufficient with increased self-government. The territories consider their political status "colonial" under the U.S. Each one believes that in this day and age, the U.S. should and must shed itself from its status as a colonial empire.

Who defines U.S. territorial policies? Is it the Congress, or the president, or both? Shouldn't the territorial governments be involved in defining U.S. territorial policies? It's a question that is frequently asked, not only because the territories find themselves not being involved, but even if they were, it is not clear what guiding principles the federal government would be guided by in the formulation of territorial policies. This is likely the reason for the absence of a consistent and clear policy. Thus, it is the view of this writer that the formulation of territorial policies should be guided by the following principles.

1. Increasing the Interior department's control over the insular areas is inconsistent with the goal of self-government.
2. Self-government empowers the insular area governments.
3. All departments of the federal government should become aware of their respective responsibilities for programs in the insular areas.

4. The economic and social development of the insular areas is paramount.
5. A disenfranchised community of people within the American political family is inconsistent with U.S. democratic values.

Roles of the Interior department:

The Department of the Interior was created in March 1849 by Congress as the "home department" with the responsibility of advancing U.S. domestic interests. Some 130 years later, the Carter Doctrine announced a framework for a comprehensive federal territorial policy towards Guam, American Samoa, the U.S. Virgin Islands and the CNMI. The policy announcement was a commitment of the federal government to encourage the self-determined political, economic and social development of the territories. The same year, the Office of Territorial and International Affairs was created within the Interior department, headed by an Assistant Secretary. This Assistant Secretary served as the principal advisor to the Secretary on all insular matters.

Governor Babauta and Deputy Assistant Secretary of the Interior for Insular Affairs David B. Cohen in March 2004 sign a grant agreement of $11 million for Capital Improvement Projects in the CNMI for FY 2004. Also in the picture from the CNMI are Resident Representative Pedro A. Tenorio and, L to R, Senators Joseph Mendiola, Henry H. San Nicolas, Thomas P. Villagomez, Luis P. Crisostimo, and Joaquin G. Adriano.

President Ronald Reagan issued Executive Order 12572 on November 3, 1986, on "Relations with the Northern Mariana Islands." It read in part, "The relations of the United States with the Government of the Northern Mariana Islands shall, in all matters not the program responsibility of another Federal department or agency, be under the general administrative supervision of the Secretary of the Interior."

Factors that Play a Role in Determining U.S. Territorial Policy:

A. Geographical location, size, culture and political history of the territory.

American Samoa is an unincorporated and unorganized territory. Because it is unincorporated, not all U.S. Constitutional provisions apply. According to the 1999 Report on the State of the Islands prepared by the Interior department, American Samoa is an unorganized territory because the Congress has not provided American Samoa with an Organic Act similar to that of Guam. The American Samoans are nationals of the United States but not U.S. citizens. Congress defines by legislation the relationship between American Samoa and the federal government. By law, the Secretary of the Interior has plenary authority over American Samoa. The American Samoan Constitution can be amended only through an act of Congress. This is different when compared to the CNMI; the CNMI Constitution can be changed by the people of the Northern Marianas through different ways, as specified in the CNMI Constitution.

The American Samoan economy relies in part on Section 936 of the federal tax code. Section 936 is an exemption from paying federal income taxes that is extended to corporations which invest in American Samoa, similar to the exemption that applied to Puerto Rico before 1996. Tourism in American Samoa is very small compared to the other territories. American Samoa is looking to diversify its economy due to the decline of its tuna cannery industry. American Samoa is still the most traditional in culture among the territories.

The political relationship between the Northern Mariana Islands and the United States is defined in Article I, Sections 101 through 105, and in Section 501 of the Covenant. That relationship is such that, as stated in Sections 101, 102 and 104, the CNMI is under U.S. sovereignty, and the CNMI is bound by the Covenant and certain provisions of the U.S. Constitution, treaties, and laws. The Covenant in Sections 103, 105 and 201 grants and respects the right of local self-government under a constitution of the CNMI's own making. However, Article II, Sections 201 to 204, and Sections 501 and 805 of the Covenant impose certain requirements on the contents of the CNMI Constitution. And, as stated in Section 105 of the Covenant, while the U.S. Congress can enact legislation applicable to the CNMI, if such legislation cannot also be made applicable to the states, the CNMI must be specifically mentioned for the legislation to be effective in the CNMI. Congress gave up some of its legislative power by agreeing to the mutual consent requirement in Section 105 for modifying Articles I, II, and III, and Sections 501 and 805 of the Covenant. The relationship is further defined in Section 104 by entrusting to the U.S. complete responsibility for foreign affairs and defense matters affecting the Northern Mariana Islands.

The CNMI is actively being pursued by the U.S. military for more land in addition to the 7,203 hectares it has leased on Tinian. The CNMI economy relies heavily on tourism and on the projected revenue from the approved exclusive casino license on Saipan.

Pres. Reagan's Executive Order No. 12572 dealt with the relations between the U.S. Government and the Government of the Northern Mariana Islands. Thus, the relations between the two governments are, in part, under the "general administrative supervision" of the Interior department, but the CNMI Government itself is not under the same kind of supervision by that department. (See Addendum K., Executive Order 12572.)

The Spanish-American War led to the U.S. acquisition of Guam. By virtue of the Treaty of Paris of 1898 between the U.S. and Spain which ended that war, and the Organic Act of 1950, Guam is under U.S. sovereignty. Guam is an unincorporated, organized territory. Because it is unincorporated, not all of the provisions of the U.S. Constitution apply to Guam. It is organized because the Guam Organic Act enacted by Congress in 1950 provides for the establishment of the territory's governmental institutions. The Organic Act was amended by P.L. 90-497, which Congress passed on September 1, 1968, giving the voters of Guam, beginning in 1970, the right to elect their own governor and lieutenant governor to four-year terms, with a limit of two successive terms.

Politically, Guam is still pursuing a status that would be based on self-determination. Guam has always felt that its current political status is not of its own choosing. In his 1975 article, "The Applicability of Federal Law to Guam," Leibowitz stated that the Guam Organic Act "is the basic document setting forth the relationship between Guam and the federal government. The Organic Act does not even in theory take its powers from the people of Guam." Thus, the Guam Commission on Self-Determination was established in 1997 to examine the territory's future political status options, and to support greater self-government for Guam. It has now been nearly 20 years since the commission was established, but thus far, its efforts have not led to a status plebiscite. Whatever the reason for this, the people of Guam will not rest until they feel that they had their say, as far as their political future is concerned, by exercising their right of self-determination.

Guam's economy is driven, in part, by the island's expanding military presence; the military already holds about one-third of the land on Guam. In addition to the military presence, the growing tourism industry continues to play a vital role in Guam's economy.

The Spanish-American War also led to the U.S. acquisition of Puerto Rico. The Treaty of Paris of 1898, which ended that war, placed Puerto Rico (and Guam and the Philippines) under U.S. sovereignty. The Foraker Act, officially known as the Organic Act of 1900, established a civil government for Puerto Rico, giving the island its status as an organized territory. In the case of Downes v. Bidwell (1901), the U.S. Supreme Court ruled that Puerto Rico was an unincorporated U.S. territory. The Jones Act of 1917 granted U.S. citizenship to all persons born in Puerto Rico.

Puerto Rico is the largest and most populated of all the territories. It is also the most politically active in its quest for a permanent political status. Like other territorial jurisdictions, the political movement for change in Puerto Rico is for increased autonomy. The political status options Puerto Ricans are considering are independence, commonwealth and statehood.

Under the Puerto Rico Commonwealth Government beginning in the 1950s, because of Section 936 of the U.S. Tax Code, the Puerto Rico branches of U.S. companies were exempted from paying U.S. corporate income taxes. As a result, manufacturing – especially in pharmaceuticals, medical equipment, and electronics – expanded greatly. These "936 companies" included Johnson & Johnson, and Abbott Laboratories. However, because of a law signed by Pres. Clinton in 1996, the exemptions were scheduled to be eliminated over a nine-year period that began in 1996 and ended in 2005. The ending of these tax breaks contributed significantly to a recession in Puerto Rico that has not ended.

The Virgin Islands are an unincorporated, organized territory of the United States. Because it is unincorporated, not all federal laws and not all the parts of the U.S. Constitution apply. It is governed by The Organic Act of the Virgin Islands of the United States of 1936, passed by Congress on June 22, 1936. As with the other U.S. territories, the Virgin Islands are also under U.S. sovereignty. A distinguishing difference is that the Virgin Islands are the only insular territory that the U.S. actually purchased.

Persons born in the Virgin Islands are U.S. citizens. Congress amended The Organic Act of 1936 on July 22, 1954, creating a unicameral legislature for the Virgin Islands. Congress did not provide for an elected governor until 1968, when it enacted P.L. 90-496. Similar to the other territories, the Virgin Islands Commission on Status and Federal Relations, established March 22, 1988, monitors the pulse of the people pushing for a change in the territory's political status. A status referendum was scheduled for September 1993, but had to be postponed due to a hurricane that struck on September 17. When the referendum was finally held on October 11, it was deemed inconclusive because it had not garnered the required percentage of eligible voters required by referendum rules.

The Virgin Islands rely heavily on tourism. But as with the rest of the territories, there is an inherent weakness in relying solely on the visitor industry. Maintaining and improving the tourism industry is important, but the Virgin Islands want to find new ways to foster greater economic stability.

B. Strategic military and other strategic interests.

Should the U.S. relinquish control over the vast area of the Western

Pacific? It's a rhetorical question intended to generate discussion, not on whether the U.S. should actually give it up or keep it, but on the question of why the U.S. might want to keep it, for other than military interests. The U.S. has been interested in the Marianas for military purposes since at least the Spanish-American War in 1898. The value of the island chain is that it provides strategic stepping stones in the Western Pacific relative to the Philippines, Japan and China. After World War II, the U.S. drafted the Trusteeship Agreement to retain complete control of the region, used the Marshall Islands for nuclear bomb testing, and used Guam as a B-52 base for air bombing raids in Vietnam and Cambodia during the Vietnam War. Military value was the primary U.S. concern during the Northern Marianas Covenant negotiations, not economic value. It is a strategic denial of the region to any other power, and the ability to use the islands for military exercises, such as bombing on Farallon de Medinilla, using Tinian as an island amphibious invasion tactics practice area, and the U.S. right of eminent domain anywhere in the CNMI, a right specifically and deliberately written in Section 806 of the Covenant. In the post-Cold War period, U.S. military needs changed, but the strategic value of the Marianas, including Guam, remained extremely important for contingency purposes to replace military bases lost in Southeast Asia. The Marianas, including Guam, also have strategic military value for U.S. actions opposing China's claims of sovereignty over most of the South China Sea. Tinian also serves U.S. strategic needs by hosting the Voice of America transmitter on the island.

Was the U.S. overly anxious to resolve the Micronesian Trusteeship issues to the detriment of self-government? It would be a stretch to argue this point to the contrary. In the article, "The Northern Mariana Islands: Where America's Day Begins," Retzler (1996) writes,

> "In classified memos and interviews, many key military officials noted that denying the islands to other countries was a crucial incentive for affiliation [with the U.S.]. For example, in an appeal to the Senate shortly after WWII, General Dwight D. Eisenhower referred to Micronesian islands as sandpits, but added that it was important to make them our sandpits."

The central problems are economic. A strong economic base is a constant challenge for the political and social development of the insular areas. Without it, there will always be questions raised about their political future and their relationships with the U.S. Insufficient social development also undermines the credibility of the relationship. In the CNMI and Guam, the presence of the military is part of the economic puzzle that remains an option. To other insular areas, a military-driven economy is not an option, because of their geographic location. In American Samoa, for example, the military has no strategic interest in that part of the world. In the CNMI, the military controls two-thirds of the island of Tinian, but there is no active military presence to support the local economy in a meaningful way. This could change, however, if the military is successful in its expressed interest in acquiring the island of Pagan, just 70 miles north of Saipan. But this endeavor is creating anxiety among CNMI residents. There is a growing concern that they are losing control over their islands, and especially control over ownership and use of land. Furthermore, the people in the CNMI want jobs, but there is concern that Pagan may end up like Tinian, creating no jobs on which to build an economy.

C. Develop a uniform policy for all territories and commonwealths.
Free Association status for all, and end colonialism. From an international perspective, the U.S. should have supported a freely associated status for all of Micronesia. Free association status would save U.S. taxpayers from concerns regarding funding.

Economic self-reliance should be made a uniform policy for all, and be the top policy priority. If self-reliance is made the No. 1 priority for all the insular areas, should they not be placed under the administrative oversight of the Economic Development Administration of the U.S. Department of Commerce?

D. What should Congress focus on?
  1. Self-government, with voting representation in Congress. The question associated with the representation issue is whether the U.S. Constitution follows the flag. U.S. courts and the Congress have interpreted the Constitution to mean that incorporation as a territory implies a promise of statehood. Is voting representation so preciously tied to statehood that maintaining colonial status is better than giving the territorial delegates in the House of Representatives voting rights? How can the flag of the U.S. fly proudly in sovereign dominion over the territories, but not be accompanied by all provisions of the Constitution? How can the territories belong to the U.S., but not be part of the U.S.? How can the United States create a system of dominion over the territories with a clear conscience? Is the incorporation of the territories a threat to the way of life enjoyed by the 50 states? If the brave men at Gettysburg and on other battlefields during the Civil War who died so that this nation might live, why is that any different from the brave men from the insular territories who also died in wars so that this nation might live?
  2. Extension of Voting Rights. The Congress can extend voting rights to the residents of the insular areas in the same way that it

extended voting rights to the residents of the District of Columbia. The 23rd Amendment to the Constitution gave the D.C. residents the right to vote in presidential elections. That voting right was ratified in 1961, and the residents exercised this right for the first time in 1964. If the insular areas get that voting right, this would not have to upset CNMI relations with the U.S. under the Covenant.

3. Establishment of a Constitution that is the making of each territory.
4. Economic development and job training in the private sector. The CNMI is especially vulnerable in both these areas. Tourism is currently the mainstay of the CNMI economy, but the seasonal nature of the industry is such that the Commonwealth cannot depend on it on a sustained and consistent basis. Thus, the CNMI gambled its economic future on the exclusive casino license on Saipan, which many in the CNMI, as well as outside, feel has an uncertain future. It is as unpredictable as the casino industry in Atlantic City, New Jersey. The future of the casino industry in the CNMI is an important topic in discussions between the federal government and the CNMI in regards to training local U.S. citizens to replace all the nonresident workers holding CNMI-only CW-1 work permits. (P.L. 113-235 requires that this CW-1 program end in December 2019.) With the removal of the discretionary authority of the Secretary of Labor to extend the CW-1 program in the CNMI, the future of the CNMI-only CW-1 work permit program is in the hands of Congress.

Eighteen months after the U.S. Secretary of Labor on June 3, 2014, extended the CW-1 program for five years, it still was not clear how much the CNMI had to report on the training of U.S. eligible workers to replace the CW-1 nonresident workers. Even if the next president's Administration were to agree to extend the CW-1 program beyond December 2019 for another five years, there is nothing the president could do unless Congress acts. Observers in the CNMI believe that the current (114th) Congress is unlikely to act, given the political climate in Washington over immigration reform and the prospects of a power shift in the White House (after the 2016 elections). Given this scenario, Congress would expect the CNMI to bring in U.S. citizens to replace the nonresident workers. It is a legitimate expectation, because even if every U.S. eligible worker in the CNMI were hired, it wouldn't be enough to fill all the jobs that would be vacated by the nonresident workers. The question is whether it is reasonable to recruit from the U.S. mainland when wages are much lower in the CNMI.

E. Federal policy options for the territories.
 1. Place all the territories under the U.S. Department of Commerce.
 2. Place all the territories under the White House, handled by an assistant to the president. An October 2008 report prepared for the CNMI Government and funded by the Interior department entitled Economic Impact of Federal Laws on the Commonwealth of the Northern Mariana Islands, stated,

 > "The territories' access to and participation in Executive Branch policy-making is limited and fragmented. The Executive Branch's ability to articulate and follow consistent policies to promote economic development and self-reliance in the territories has been narrow and inadequate to the task at hand."

 Furthermore, the report stated, "Congress regularly deals with trade and investment policies in ways that harm the economic development prospects of the territories." Obviously, Congress pays little attention to the territories. The Interior department sponsors conferences and provides technical assistance that take the territories nowhere. The Commerce department's Economic Development Administration, having no focus on the territories, is interested only in world economic competitiveness. The Defense department, though very focused on certain territories, namely the CNMI and Guam, is in those territories only to take away more lands from the natives for military purposes. Furthermore, not one U.S. president has ever visited the CNMI since the termination of the Trust Territory of the Pacific Islands. It is for these reasons, and more, that a political status referendum for all the territories should be conducted every 15 years. This may be the only way to get Washington's attention.
 3. Stop the policy of the territories being beholden to Washington because Washington controls the funding and the policies that affect the territories.
 4. Establish a federally mandated funding formula for all the territories: 70% federal funding share for all programs the 50 states are eligible for, i.e., highway funding, food stamps, Supplemental Security Income (SSI), and so forth. The territories will deal with the remaining 30%. The motive behind this recommendation is borne from the not-so-often-asked question: When is the benefit of the Covenant going to get greater than the cost to the United States?
 5. Establish a CNMI Covenant Section 902 consultation process for all territories, in which all discussions are held with a presidential appointee. To some, this approach may be impractical, but it

elevates the territories beyond their colonial status. This point was made clear at the February 1993 "A Time of Change" conference in Washington, D.C., when Guam Gov. Joseph F. Ada introduced himself as the Governor of the American Colony of Guam. Section 902 of the Covenant provides the opportunity for direct consultation between a representative appointed by the president and a representative appointed by the CNMI governor. Unfortunately, some federal officials don't really understand this status, perhaps because the CNMI doesn't use the Section 902 consultation process as often as it should. The CNMI has the authority under Section 902 to request the president to appoint his special representative to discuss matters of mutual concern. The 902 consultations serve as an excellent forum for finding solutions to local-federal problems, especially on issues of disagreement. Misunderstanding of the 902 process extends within the CNMI, as well. And misunderstanding can lead to disappointment and frustration. The 902 process is one of consultation, not negotiation. The special representatives only recommend solutions. For that reason, we need to strengthen the links between the governor and the president and their special representatives. Furthermore, with such a mechanism in place, high-level discussions affecting the federal-territorial relationship would be held without the administrative oversight of the Interior department.

6. Conduct a federally mandated political status referendum in each territory every 15 years. This is one way to keep Congress and the Executive Branch informed about what is going on in the territories.

Chapter 8: The People Who Shaped Me

Pete A. Tenorio

After college, I returned to the CNMI with plans to be a teacher. I never dreamed that I would be involved in politics, let alone run for public office. One of the first persons that I got acquainted with was Pete A. Tenorio. At the time I got to know Pete Tenorio, he was a candidate for public office and I got involved in his campaign. Pete Tenorio introduced me to politics. He was my political mentor and changed my career path for good.

Diego T. Benavente

Diego Benavente served the people of the CNMI with honor and distinction, especially when he was lieutenant governor. Our working relationship as governor and lieutenant governor was based on mutual respect. We shared the same vision on education, the economy, and politics. He taught me a lesson or two about loyalty to family and friends, and most importantly, to the people.

Francisco DLG. Camacho

From the time Frank married my oldest sister, Vicky, he became more than just a brother-in-law. He became a trusted friend and confidant. Throughout my entire political life, he served as my cook, recordkeeper, organizer, event coordinator, advisor, financier, negotiator, speech writer and a facilitator for just about everything that needed to be done in order to achieve a successful outcome in every election that I was involved in. He stood by me through the toughest of times and never wavered. His passing in September 2010 was so sudden. I never got a chance to tell him how much he meant to me, and to give him a hug to thank him for devoting so much of himself and his family to my personal and political life. I am indebted to him for the rest of my days.

Edward DLG. Pangelinan

Edward Pangelinan is more than just a friend; he is my mentor on CNMI-federal relations. His perspectives on the Covenant were reassuring and invaluable. He has greatly influenced my perception and understanding of CNMI-federal relations. The more time I spend with Ed Pangelinan discussing CNMI-federal issues, the more I learn.

Jose C. Tenorio (Joeten)

As my secret advisor on the economy, government and the garment industry, Joeten was a God-send. His advice to me was immeasurable.

F. Haydn Williams

I got to know Haydn Williams at a personal and professional level during my 12 years as Resident Representative. He shared with me his behind-the-scenes insight on what took place, and why, during the Covenant negotiations between the NMI representatives and the U.S. He was candid about what he knew, and he went out of his way to share it with me. On the applicability of the Territorial Clause, he said, "Let there be no confusion that the Territorial Clause applies to the NMI. I don't know what the fuss is all about with the current leaders in the CNMI saying that it doesn't apply." On land alienation in section 805 of the Covenant, he said, "The NMI Delegation did not want it. It was the U.S. Delegation that put it in." Our many meetings together always ended with him saying, "When can we meet again?"

Governor Carlos S. Camacho

Gov. Camacho was very close to my paternal grandmother. That is how I met and got to know him. He facilitated much of my success in my second round of graduate school by encouraging me to complete my studies in health care administration and planning, so that I could return to the CNMI and serve the people by working in the early years of the newly-formed government. If it weren't for him, I would have accepted a job offer by the Department of Health in the state of New Mexico rather than return home immediately.

George Miller

George Miller had a hand in shaping the future of the CNMI. He was especially critical of the local leaders whom he perceived as being beholden to, and in the pockets of, the garment industry. He saw widespread violations of human rights and U.S. labor laws applicable to the CNMI. His critics said that he was anti-garment in the CNMI to protect the same industry in his Congressional district in California. I worked with Mr. Miller for nearly all the 12 years I was in Washington as Resident Representative, but I did not see that in him. I saw a man who was genuinely concerned about the poor working conditions in the factories and the violations of the workers' rights. In that respect, he believed that U.S. labor laws applicable to the CNMI should be vigorously enforced. While there were some in Congress, mostly Republicans, who wanted to save the garment industry at any cost, I wanted to save the Commonwealth. Working with Mr. Miller, I was perceived for political consumption at home as a Democrat wearing a Republican hat. Nothing could be further from the truth.

Adam Turner

When I was elected Resident Representative in 1989, Adam Turner was finishing a zoning project that Gov. Lorenzo I. Deleon Guerrero had hired him to do. Adam once worked as an aide for a U.S. senator and because of that experience and his knowledge of the CNMI, I hired him to work with me in Washington. He was an invaluable advisor and became a trusted personal friend. He knew the ways of Washington, and I attributed much of the success of the Office of the Resident Representative to his efforts.

Paul A. Manglona

Known as Senator Paul, he is always looking for fresh new ideas. He cared deeply, not just for the people of Rota whom he served, but for the entire CNMI. His challenge was balancing the two. His perceived good for the CNMI was not always perceived as directly benefitting Rota. Politics is his passion. He loved the Senate, where he spent nearly half his life. He believed in the dignity and splendor of the Senate. No matter how bad things looked, he was always optimistic about the future of Rota and its people. As he literally aged serving as senator, he turned his focus to the youth to ensure a secure and prosperous future for them. He mastered the art of politics; he is a giver and a taker. Senator Paul is a lifelong friend and confidant. He gave me guidance when no one else would.

Pete P. Reyes

Senator Pete P. Reyes is an ardent proponent of the First Amendment Right to Freedom of Speech. Why not? Senator Reyes is a leader you would want on your side. In 1996, when the Occupational Safety and Health Administration (OSHA) threatened to cease funding OSHA workshops in the CNMI, he asked me as Resident Representative to intercede. OSHA, he said, could not expect us to comply without our being properly educated on all the requirements. The OSHA workshops had benefitted more than 1,500 people, and the rise in voluntary compliance with OSHA regulations was good business practice for the CNMI.

Sen. Reyes was an outspoken critic of my Administration as governor. On one of a number of issues, he opposed my appointee to the position of Attorney General and even camped outside of my office in protest of the appointment. He surely practiced his First Amendment right as expected. He impressed upon me the importance of listening to dissenting views, especially in the early stages of the new and young government we had.

Benigno T. Fejeran

"Ben" Fejeran is a lifelong friend. The old adage that says that in time of need or controversy, you find out who your true friends are, holds true with Ben. When the heat was on, and at the end of the day, he was always standing right next to me.

Robert Schwalbach

"Bob" Schwalbach was an invaluable member of my staff all of my 12 years in Washington and when I served as governor. His views and insights on the CNMI are reflective of his own personal views, values and ideology. Much of those views were reflected in the policy statements and position papers that the Office of the Resident Representative worked on, and in his work for the four years he served as Senior Policy Advisor during my term as governor.

Francisco I. Taitano

Francisco and I grew up together in Tanapag. For schooling, he went to Montana and I went to Vermont. We met back in Saipan working for the same cause: serving the community we had left behind for a number of years. Frank served on my staff when I was a senator, Resident Representative, and governor. In those 20 years together, he was my closest confidant. Francisco has this magical ability to work with people. He taught me how to work with everyone, even with those so-called "impossible people." It's an ability I lacked. There is much I learned from him. He is truly a friend, one whose friendship I cherish and will take to my grave.

Luis P. Crisostimo

Senator Luis P. Crisostimo was driven with a passion to bring about positive changes to the benefit of all, regardless of who you were or your party affiliation. He never retreated from challenges or hard work. He believed that through hard work, change would emerge. I was privileged to have spent time with him when he was battling cancer. Although his body was weakening, his mental capacity remained focused on what he loved doing best – serving the people of the CNMI in his capacity as senator. Despite the agonizing pain he endured due to his illness, he never once retreated to feel sorry for himself. When he lost more than 100 pounds within six months, he said to me, "Now I have to take all my pants to the tailor shop and have them retrofitted." If only I had half the courage he had.

Pamela Brown

Pam is a champion for justice, especially for the disadvantaged and the oppressed. She represented clients in discrimination lawsuits against the CNMI Government. Her persona is "Give me your Tired, your Poor…." Pam was the first Federal Ombudsman named by the Secretary of the Interior to serve in the CNMI as a liaison between the local and federal governments on enforcement of labor and immigration laws. As governor, I first hired her as my legal counsel, and later appointed her the Attorney General. My only request of her was to clean up the labor and immigration mess by working closely with the federal government. I was inspired by her devotion to the dignity of every individual, regardless of who they were.

Benjamin T. Manglona

I know a true public servant when I see one. Hands down, I saw that in Benjamin T. Manglona. His whole life was devoted to public service. He and I worked closely on federal issues, especially when he was the lieutenant governor and I was the Resident Representative. We served together as panelists at congressional hearings in Washington, D.C., and as special representatives in the Section 702 financial negotiations and the Section 902 consultation talks with the federal government. We served together as senators in the 5th and 6th Legislatures. He was tough in everything that we worked on together, and especially in our dealings with the federal government. He loved the CNMI, but Rota even more. In the times we worked together, I dared not stand between him and the people of Rota. He had a vision of an economically prosperous Rota. He wanted more planes servicing Rota and bringing in loads of tourists, more investors, more cars on the streets, more restaurants, and more. On a personal note, he would spend his last penny on a cup of coffee, breakfast, lunch or dinner for you. I was inspired by his vision, his tenacity, and his intelligence.

Chiaki Mukai

To personally get to know one of the astronauts from spaceflight STS-95 on the Space Shuttle Discovery in 1998 was a rare opportunity. I didn't get to know Ms. Mukai that well, but well enough to be inspired by her about getting our students excited about learning and the importance of education. My way of doing that was to invite the astronaut to Saipan to visit the schools and meet the students. Her slogan was, "If you can dream it, you can do it." I am still inspired to this day.

Dwight C. Ovitt

Dwight Ovitt served his two-year term as a Peace Corps volunteer on Saipan. In 1968, Dwight lived in Tanapag village, next to my parents' house. He taught agriculture at Mt. Carmel High School. As neighbors in Tanapag, we hung out together a lot. With my parents' permission, he petitioned the Court to serve as my legal guardian and then we were off to Vermont, where I finished high school. The journey I took with him by way of the Micronesian Islands, Los Angeles, Washington, D.C., New York City, and finally to Vermont, forever changed my life. It was the journey of a lifetime.

Scott Rutter

Scott Rutter is a retired Army lieutenant colonel who, while still on active duty, wrote to me as Resident Representative in 1999, volunteering his services on CNMI-federal relations. In addition to the letter, he personally showed up at my office to meet with me on his offer to do as I saw fit. His interest in the CNMI stemmed from his experience of having visited Saipan on several occasions while he was stationed in Korea. I took immediate interest in his offer and assigned him the task of securing recognition of the NMI Marine Scouts – recruited, trained, equipped by, and who fought alongside, U.S. Marines on Saipan and the Northern Islands during World War II – as U.S. Marine Corps veterans. His expertise and knowledge of the military bureaucracy were invaluable. Lt. Col. Rutter's yearlong assignment resulted in the Defense department's formal recognition of the Marine Scouts in 2000.

Important Dates and Events in NMI History

Selected and prepared by Juan Nekai Babauta
October 2016

1787   The Northwest Ordinance was enacted for the development and government of the Northwest Territory, which was the incorporated U.S. territory north and the west of the Ohio River. This Ordinance was approved by the U.S. Congress under the Articles of Confederation 229 years ago. The ordinance gave this territory a nonvoting delegate in the U.S. Congress.

1849   March 3 – The Department of the Interior was created by Congress as the "Home Department." The Department of the Interior was charged with the responsibility of advancing the domestic interests of the people of the United States.

1944   U.S. Forces attacked and occupied Saipan and Tinian and recaptured Guam.

1947   April 2 – The Trusteeship Agreement for the Trust Territory of the Pacific Islands was approved by the United Nations Security Council.

July 18 – The Trusteeship Agreement between the United Nations Security Council and the U.S. became effective by President Harry S. Truman signing into law a Joint Resolution that approved the Trusteeship Agreement with the U.S. as the Administering Authority of the Trust Territory. President Truman issued Executive Order No. 9875, which placed the Trust Territory under the administration of the U.S. Navy.

1950   July 28 – Secretarial Order 2577 created the Office of Territories. The objectives of the Office of Territories were to promote the economic, social, and political development of the territories, leading toward a goal of self-government for each of them.

August 1 – President Truman signed into law the Organic Act of Guam. The Act conferred U.S. citizenship on the people of Guam and defined Guam as an unincorporated territory. Prior to 1950, the Secretary of the Navy served as the administering authority in Guam.

1951   June 29 – President Truman issued Executive Order No. 10265, which transferred administration of the Trust Territory from the U.S. Navy to the Department of the Interior.

1952   November 10 – President Truman issued Executive Order No. 10408, which turned over Saipan and Tinian to the Navy Administration effective January 1, 1953.

1953   July 17 – President Dwight D. Eisenhower issued Executive Order No. 10470, which turned over islands north of Saipan to the Navy Administration, leaving Rota the only island in the Northern Marianas under the Department of the Interior.

1957   The Popular Party was established on Saipan. This political party then advocated the reintegration (reunification) of the NMI and Guam. In 1977, the Popular Party became the Democratic Party.

1961   First plebiscite in NMI for reintegration with Guam. NMI said yes.

1962   May 8 – President John F. Kennedy issued Executive Order No. 11021, which transferred the administration of the NMI (except Rota) from the Navy to the Department of the Interior. Rota was already under the administration of the Department of the Interior.

1963   Second plebiscite in NMI for reintegration with Guam. NMI said yes for the second time.

Vicente N. Santos was elected to the unicameral Mariana Islands District Legislature and served as the President of that legislative body from its inception in 1963 until the Northern Marianas achieved a new political status with the United States. Santos was one of the driving forces behind a political union with the United States and reintegration of the NMI and Guam.

1964   January 30 – Secretarial Order 2876 set forth the extent and nature of the authority of the Government of the Trust Territory of the Pacific Islands and the manner in which that authority was to be exercised.

September 28 – Secretarial Order 2882 created a locally elected bicameral legislature (Congress of Micronesia) for the Trust Territory of the Pacific Islands.

1965   February 16 – Legislative authority for the Trust Territory was transferred from the U.S.-appointed High Commissioner to the newly established Congress of Micronesia (COM), subject to veto by the Department of the Interior under Secretarial Order 2882 of September 28, 1964. Also on this date, the Congress of Micronesia was established.

1967   May 10 – U.S. Public Law 90-16 provided that the High Commissioner of the Trust Territory of the Pacific Islands would be appointed by the President with the advice and consent of the Senate. The Deputy High Commissioner would continue to be appointed by the Secretary of the Interior. Prior to the enactment of U.S. P.L. 90-16, the High Commissioner was appointed by the Secretary of the Interior.

August 5 – The Congress of Micronesia established its first commission to explore future political status options, the Joint Committee on Future Political Status (JCFS).

1968   September 11 – The Organic Act of Guam, approved in 1950, was amended to extend various provisions of the U.S. Constitution to the people of Guam. The amendments also included the Elective Governor Act (U.S. P.L. 90-497) that gave the voters of Guam the right to vote for their own Governor and Lieutenant Governor. Prior to 1968, the Governor of Guam was appointed by the President of the United States.

December 27 – Secretarial Order 2918 superseded Secretarial Orders 2876 and 2882 and formed the basic governmental charter for the Trust Territory of the Pacific Islands. Thus, the Executive authority of the Government of the Trust Territory of the Pacific Islands, and the responsibility for carrying out the international obligations of the United States with respect to the Trust Territory of the Pacific Islands, were vested in the High Commissioner of the Trust Territory of the Pacific Islands. For administrative purposes, the Trust Territory of the Pacific Islands was divided into six districts: Mariana Islands, Marshall Islands, Palau, Ponape, Truk, and Yap. Each district was under a District Administrator who was responsible to the High Commissioner.

1969 August 29 – The Congress of Micronesia created the Micronesian Political Status Delegation to negotiate future political status with the U.S.

October 1-17 – The First Round of Micronesian Status Negotiations between the U.S. and the Micronesian Political Status Delegation.

November – In a referendum, a majority of the voters of Guam rejected the political unification of Guam and the Northern Mariana Islands.

Francisco C. Ada became District Administrator for the Marianas District. The position was the highest administrative position in the Marianas District. Mr. Ada reported only to the Commissioner of the Trust Territory of the Pacific Islands. There were five other District Administrator positions, one each for the districts of Palau, Yap, Ponape, Truk, and the Marshall Islands.

1970 May 4-8 – The Second Round of Micronesian Status Negotiations between the U.S. and the Micronesian Political Status Delegation. The JCFS, on behalf of all of Micronesia, rejected Commonwealth status in favor of a looser relationship with the U.S.

1971 February 19 – The Marianas Islands District Legislature approved the political separation of the NMI from the rest of Micronesia.

February 20 – The Congress of Micronesia's Legislative Chambers on Saipan were burned down.

March 13 – President Richard Nixon appointed Franklin Haydn Williams as his Personal Representative for the Micronesian political status negotiations.

May – The Congress of Micronesia's special session in Truk was boycotted by the NMI.

October 4-12 – The Third Round of Micronesian Status Negotiations was held between the U.S. and the Micronesian Joint Committee on Future Status. The members of this joint committee were appointed by the Congress of Micronesia. This committee had two representatives from the NMI.

1972 April – The Fourth Round of Micronesian Status Negotiations was held between the U.S. and the Micronesian Joint Committee on Future Status. In this round, at the request of the two NMI representatives, the U.S. agreed to separate status negotiations between the NMI and the U.S.

April 12 – U.S. agreed to NMI's request for separate political status negotiations from the rest of Micronesia.

May 19 – The Mariana Islands District Legislature and Francisco C. Ada, the Mariana Islands District Administrator, approved a bill to establish a Marianas Political Status Commission of 15 members to represent the NMI in political negotiations with the U.S.

August 16 – The 15 members of the Marianas Political Status Commission were chosen. The members from the Marianas Islands District Legislature were Vicente N. Santos and Felipe A. Salas; from the Congress of Micronesia were Edward DLG. Pangelinan and Herman Q. Guerrero; from the Rota Municipal Council were Benjamin T. Manglona and Joannes R. Taimanao; from the Tinian Municipal Council were Herman M. Manglona and Francisco A. Hocog; representing the Northern Islands was Olympio T. Borja; the Popular Party was represented by Joaquin I. Pangelinan; the Carolinians were represented by Felix F. Rabauliman, and representing the business community was Jose C. Tenorio (Joeten) from the Chamber of Commerce. These were the original members, but there were changes later on in the composition of the membership during the negotiation process.

September 7 – The first meeting of the Marianas Political Status Commission was held. At this meeting, the commission elected Edward DLG. Pangelinan as its Chairman, and Vicente N. Santos as its Vice Chairman. Pangelinan was a Senator in the Congress of Micronesia. Santos had been the President of the Mariana Islands District Legislature since 1963.

December 13-14 – The First Round of the Northern Marianas Status Negotiations between the U.S. and the Marianas Political Status Commission was held. Edward DLG. Pangelinan was the Chairman and spokesman of the Commission. The opening session of the negotiations was held in the auditorium of Mt. Carmel School. The rest of the sessions were held at the Royal Taga Hotel.

1973 May 15-June 4 – The Second Round of the Northern Marianas Status Negotiations between the U.S. and the Marianas Political Status Commission was held on Saipan.

September – Pedro A. Tenorio replaced Jose C. Tenorio (Joeten) as the representative of the business community on the Marianas Political Status Commission.

December 6-19 – The Third Round of the Northern Marianas Status Negotiations between the U.S. and the Marianas Political Status Commission was held on Saipan.

1974 May 15-31 – The Fourth Round of the Northern Marianas Status Negotiations between the U.S. and the Marianas Political Status Commission was held on Saipan.

December 5-19 – The First Part of the Fifth Round of the Northern Marianas Status Negotiations between the U.S. and the Marianas Political Status Commission was held on Saipan. In this part of the Fifth Round, the two sides reached a tentative agreement on a draft version of the Covenant.

1975 February 8-11 – The Second Part of the Fifth Round of the Northern Marianas Status Negotiations between the U.S. and the Marianas Political Status Commission was held. In this part of the Fifth Round, the major issues decided were establishing a bicameral Commonwealth Legislature, having equal representation in one house of this Legislature for each of the three municipalities (Saipan, Tinian, and Rota), and requiring approval of the Covenant by at least 55% of the votes cast in a plebiscite in order for the Covenant to be approved by the people of the NMI.

February 12 – The Marianas Political Status Commission met and voted 14-0 to approve the Covenant.

February 15 – The Covenant was signed by Ambassador Franklin Haydn Williams for the U.S. and by 13 of the 15 members of the Marianas Political Status Commission. The signing ceremony took place in the Mt. Carmel School Auditorium. The two commission members who did not sign the Covenant were Felix F. Rabauliman and Oscar C. Rasa.

February 20 – The Covenant was approved by the Marianas Islands District Legislature by a unanimous vote.

February 28 – The Marianas Islands District Legislature requested the U.S. to set a date for a plebiscite to approve the Covenant.

June 17 – The Covenant was approved by 78.8% of the people of the NMI who voted in the plebiscite for the approval of the Covenant in accordance with Section 101 of the Covenant. The voter turnout in this plebiscite was 92%.

July 1 – President Gerald R. Ford sent the Covenant to Congress for approval.

July 10 – Representative Philip Burton of California introduced in the House of Representatives House Joint Resolution 549 to approve the Covenant. This Joint Resolution included the text of the Covenant. Philip Burton was the Chairman of the Subcommittee on Territorial and Insular Affairs of the House Committee on Interior and Insular Affairs.

July 1 – The House Subcommittee on Territorial and Insular Affairs held a hearing on House Joint Resolution 549.

July 16 – The House Committee on Interior and Insular Affairs approved House Joint Resolution 549 by a vote of 30-0.

July 21 – The House of Representatives approved House Joint Resolution 549 by a voice vote under suspension of the rules.

July 24 – The Senate Committee on Interior and Insular Affairs held a hearing on House Joint Resolution 549.

October 3 – The Senate Committee on Interior and Insular Affairs approved the Covenant by a unanimous vote.

November 5 – The Senate Committee on Foreign Relations held a hearing on House Joint Resolution 549.

November 17 – The General Legislation Subcommittee of the Senate Armed Services Committee held a hearing on House Joint Resolution 549.

1976 January 20 – The Senate Committee on Foreign Relations approved House Joint Resolution 549 by a vote of 7-4.

January 27 – The Senate Armed Services Committee approved House Joint Resolution 549 by a vote of 9-6.

February 24 – The Senate approved House Joint Resolution 549 by a vote of 66-23.

March 11 – The House of Representatives voted to approve the Senate version of House Joint Resolution 549.

March 24 – President Ford signed into law House Joint Resolution 549. This Joint Resolution became U.S. Public Law 94-241. The Covenant, which was enacted into U.S. law as Public Law 94-241, is now found in 48 U.S.C. Sections 1801-1805 in the U.S. Code. With President Ford's signing into law House Joint Resolution 549, the parts of the Covenant that are listed in Section 1003(a) of the Covenant went into effect.

April 1 – U.S. administration of the NMI was separated from the rest of the Trust Territory by U.S. Department of the Interior Secretarial Order No. 2989 of March 24, 1976, which was effective on April 1, 1976. The administration of the NMI was headed by a Resident Commissioner appointed by the Secretary of the Interior.

April 17 – Erwin D. Canham took over as the Resident Commissioner and Francisco C. Ada as the Deputy Commissioner.

August 23 – By Proclamation, the Resident Commissioner for the NMI transitional government, Erwin D. Canham, established a Northern Marianas Community College (NMCC).

October 18-December 6 – The First NMI Constitutional Convention met to write and approve the Constitution pursuant to Sections 201-203 of the Covenant.

December 5 – The original NMI Constitution was approved and signed by members of the First Constitutional Convention.

December 6 – The First Constitutional Convention officially approved a section-by-section analysis of the original NMI Constitution.

1977 March 6 – The original NMI Constitution was approved by 93% of the votes in a referendum.

April 21 – The original NMI Constitution was officially submitted to President Jimmy Carter for his approval pursuant to Sections 202 and 203 of the Covenant.

October 24 – President Carter issued Presidential Proclamation 4534 that declared that (1) the NMI Constitution was in agreement with the Covenant, (2) the Covenant was approved by the U.S. Government, (3) the NMI Constitution would come into full force and effect on January 9, 1978, (4) those parts of the Covenant that are listed in Section 1003(b) of the Covenant would come into full force and effect on January 9, 1978. (Note: On November 3, 1986, President Ronald Reagan issued Presidential Proclamation 5564 that declared that, effective November 4, 1986 (Marianas time), all parts of the Covenant would be in full force and effect. (See November 4, 1986.)

December 3 – Carlos S. Camacho and Francisco C. Ada of the Democratic Party were elected as the first Governor and Lt. Governor of the CNMI. They defeated the Territorial Party ticket of Jose C. Tenorio (Joeten) and Olympio T. Borja. Edward DLG. Pangelinan was elected as the first Resident Representative to the United States and served in that position from 1978 to 1986.

1978 January 9 – Carlos S. Camacho and Francisco C. Ada were sworn in as the first Governor and Lt. Governor of the CNMI. Also on this date, at 11 a.m., the Constitution of the NMI went into full force and effect. The Constitution provided for a republican form of government with separate executive, legislative and judicial branches and a bill of rights. Article XV of the Constitution mandated that there be higher education and adult education in the NMI as provided by law.

1979 February – Herbert Soll was nominated to be a judge, and with the advice and consent of the NMI Legislature, he was confirmed as the first Commonwealth Trial Court judge of the CNMI.

1980 January 18 – P.L. 1-43 established the Northern Mariana Islands Retirement Fund (NMIRF) as an autonomous public corporation effective October 1, 1980.

1981 March 12 – Governor Carlos S. Camacho issued Executive Order 25, placing the NMCC within the Department of Education under the control and supervision of the Board of Education.

November – Pedro P. Tenorio and running mate Pedro A. Tenorio, under the newly formed Republican Party, were elected as the second Governor and Lt. Governor of the CNMI. They defeated Carlos S. Camacho and Lorenzo DLG. Cabrera under the Commonwealth Popular Democratic Party, and Herman R. Deleon Guerrero and Froilan C. Tenorio under the Democratic Party.

1982 January – Pedro P. Tenorio and Pedro A. Tenorio were sworn in as the second Governor and Lt. Governor of the CNMI.

October – NMCC applied to become a candidate for accreditation to the Accrediting Commission for Community and Junior Colleges (ACCJC) of the Western Association of Schools and Colleges. The application was submitted by the Chairman of the Board of Regents, Juan Nekai Babauta.

December – The Accrediting Commission made a site visit to NMCC for the first time and issued 17 tasks requiring action by NMCC.

(Note: The Gross Island Product for 1982 was estimated at $165 million. Tourism was the principal industry, with more than 80% of all visitors originating from Japan.)

1983 January 19 – CNMI P.L. 3-43, the Education Act of 1983, vacated Governor Carlos S. Camacho's Executive Order 25 and established the Northern Marianas College (NMC) as a public, not-for-profit corporation, with the Board of Education as its governing body and headed by a President appointed by the Board.

March 10 – President Reagan issued Presidential Proclamation 5030, which claimed for the United States an Exclusive Economic Zone (EEZ) beyond the territorial sea and within 200 nautical miles of the coasts "of the United States, Puerto Rico, NMI, and the United States overseas territories and possessions."

1984 February – NMC launched a Comprehensive Institutional Self-Study.

April – The Accrediting Commission (ACCJC) made its second on-site visit to NMC. NMC reported on the 17 tasks issued by the Commission.

1985 The Second NMI Constitutional Convention was held. Constitutional Amendment 38 directed the Legislature to establish by law, a Northern Marianas College to be headed by a President chosen by the Board of Regents. Amendment 38 also established an elected Board of Education, whose members serve four-year terms, to formulate policy for and exercise control of the Public School System, which provides free public elementary and secondary education.

March 28 – P.L. 4-34, the Postsecondary Education Act of 1984, abolished the responsibility of the Board of Education for NMC and provided a transition for a new Board of Regents for NMC appointed by the governor. The Postsecondary Education Act of 1984 dissolved the responsibility of the Board of Education for NMC and provided a transition for a new Board of Regents.

April – The ACCJC On-site Evaluation Team met with the Board of Regents, the Governor, and other NMI leaders.

May – NMC received the report from the ACCJC On-site Evaluation Team.

June – NMC was granted full accreditation for the first time by the ACCJC.

November – Froilan C. Tenorio was elected the second Resident Representative to the United States. He served in that position from 1986 to 1990. Also, Pedro P. Tenorio and Pedro A. Tenorio were re-elected Governor and Lt. Governor of the CNMI. They defeated Carlos S. Camacho and Juan B. Tudela under the Democratic Party.

November – The voters ratified all 44 constitutional amendments that had been approved by the Second Constitutional Convention.

1986 January 1 – Under U.S. P.L. 86-788, the CNMI was required to elect for coverage under the U.S. Social Security System, but the CNMI did not do so.

Therefore, CNMI government employees were not covered under the Social Security system. On this same date, Social Security coverage of private sector employees became effective.

January 9 – Pedro P. Tenorio and Pedro A. Tenorio were sworn in again as the Governor and Lt. Governor of the CNMI.

January 14 – The U.S. Congress approved and President Reagan signed into law P.L. 99-239, the Compact of Free Association Act of 1985, which approved the Compacts of Free Association between the U.S. and the Federated States of Micronesia (FSM) and the Republic of the Marshall Islands (RMI).

October 15 – The U.S. and the RMI agreed that the effective date of their Compact would be Oct. 21, 1986.

October 16 – The U.S. Congress approved the Compact of Free Association with the Republic of Palau.

October 24 – The U.S. and the FSM agreed that the effective date of their Compact would be Nov. 3, 1986.

November 3 – President Reagan issued Presidential Proclamation 5564 which declared that, effective November 4, 1986 (Marianas time), (1) all parts of the Covenant were in full force and effect; (2) the Commonwealth of the Northern Mariana Islands officially came into existence; (3) the legal residents (domiciliaries) of the NMI who had been citizens of the Trust Territory of the Pacific Islands, and those persons who had been legal residents of the NMI continuously since before January 1, 1974 but who were not citizens of the Trust Territory of the Pacific Islands and who were not already U.S. citizens, became U.S. citizens pursuant to Section 301 of the Covenant; (4) the Trusteeship Agreement for the Trust Territory of the Pacific Islands was terminated for the CNMI, the Republic of the Marshall Islands, and the Federated States of Micronesia. (Termination of the Trusteeship for Palau came later).

November 4 – Sections 101, 104, 301, 302, 303, 506, 806, and 904 of the Covenant, which deal with U.S. citizenship and U.S. sovereignty, became effective at 12:01 a.m. on this date, Northern Mariana Islands local time. NMI legal residents became U.S. citizens, in accordance with Section 301 of the Covenant.

1989 May 2 – CNMI Public Law 6-25, the Commonwealth Judicial Reorganization Act, created the CNMI Supreme Court and changed the name of the Commonwealth Trial Court to the Commonwealth Superior Court. The significance of the Commonwealth Judicial Reorganization Act is that it transferred all local appellate jurisdiction to the newly established CNMI Supreme Court.

May 15 – Jose S. Dela Cruz was sworn in as the first Chief Justice of the CNMI Supreme Court. Ramon G. Villagomez also was sworn in as the first Associate Justice of the CNMI Supreme Court.

October 24 – Jesus C. Borja was sworn in as the third Justice of the Supreme Court. This third appointment to the Supreme Court made the composition of the Supreme Court complete to conduct business.

November – Juan Nekai Babauta was elected as the third Resident Representative to the United States. He served as Resident Representative from 1990 to 2002. Lorenzo I. Deleon Guerrero and Benjamin T. Manglona under the Republican Party were elected Governor and Lt. Governor of the CNMI. They defeated Froilan C. Tenorio and Victor B. Hocog under the Democratic Party.

1990 January – Lorenzo I. Deleon Guerrero and Benjamin T. Manglona were sworn in as the third Governor and Lt. Governor of the CNMI.

1991 April 4 – The larger-than-normal flag of the CNMI was installed in Washington, D.C., at the Kennedy Center for the Performing Arts in the Hall of States, where the flags of the 50 States and the territories are displayed.

1992 The U.S. Congress enacted authorization for NMC to be designated a Land Grant Institution. The funds were not immediately appropriated.

1993 November 6 – Froilan C. Tenorio and Jesus C. Borja under the Democratic Party were elected Governor and Lt. Governor of the CNMI. They defeated incumbents Lorenzo I. Deleon Guerrero and Benjamin T. Manglona under the Republican Party. Juan N. Babauta was re-elected to a second term as Resident Representative to the United States.

1994 The Third Constitutional Convention was approved by the voters.

January – Froilan C. Tenorio and Jesus C. Borja were sworn in as the fourth Governor and Lt. Governor of the CNMI.

October 1 – The U.S. Congress approved the Compact of Free Association with Palau, which had already been declared a constitutional republic 13 years earlier.

1995 August 2 – The Third Constitutional Convention approved 19 proposed amendments to the NMI Constitution and a section-by-section analysis of the Constitution.

1996 March 2 – CNMI voters rejected all of the 19 proposed amendments to the Constitution that had been approved by the Third Constitutional Convention.

Guam sued the federal government to require it to issue a Compact Impact Report.

April 26 – President Bill Clinton signed a law giving NMC a Land Grant endowment of $3 million.

September 30 – The Land Grant funding for NMC was finally appropriated.

(Note: The population of the Northern Mariana Islands at this time was 67,212.)

1997   The U.S. District Court for Guam ordered the Department of the Interior to provide to the Government of Guam the Compact Impact report.

November 1 – Pedro P. Tenorio and Jesus R. ("Pepero") Sablan under the Republican Party were elected Governor and Lt. Governor of the CNMI. They defeated Froilan C. Tenorio and Jesus S. Deleon Guerrero under the Democratic Party, and the Independent team of Jesus C. Borja and Benigno M. Sablan. Also, Juan N. Babauta was re-elected to a third term as Resident Representative to the United States. Also on this date, House Legislative Initiative 10-3, which was passed by the CNMI Legislature, was approved by voters to establish the CNMI Supreme Court and the Superior Court constitutionally, rather than by statute, as had been the case in P.L. 6-25.

1999   June 13 – Dr. Chiaki Mukai, the astronaut from Japan who flew with Senator John Glenn aboard the STS-95 Shuttle Discovery in 1998, arrived on Saipan for a three-day, historic visit by invitation of Juan N. Babauta, Resident Representative to the United States. Astronaut Mukai's visit was intended to inspire the students of the NMI on the importance of education. Her message to the students was, "If you can dream it, you can do it." She met with NMI leaders, students, and the people of the NMI. Dr. Mukai was the keynote speaker for the 1,200 nurses attending the American Pacific Nursing Leaders Council Conference on Saipan. She also was the commencement speaker at the Hopwood Junior High School graduation and at the Marianas High School graduation, and visited several elementary schools to speak to the students.

2000   January 31 – The Marianas Marine Scouts were officially recognized as U.S. veterans. The Marianas Marine Scouts were a selected group of about 50 Chamorro and Carolinian men placed under the command of the 6th Provisional Military Police Battalion of the United States Marine Corps in July 1945 to assist in the mop-up operations in the Northern Mariana Islands. Even though the islands were declared secure by U.S. forces, several hundred Japanese soldiers remained hidden in the jungles and caves of Saipan and the Northern Islands, killing American soldiers with sniper attacks. The Marianas Marine Scouts were issued Marine Corps uniforms, trained to use rifles and grenades, and instructed in hand-to-hand combat. The Marianas Marine Scouts were forgotten for more than 50 years. They wanted nothing more than to be recognized for their service. In a special ceremony on January 31, 2000, the governments of the United States and the Commonwealth of the Northern Marianas Islands paid tribute to 63 Marine Scouts who became honored veterans of the United States.

March 24 – Benigno R. Fitial, who was then Speaker of the House, founded the Covenant Party after leaving the Republican Party of the Northern Mariana Islands. Fitial rejoined the Republican Party on January 5, 2011.

December 1 – Governor Pedro P. Tenorio signed into law P.L. 12-32, the "Investment Incentive Act of 2000," which established the Qualifying Certificate (QC) Program. The QC Program provided for the reduction or the elimination of the majority of CNMI taxes (Business Gross Revenue Tax, Income Tax, Excise Tax, etc.) for qualified new investments for a period of up to 25 years. The belief was that the QC program would provide a stimulus for additional investments in the CNMI.

2001 November 3 – Pedro A. Tenorio was elected the fourth Resident Representative to the United States. He served in that position from 2002 to 2008. Juan N. Babauta and Diego T. Benavente under the Republican Party were elected Governor and Lt. Governor of the CNMI. They defeated Jesus C. Borja and Brigida DLG. Ichihara under the Democratic Party, Benigno R. Fitial and Rita H. Inos under the Covenant Party, and Froilan C. Tenorio and David C. Sablan under the Reform Party.

2002 January – Juan N. Babauta and Diego Tenorio Benavente were sworn in as the sixth Governor and Lt. Governor of the CNMI.

An Honorable Accord: The Covenant between the Northern Mariana Islands and the United States was published by the University of Hawaii Press. This book was written by Howard P. Willens and Deanne C. Siemer. In the words of the authors, "Our intention throughout this project has been to describe as accurately as possible the process by which the Northern Mariana Islands became part of the United States."

2003 May 10 – The volcano on the island of Anatahan erupted, sending huge plumes of ash and smoke into the sky. According to reports from the U.S. Geological Survey, the volcano continues to erupt sporadically to this day. Governor Juan N. Babauta declared a state of emergency for the Commonwealth as a result of the eruption, and several commercial flights out of, and into Saipan were cancelled for a period of time.

November – Juan Tudela Lizama was the first judge in the CNMI to be retained as a judge by voters. (The CNMI Constitution requires that the retention of judges and justices be put to a vote in a general election before the end of the judge's or justice's term.)

2005 March 29 – The Saipan International Airport was renamed the "Francisco C. Ada/Saipan International Airport." Francisco C. Ada, the first Lt. Governor of the CNMI, was recognized by the 13th Northern Marianas Commonwealth Legislature and Governor Juan N. Babauta with the passage of Saipan Local Law No. 13-10. (See Addendum L., Letter from former Lt. Gov. Francisco C. Ada.)

June 28 – Their Majesties Emperor Akihito and Empress Michiko of Japan arrived on Saipan for an historic visit to mourn the estimated 40,000 Japanese soldiers killed in the NMI during World War II. They had come also to memorialize the thousands of American, Korean and Chamorro soldiers who sacrificed their own lives in the fighting. Upon the Imperial Couple's arrival on Saipan, they were greeted with a warm welcome by Juan N. Babauta, Governor of the CNMI. During the Imperial Couple's visits at several memorial sites on the northern side of the island, they offered prayers and flowers honoring not only the Japanese who died on Saipan during World War II, but also the U.S. soldiers. In an unscheduled stop, the Imperial Couple also paid their respects at the Korean World War II memorial. The Imperial Couple visited Suicide Cliff, Banzai Cliff, the Japanese memorial, the Korean memorial, and the American Memorial Park in Garapan. In their attempt to reach out to the local community, the Imperial Couple also visited the Aging Center (Manamko' Center) in Garapan, where they were greeted by an enthusiastic crowd singing local and Japanese songs. Governor Babauta described the entire experience in one word, "Excellent."

July – An accreditation warning on financial issues was issued to NMC by the Accrediting Commission (ACCJC).

November 5 – Benigno R. Fitial and Timothy P. Villagomez under the Covenant Party were elected Governor and Lt. Governor of the CNMI. They defeated incumbents Juan N. Babauta and Diego T. Benavente under the Republican Party, Froilan C. Tenorio and Antonio A. Santos under the Democratic Party, and the independent team of Heinz S. Hofschneider and David M. Apatang.

December – The construction of the CNMI Veterans Cemetery n Saipan was completed. In early 2005, the CNMI received a $1.7 million grant from the U.S. Department of Veterans Affairs for the design and construction of the cemetery. The cemetery is situated on nearly five acres of land with about 1,200 gravesites, a committal shelter, paved roads, drainage, and an irrigation system.

2006 January 9 – Benigno R. Fitial and Timothy P. Villagomez were sworn in as the seventh Governor and Lt. Governor of the CNMI.

NMC issued a Self-Study for Reaffirmation of Accreditation.

October 16-19 – The ACCJC On-site Evaluation Team for Accreditation visited NMC.

November 21 – Gregorio Camacho Cabrera became the first veteran to be buried at the newly constructed CNMI Veterans Cemetery.

2007 January – The ACCJC placed NMC on Probation status.

May 25 – The minimum wage in the CNMI was federalized under U.S. Public Law 110-28, The U.S. Troops Readiness, Veterans' Care, Katrina Recovery, and Iraq Accountability Appropriations Act. The law included the application of the Fair Labor Standards Act (FLSA) wage rates by gradual increases in the CNMI and American Samoa.

2008 January 31 – The ACCJC placed NMC on "Show Cause" status.

May 8 – President George W. Bush signed into law S. 2739, the Consolidated Natural Resources Act of 2008, which became U.S. Public Law 110-229. Title VII of this Act: (1) added a Section 6 to the CNMI Covenant to provide for federal takeover of control over immigration in the CNMI pursuant to Section 503(a) of the Covenant. This new Section 6 of the Covenant is in 48 U.S.C. 1806-1808 in the U.S. Code; (2) repealed Section 506 of the Covenant. This section dealt with immigration matters; (3) made the CNMI

Resident Representative to the U.S., as established by Section 901 of the Covenant, an elected nonvoting Delegate to the U.S. House of Representatives.

November 4 – Gregorio C. Sablan was elected the first Delegate to the U.S. Congress from the CNMI.

2009 April 24 – Lt. Governor Timothy P. Villagomez resigned from office following his conviction on federal criminal charges related to fraud.

May 1 – Eloy S. Inos was sworn in as the first unelected Lt. Governor of the CNMI after being nominated by Governor Benigno Fitial to fill the Lt. Governor vacancy following the resignation of Timothy P. Villagomez.

November 7 and 23 (run-off) – Benign R. Fitial and Eloy S. Inos under the Covenant Party were elected Governor and Lt. Governor of the CNMI. They defeated Heinz S. Hofschneider and Arnold I. Palacios under the Republican Party, the independent team of Juan T. Guerrero and Joseph N. Camacho, and the independent team of Ramon S. (Kumoi) Deleon Guerrero and David M. Borja.

2010 January – Benigno R. Fitial and Eloy S. Inos were sworn in as Governor and Lt. Governor. Eloy S. Inos was sworn in as Lt. Governor to serve his first term. They were elected in November 2009 to a one-time, five-year term because of Senate Legislative Initiative 16-11, which extended their terms to five years in order for all future CNMI elections to coincide with U.S. national elections.

2011 July 30 – CNMI Superior Court Judge Ramona Villagomez Manglona was sworn in as the Chief Judge of the U.S. District Court for the NMI.

September 26 – The Rota International Airport was renamed the "Benjamin Taisacan Manglona International Airport" in honor of the former Lt. Governor.

October 24 – The CNMI Government implemented Public Law 16-51 a little more than two years and 10 months after the legislation was signed into law on January 15, 2009 by Governor Benigno R. Fitial. Public Law 16-51 established the Commonwealth Healthcare Corporation (CHCC), a public corporation, as a successor to the Department of Public Health. The CHCC is now the operator of the Commonwealth's healthcare system and the primary provider of healthcare- related public health services in the CNMI.

2012 November 6 – Gregorio C. Sablan was re-elected to a third term as Delegate to the U.S. Congress. On this date also, President Barack Obama was re-elected to a second term as President of the United States, defeating former Massachusetts Governor Mitt Romney.

2013 February 11 – Governor Benigno R. Fitial was impeached by the House of Representatives by a vote of 16-4. The House approved 13 articles (charges) of impeachment.

February 20 – Benigno R. Fitial resigned from office as Governor of the CNMI. He was the first Governor of the CNMI to resign. That afternoon,

Lt. Governor Eloy S. Inos was sworn in as Governor, and Senate President Jude U. Hofschneider was sworn in as Lt. Governor.

September 11 – President Barack Obama nominated Esther P. Kia'aina to be Assistant Secretary for Insular Affairs in the Department of the Interior. The nomination was approved by the U.S. Senate Committee on Energy and Natural Resources on December 19, 2013. Kia'aina was confirmed by the Senate on June 26, 2014. The Office of Insular Affairs coordinates federal policy for the territories of American Samoa, Guam, the U.S. Virgin Islands, and the Commonwealth of the Northern Mariana Islands. The Assistant Secretary also administers and oversees U.S. federal assistance provided to the Federated States of Micronesia, the Republic of the Marshall Islands, and the Republic of Palau under the Compacts of Free Association.

2014   November 4 and 21 (run-off) – Eloy S. Inos and Ralph DLG. Torres were elected Governor and Lt. Governor of the CNMI under the Republican Party. They defeated Edward M. Deleon Guerrero and Daniel O. Quitugua under the Democratic Party, the independent team of Heinz S. Hofschneider and Ray N. Yumul, and the independent team of Juan N. Babauta and Juan S. Torres. Edward D. Manibusan was elected as the first elected CNMI Attorney General. Gregorio C. Sablan was elected to a fourth term as Delegate to the U.S. Congress.

2015   August 2 and 3 – Super Typhoon Soudelor passed over Saipan late Sunday night at around 11 p.m. (August 2) and early Monday at around 1 a.m. (August 3) and left Saipan in a "state of disaster." It was the worst storm to hit Saipan in nearly 30 years.

August 6 – President Barack Obama declared the Northern Mariana Islands a federal disaster area, allowing the residents to receive federal government aid.

December 29 – Governor Eloy Songao Inos passed away in Seattle, Washington, after a long illness complicated by diabetes. Lt. Governor Ralph Deleon Guerrero Torres was sworn in as Governor of the CNMI. Senate President Victor B. Hocog was sworn in as Lt. Governor of the CNMI.

2016   March 28 – The U.S. District Court for the Northern Mariana Islands struck down as unconstitutional the two subsections in Title 6 of the CNMI Code that banned handguns and handgun ammunition. Chief Judge Ramona V. Manglona ruled that 6CMC 2222(e) and 2301(a)(3) in the CNMI Code, which banned handguns and handgun ammunition, were in violation of Covenant Section 501(a), the Second Amendment of the U.S. Constitution, and the Due Process and Equal Protection clauses of the 14th Amendment of the U.S. Constitution. The case in this matter involved a lawsuit filed by U.S. Navy veteran David J. Radich and his wife, Li-Rong, against the CNMI Department of Public Safety and the Department of Finance for refusing to process the couple's applications to possess and import handguns and handgun ammunition in the CNMI. In her ruling, Chief Judge Ramona Manglona said "the Second Amendment as well as the Due Process Clause and Equal Protection Clause of the Fourteenth Amendment, are the law of the land in the CNMI as if it were a state."

April 11 – Governor Ralph Torres signed into law P.L. 19-42, the "Special Act for Firearms Enforcement" (the SAFE Act) "for the regulation and control of firearms and ammunition in the Commonwealth" in order to provide "the greatest possible degree of protection to the people of the Commonwealth and its guests."

April 24 – Former Lt. Governor Benjamin T. Manglona died at the age of 78. He was Lt. Governor from January 1990 to January 1994, and he was the Mayor of Rota from January 1998 to January 2006.

April 26 – Governor Ralph Torres signed into law P.L. 19-63, the "Second Marianas Political Status Commission Act," to establish the Second Marianas Political Status Commission "to examine whether the people desire continuing in a political union" with the U.S. "pursuant to the Covenant, … or whether some other political status would better enable them to fulfill their aspirations of full and meaningful self-government."

Addendums

A. October 19, 1993 invitation from Close Up Foundation to serve on Board of Advisors.

Robert A. Malson
Executive Vice President &
Chief Operating Officer

October 19, 1993

The Honorable Juan N. Babauta
Resident Representative to the United States
2121 R Street, N.W.
Washington, D.C. 20008

Dear Representative Babauta:

On behalf of all of us at the Close Up Foundation, I would like to offer our sincere appreciation for your commitment to our work with the young people of the Commonwealth of the Northern Mariana Islands.

As a member of the Board of Advisors you have joined a distinguished list of elected officials, educators, and business leaders who realize that democracy is more than a spectator sport. In order for democracy to survive, it is our belief that we must all become active and informed citizens. You, however, serve as a role model for all.

The time you have spent working to ensure that the Close Up program is available to as many young people from the CNMI as possible, and the interest you show in meeting them here in Washington is much appreciated.

As you know, Close Up provides week-long educational seminars in Washington, D.C. for high school students and educators from across the country. During their stay here in Washington, the students have the opportunity to go behind the facades of buildings they often see only on television and meet with people who make and direct policy which affects their lives. Many of the CNMI students also participate in sessions on the Pacific Basin which are held in Honolulu or in international affairs sessions held in Philadelphia and New York.

In addition, Close Up also provides teacher training institutes and materials for teachers throughout the Pacific.

We are pleased that more than 150 Northern Mariana high school students and teachers have been involved in Close Up since the program was introduced there in 1985. We are equally pleased that you will now be included on our Board of Advisors. Welcome aboard.

Sincerely,

[signature]

20 Years of Education for Democracy
44 Canal Center Plaza   Alexandria, Virginia 22314   (703) 706-3333   FAX (703) 706-3329

B. In Recognition of Work with the Close Up Foundation, by Guam Del. Robert A. Underwood in the U.S. House of Representatives on April 24, 2001. Congressional Record, Washington, D.C.

Congressional Record

United States of America

PROCEEDINGS AND DEBATES OF THE *107th* CONGRESS, FIRST SESSION

Vol. 147 — WASHINGTON, TUESDAY, APRIL 24, 2001 — No. 52

CONGRESSIONAL RECORD — *Extensions of Remarks* — April 24, 2001

IN RECOGNITION OF JUAN NEKAI BABAUTA AND HIS WORK WITH THE CLOSE UP FOUNDATION

HON. ROBERT A. UNDERWOOD
OF GUAM
IN THE HOUSE OF REPRESENTATIVES
Tuesday, April 24, 2001

Mr. UNDERWOOD. Mr. Speaker, I take this opportunity today to recognize my friend Juan Nekai Babauta, the Resident Representative to the United States from the Commonwealth of the Northern Mariana Islands (CNMI), for his efforts on behalf of the Close Up Foundation. I particularly commend Mr. Babauta for his continued commitment to the issue of civic education for young people and especially for his diligent work with the Close Up Foundation, the nation's largest nonprofit, nonpartisan citizenship education organization.

Mr. Speaker, as many of my colleagues know, the CNMI became a territory of the United States and an American commonwealth in 1976. Since then the citizens of the CNMI, with whom my constituency, the people of Guam, share indigenous identity and Chamorro heritage, have elected a Resident Representative to serve them in the Nation's capital. To date the CNMI is the only American jurisdiction that has not been afforded representation in Congress, thus I often feel compelled to offer remarks here in the House for Guam's Pacific neighbors.

As you know, Mr. Speaker, many of the islands of Oceania face daunting challenges in the area of economic stability and growth. Their relatively limited size, small population and extended distance from major markets, makes building a strong and sustainable economy among the most difficult tasks facing contemporary government. With the competing needs of various sectors of society, the government is forced to make tough choices. Roads must be maintained and airports must be modernized, hospitals must be improved and schools must be expanded and repaired, health care must be available to all and social safety nets must be in place for the neediest citizens. Pressing demands on an island's resources must be balanced with an eye towards meeting the needs of the day, while not ignoring future needs. Public servants like Juan Nekai Babauta make invaluable contributions to the extremely difficult balancing act between available resources and societal needs.

All of the islands of the Pacific are also confronting numerous problems when it comes to their youth. In CNMI, as is also the case in Guam, the government must find ways to combat apathy and cynicism among their young people. There is a constant concern with ensuring that young people will enter adulthood committed to being active, contributing citizens of their communities. For public servants like Juan Nekai Babauta, there is a recognition that preparing the next generation of leaders is a priority for the future welfare of the islands. Throughout his years of service, Mr. Babauta has been a champion for education and a strong advocate for young people. As the Resident Representative for CNMI, he has aggressively and successfully lobbied this Congress to provide $3 million in federal funds for an endowment at the Northern Marianas College. He also achieved success in his attempt to open admission to our U.S. service academies to CNMI students. These and other pursuits demonstrate Mr. Babauta's effectiveness and his work on behalf of his constituency.

Throughout his career, Mr. Babauta has recognized that preparing the next generation of leaders must include preparation through a focus on civic education. His commitment to this end is evidenced through his unwavering support of the Close Up Foundation's program in the Pacific Islands.

Mr. Speaker, as you and my other colleagues in the House know well, the Close Up Foundation operates one of the most successful and innovative civic education programs in the country. Most of us have had the privilege of meeting students who are in Washington for an intensive course of study about the federal government. Annually, I personally meet with students and teachers from Guam who are participants in Close Up's civic education program that is specially designed for Pacific Islands students and educators. As an educator by profession, I have been personally impressed with Close Up's Island-based activities, including their development of island-specific curricular materials, teacher training seminars and programs related to teaching young people about the merits of community service.

Mr. Babauta, when back home in Rota and Saipan has encouraged students and teachers to participate in the program. He has used his position and contacts to assist educators and schools to raise funds that would allow students to participate in the Close Up program, including taking advantage of local media outlets to promote the program. Mr. Babauta even assists students and teachers with the process for obtaining passports and other travel documents that will allow them to travel to Washington for the Close Up program. All of these activities speak to his deep belief in the importance of civic education to CNMI students, including the need for them to explore the historic ties between the United States and the Pacific Islands. Equally important, Mr. Babauta's support for the Close Up program signals his conviction that for the CNMI and other Pacific Islands to secure a future of engaged citizenry committed to democratic government, it is important that they be educated in how democracy is reliant upon the involvement and input of the people.

In closing, Mr. Speaker, I wish to thank Mr. Babauta for his work with Close Up Pacific Islands program. His efforts over the years demonstrate his commitment to the welfare of the young people of the Pacific, and his conviction that educating young people about democracy, the importance of community service, and the rights and responsibilities of citizenship is indispensable for the future of the CNMI and other Pacific Islands.

C. Statement by Juan N. Babauta before the Navajo Code Talkers at the Navajo Code Talkers Ceremony
Window Rock, AZ
March 10, 1994

I am Juan Nekai Babauta from Saipan. A native Carolinian and Chamorro, I am a child of the generation you saved in your July 1944 effort to liberate Saipan and Tinian. I am humbled by this privilege to be a part of this very special occasion.

World events in 1944 and the critical role you, the Navajo Code Talkers, played have inextricably changed the course of our CNMI history. From the end of World War I until the liberation by the United States nearly 50 years ago, we were under the Japanese administration. Since our liberation, we were under the Naval Administration, the Trust Territory Administration under the auspices of the United Nations and then became part of the U.S. family by becoming an American Commonwealth in 1978. In 1986, our people gained full U.S. citizenship rights, which we had fervently pursued for decades.

World War II, and every war, extracts an immeasurable price on the soul of humankind. Sometimes too easily overshadowed by the sadness of those days of war are the memories of friendships made and personal acts of human kindnesses. I humbly stand here to say that you and your deeds have not been forgotten by the peoples of Saipan, Tinian and the rest of the Northern Mariana Islands. Permit me, especially on behalf of those future generations you liberated, to say again a very humble thank you very, very much, to each and every Navajo Code Talker.

D. Letter from U.S. Pres. William Jefferson Clinton

THE WHITE HOUSE

WASHINGTON

August 19, 1994

Mr. Juan N. Babauta
Resident Representative
Commonwealth of the Northern
 Mariana Islands
2121 R Street, N.W.
Washington, D.C. 20008

Dear Juan:

    Thank you for sharing your memorial booklet. It meant a lot to me.

    As we remember the fiftieth anniversary of the crucial World War II battles for Saipan and Tinian, it is fitting to honor those who made the ultimate sacrifice. Your booklet will ensure that those brave men who fought so fiercely on the islands of Saipan and Tinian, particularly those who lost their lives, will long be remembered.

    Thanks again for sending the moving tribute.

Sincerely,

Bill Clinton

E. Use of General Headnote 3(a).

Why the CNMI is still permitted to use General Headnote 3(a): "On July 18, 1947, the United States became the administering authority of the Trust Territory of the Pacific Islands, which included the Northern Mariana Islands (Trusteeship Agreement, 61 Stat. 3301, T.I.A.S. No. 1665, 8 U.N.T.S. 89). In accordance with provisions of the Trusteeship Agreement to promote self-government of the people of the Trust Territory, the U.S. signed a Covenant on March 24, 1976, to establish a Commonwealth of the Northern Mariana Islands in Political Union with the United States, which became fully effective on November 4, 1986 (Public Law 94-241, 90 Stat. 263).

"Article VI, Section 603 (c) of the Covenant provides that imports from the Northern Mariana Islands into the Customs territory of the United States will be subject to the same treatment as imports from Guam into the Customs territory of the United States. Products from Guam are eligible for duty-free treatment under General Note 3(a) (iv), Harmonized Tariff Schedule of the United States, if they meet certain qualifications. Therefore, products from the Northern Mariana Islands are eligible for this same duty-free treatment provided they meet the same qualifications.

"General Note 3(a) (iv), of the Harmonized Tariff Schedule of the United States, provides for the duty free treatment of goods imported from an insular possession if they are the growth or product of the possession; do not contain foreign materials which represent more than 70 percent of the goods' total value (or more than 50 percent when considering textile and apparel articles subject to textile agreements, and other goods described in Section 213 (b) of the Caribbean Basin Economic Recovery Act) and they are imported directly into the Customs territory of the United States from the possession.

"In order to be considered a product of the Northern Mariana Islands, textile apparel must meet the requirements in Section 12.130 of the Customs Regulations (19 CFR 12.130). This section provides the criteria which are used for determining the country of origin for all imports of textile products imported into the United States for the purposes of duty, marking and quota/visa applicability. Generally, a product will be considered to be a product of a particular foreign territory or country, or insular possession, if it is wholly the growth, product, or manufacture of that foreign territory or country, or insular possession. If the textile product is produced or derived from, or processed in more than one foreign territory or country, or insular possession, the actual country of origin is based on where it last underwent a substantial transformation.

"Prior to a textile good qualifying for duty-free entry, the merchandise must not only have to be a product of the NMI, but it must contain less than 50 percent foreign material of the total value of the imported item. Little or no fabric is produced in the NMI. However, an apparel product produced from foreign fabric which has undergone a double substantial transformation in the NMI is considered a product of the NMI. Thus, apparel products which are both cut and then assembled in the NMI would be considered a product of the NMI…

"With regard to the issue of the proper marking, Section 304 of the Tariff Act of 1930, as amended (19 U.S.C. 1304), provides that, unless excepted, every article of foreign origin imported into the United States shall be marked in a conspicuous place as legibly, indelibly, and permanently as the nature of the article (or container) will permit, in such a manner as to indicate to the ultimate purchaser in the United States the English name of the country of origin of the article. ... On July 25, 1984, the U.S. Customs Service ruled that products of Guam are exempted from the country of origin marking requirements of 19 CFR 134.32 (1), as products of the possessions of the United States. [The U.S.] Customs [Service] has ruled that the NMI is a territory or possession of the United States and products therefrom would also be excluded from the country of origin marking requirements under 19 U.S.C. 1304.

"However, the Federal Trade Commission (FTC) has jurisdiction over the marking requirements for all textile products including wearing apparel, whether or not imported. Pursuant to rules and regulations published by the FTC and issued under the authority of the Textile Fiber Product Identification Act, the term "United States" means the several States, the District of Columbia, and the Territories and possessions of the United States. Thus, for all merchandise considered to be a product of the Northern Mariana Islands, the FTC would permit the use of 'Made in USA of Imported Fabric'. In support of this the FTC stated in a staff opinion letter that garments made in the Northern Mariana Islands of imported fabric should be labeled 'Made in USA of Imported Fabric'.

"Thus, clothing imported into the United States, which is considered a product of the Northern Mariana Islands must be marked with labels showing, 'Made in the U.S.A. of Imported Fabric,' or 'Made in the U.S.A.', depending on the origin of the actual fabric used to produce the garments." William D. Slyne, director of the Trade Programs Division, U.S. Customs Service, in testimony before the Insular and International Affairs subcommittee, House Committee on Interior and Insular Affairs, July 30, 1992 Oversight Hearing on the Northern Mariana Islands' Garment Industry, Serial No. 102-95, p. 270-272.

In an effort to improve the CNMI Customs Service on the issue of textile transshipment, I wrote a letter, as governor in August 2003, to the U.S. Customs and Border Protection, Department of Homeland Security, requesting technical assistance to institute new policies and regulations on textile exports to the U.S. and General Headnote 3(a). Four months later, Robert C. Bonner, the commissioner of Customs and Border Protection, agreed, and sent two individuals with expertise in the area of policy development and enforcement for the textile trade. With the Interior department's Office of Insular Affairs funding their trip, the experts conducted a weeklong seminar on Saipan in June 2004 for 12 employees of the CNMI Division of Customs Service. Francisco I. Taitano, my assistant for Customs, Quarantine, Policy, and Research, spearheaded the entire process and made all the arrangements for the seminar to take place. The training enhanced our ability to track all incoming and outgoing shipments, streamline the billing system, upgrade our network linking the CNMI's three major islands, and access a central database that could account, in real time, for all commercial goods.

However, on January 1, 2005, U.S. apparel quotas were lifted, causing garment manufacturers in the CNMI to shut down. The only remedy seen and suggested by the insular jurisdictions was to amend General Headnote 3(a) (iv) and treat U.S. insular jurisdictions like free-trade partners, by extending to all products the current requirement that calls for, at least, 30% U.S. and local content. This recommendation was presented to Congress, but never acted on.

F. Marine Induction/Discharge Ceremony
Statement of Washington Representative Juan N. Babauta
January 31, 2000

Thank you Speaker Fitial, President Manglona, Governor Tenorio, Lt. Governor Sablan, members of the Legislature, ladies and gentlemen:

Four months ago, the United States of America officially recognized as "veterans" a group of local men, who served with US forces here in World War Two.

Today, we are gathered to recognize the veteran's status of each of the individuals in that group of veterans, to present to them their discharge papers, and to pin upon them the ribbon of the Marianas Campaign.

We are honored by the presence of Marine Brigadier General Ralph Parker. But even more we are honored to be in the company of these local Marines.

Fifty four years ago the battle for the Marianas was one of the most important fought in World War II.

By July of 1944, the island of Saipan was declared secured by US forces.

Still however several hundred Japanese soldiers remained hiding in the jungle and harassed the US forces with sniper attacks.

In response, a group of Chamorro and Carolinian men were selected, put under the command of the 6th Provisional Military Police Battalion and were given responsibility for patrols against the enemy holdouts.

They were issued Marine Corps uniforms, trained to use rifles and grenades, and instructed in hand-to-hand fighting.

Once on duty, platoons of these local Marine Scouts – as they were known – combed Mt. Tapotchau, the hills of Laulau and Kagman, and the ridges of Marpi. The Scouts took part in the military expeditions on Maug and the Northern Islands.

Miraculously, none of our local men was killed in these operations. Yet their lives were clearly on the line.

The men we honor today ventured to risk their lives in the service of the faraway and largely unknown America.

I do not presume to know why these men made such an astounding decision. I imagine each individual had his own particular reasons.

But whatever their motivation may have been I do believe this: their service became one of the first essential links between our people and the people of the United States.

A link – unfortunately – America for too long failed to recognize. A link that came perilously close to being altogether forgotten.

Several years ago, my office began the process of recognition for these men.

We devoted large amounts of staff time for six to seven years 50,000 pages of military records.

By luck we found one memorandum marked top secret that contained documentation which indicated that indeed 50 + men had been recruited. That was all we needed to proceed.

We began a collaborative effort between our office and the veteran's affairs office in documenting their involvement.

The next step was the preparation of the application for recognition under US Public Law which established the US military civilian review board.

That process alone took our office 2 years to complete. It took another 12 months for the civilian military review board to review and validate the application.

At last on October 7, 1999, the Secretary of the Airforce approved the application recognizing these men for their service and that they be considered as having performed active duty for purpose of all laws administered by the US Department of Veterans Affairs.

And now, today, America is at last recognizing our men and their service.

I would like to acknowledge the work of some of those who were responsible for the US Department of Defense recognition of our men:

- The President of the US Armed Forces Veterans Association, Joseph Reyes, for his tireless efforts
- Former Representative Crispin I. Deleon Guerrero and the late Vicente C. Deleon Guerrero, in particular, who would not let our men, be forgotten.
- Both Joseph Palacios, the former Director of the Veterans Office, and Mr. Jesus C. Muna, the present director who have been very supportive.
- The support from Major Harry Blanco
- Mr. Pete Callahan, Commander of the Veterans of Foreign Wars Post 3457, who helped mobilize national recognition.
- And the legislature (10th and 11th) which passed two resolutions on behalf of our marines. Representatives Frank G. Cepeda and David M. Apatang took special interest.
- The Governors Office for all their assistance.
- I would like to recognize my staff who worked so hard on this. Mr. Emet Saures, Mr. Alex Falig, Ms. Remy Pangelinan and Mr. Edward Dlg. Pangelinan who did the research at the National Archives, the Marine Corp Historical Center, and Naval Archives.

They combed through over 50,000 pages of military records and war diaries to find the few sentences establishing that our men were, in fact, recruited by the U.S. Armed Forces.

Without that evidence the application we filed for the scouts would not have been successful.

The application that we filed which took two years to review by the Secretary of the Airforce was written and packaged by Mr. Edward Pangelinan.

Without the diligent work of two individuals over the last three months, this ceremony today would not have been possible.

They made a lot of phone calls, spoke to numerous people, wrote letters, explained to a lot of people the significance of this event, they met at the office after regular working hours to work on the discharge forms and to plan what to do the next day.

They coordinated with officials at the Pentagon, the Marine Corps Headquarters in Quantico VA, the Defense Intelligence Agency, the White House, the Marine Headquarters in Hawaii, and Okinawa. They coordinated with the DOD Civilian/Military Service Review Board at Andrews Airforce Base in Maryland.

Will these two individuals please stand up and be recognized: Mr. Edward Dlg. Pangelinan and Lt. Col. Scott Rutter

As a result of their efforts, we hope, the service of these marines will always be remembered.

Today, we honor them for the part they played in forging our bond with America.

That bond has given us the self-government we were denied through almost four centuries of colonial servitude.

That bond has given us citizenship in the United States, a nation whose principles of freedom and democracy and justice should make us proud.

So, thank you. To each of you men, each Marine, thank you. The risk you took fifty years ago has brought rich reward to all of us here, and to all who will come after.

G. Luncheon invitation from their Majesties, the Emperor and Empress of Japan

On the occasion of the Visit of
Their Majesties The Emperor and Empress of Japan
to Saipan, Commonwealth of the Northern Mariana Islands,
The Grand Steward of the Imperial Household
requests the pleasure of the company of

The Hon. Juan Nekai Babauta

at a Luncheon
by Their Majesties The Emperor and Empress of Japan
on Tuesday, June 28, 2005 from 1:15 p.m. to 2:25 p.m.
at Theater Hall, Hotel Nikko Saipan

R.S.V.P. To remind
By enclosed card
Tel : 670-323-7201/2
Fax : 670-323-8764

Dress : Lounge Suit

Guests are kindly requested to bring this card and arrive by 1:05 p.m.

H. Presidential Proclamation 5564, November 3, 1986 – Placing into full force and effect the Covenant with the Commonwealth of the Northern Marianas Islands, and the Compacts of Free Association with the Federated States of Micronesia and the Republic of the Marshall Islands.

40399

Federal Register
Vol. 51, No. 216
Friday, November 7, 1986

Presidential Documents

Title 3—   Proclamation 5564 of November 3, 1986

The President   Placing Into Full Force and Effect the Covenant With the Commonwealth of the Northern Mariana Islands, and the Compacts of Free Association With the Federated States of Micronesia and the Republic of the Marshall Islands

By the President of the United States of America

A Proclamation

Since July 18, 1947, the United States has administered the United Nations Trust Territory of the Pacific Islands ("Trust Territory"), which includes the Northern Mariana Islands, the Federated States of Micronesia, the Marshall Islands, and Palau.

On February 15, 1975, after extensive status negotiations, the United States and the Marianas Political Status Commission concluded a Covenant to establish a Commonwealth of the Northern Mariana Islands in Political Union with the United States ("Covenant"). Sections 101, 1002, and 1003(c) of the Covenant provide that the Northern Mariana Islands will become a self-governing Commonwealth in political union with and under the sovereignty of the United States. This Covenant was approved by the Congress by Public Law 94-241 of March 24, 1976, 90 Stat. 263. Although many sections of the Covenant became effective in 1976 and 1978, certain sections have not previously entered into force.

On October 1, 1982, the Government of the United States and the Government of the Federated States of Micronesia concluded a Compact of Free Association, establishing a relationship of Free Association between the two Governments. On June 25, 1983, the Government of the United States and the Government of the Marshall Islands concluded a Compact of Free Association, establishing a relationship of Free Association between the two Governments. Pursuant to Sections 111 and 121 of the Compacts, the Federated States of Micronesia and the Republic of the Marshall Islands become self-governing and have the right to conduct foreign affairs in their own name and right upon the effective date of their respective Compacts. Each Compact comes into effect upon (1) mutual agreement between the Government of the United States, acting in fulfillment of its responsibilities as Administering Authority of the Trust Territory of the Pacific Islands, and the other Government; (2) the approval of the Compact by the two Governments, in accordance with their constitutional processes; and (3) the conduct of a plebiscite in that jurisdiction. In the Federated States of Micronesia, the Compact has been approved by the Government in accordance with its constitutional processes, and in a United Nations-observed plebiscite on June 21, 1983, a sovereign act of self-determination. In the Marshall Islands, the Compact has been approved by the Government in accordance with its constitutional processes, and in a United Nations-observed plebiscite on September 7, 1983, a sovereign act of self-determination. In the United States the Compacts have been approved by Public Law 99-239 of January 14, 1986, 99 Stat. 1770.

On January 10, 1986, the Government of the United States and the Government of the Republic of Palau concluded a Compact of Free Association, establishing a similar relationship of Free Association between the two Governments. On October 16, 1986, the Congress of the United States approved the Compact of Free Association with the Republic of Palau. In the Republic of Palau, the Compact approval process has not yet been completed. Until the future political status of Palau is resolved, the United States will continue to discharge its responsibilities in Palau as Administering Authority under the Trusteeship Agreement.

On May 28, 1986, the Trusteeship Council of the United Nations concluded that the Government of the United States had satisfactorily discharged its obligations as the Administering Authority under the terms of the Trusteeship Agreement and that the people of the Northern Mariana Islands, the Federated States of Micronesia, and the Republic of the Marshall Islands had freely exercised their right to self-determination, and considered that it was appropriate for that Agreement to be terminated. The Council asked the United States to consult with the governments concerned to agree on a date for entry into force of their respective new status agreements.

On October 15, 1986, the Government of the United States and the Government of the Republic of the Marshall Islands agreed, pursuant to Section 411 of the Compact of Free Association, that as between the

United States and the Republic of the Marshall Islands, the effective date of the Compact shall be October 21, 1986.

On October 24, 1986, the Government of the United States and the Government of the Federated States of Micronesia agreed, pursuant to Section 411 of the Compact of Free Association, that as between the United States and the Federated States of Micronesia, the effective date of the Compact shall be November 3, 1986.

On October 24, 1986, the United States advised the Secretary General of the United Nations that, as a consequence of consultations held between the United States Government and the Government of the Marshall Islands, agreement had been reached that the Compact of Free Association with the Marshall Islands entered fully into force on October 21, 1986. The United States further advised the Secretary General that, as a result of consultations with their governments, agreement had been reached that the Compact of Free Association with the Federated States of Micronesia and the Covenant with the Commonwealth of the Northern Mariana Islands would enter into force on November 3, 1986.

As of this day, November 3, 1986, the United States has fulfilled its obligations under the Trusteeship Agreement with respect to the Commonwealth of the Northern Mariana Islands, the Republic of the Marshall Islands, and the Federated States of Micronesia, and they are self-governing and no longer subject to the Trusteeship. In taking these actions, the United States is implementing the freely expressed wishes of the peoples of the Northern Mariana Islands, the Federated States of Micronesia, and the Marshall Islands.

NOW, THEREFORE, I, RONALD REAGAN, by the authority vested in me as President by the Constitution and laws of the United States of America, including Section 1002 of the Covenant to Establish a Commonwealth of the Northern Mariana Islands in Political Union with the United States of America, and Sections 101 and 102 of the Joint Resolution to approve the "Compact of Free Association", and for other purposes, approved on January 14, 1986 (Public Law 99-239), do hereby find, declare, and proclaim as follows:

Section 1. I determine that the Trusteeship Agreement for the Pacific Islands is no longer in effect as of October 21, 1986, with respect to the Republic of the Marshall Islands, as of November 3, 1986, with respect to the Federated States of Micronesia, and as of November 3, 1986, with respect to the Northern Mariana Islands. This constitutes the determination referred to in Section 1002 of the Covenant.

Sec. 2. (a) Sections 101, 104, 301, 302, 303, 506, 806, and 904 of the Covenant are effective as of 12:01 a.m., November 4, 1986, Northern Mariana Islands local time.

(b) The Commonwealth of the Nothern Mariana Islands in political union with and under the sovereignty of the United States of America is fully established on the date and at the time specified in Section 2(a) of this Proclamation.

(c) The domiciliaries of the Northern Mariana Islands are citizens of the United States to the extent provided for in Sections 301 through 303 of the Covenant on the date and at the time specified in this Proclamation.

(d) I welcome the Commonwealth of the Northern Mariana Islands into the American family and congratulate our new fellow citizens.

Sec. 3. (a) The Compact of Free Association with the Republic of the Marshall Islands is in full force and effect as of October 21, 1986, and the Compact of Free Association with the Federated States of Micronesia is in full force and effect as of November 3, 1986.

(b) I am gratified that the people of the Federated States of Micronesia and the Republic of the Marshall Islands, after nearly forty years of Trusteeship, have freely chosen to establish a relationship of Free Association with the United States.

IN WITNESS WHEREOF, I have hereunto set my hand this third day of November, in the year of our Lord nineteen hundred and eighty-six, and of the Independence of the United States of America the two hundred and eleventh.

Ronald Reagan

[FR Doc. 86-25463
Filed 11-6-86; 11:17 am]
Billing code 3195-01-M

I. Japan Airlines October 26, 2005 letter on decision to pull out.

Japan Airlines Co. Ltd
2-4-11, Higashi-shinagawa
Shinagawa-ku, Tokyo
Japan 140-8637

OCT 26, 2005

The Honorable Juan N. Babauta, Governor
The Commonwealth of the Northern Marianas

Dear Governor Babauta,

Once again I would like to express my deepest appreciation to you and the peoples of the Commonwealth of the Northern Marianas for your continued support and cooperation that you have shown to JAL.

At the time of our initial investigation of the future operations of the Saipan Route, we were honored that you were able to take time out of your very busy schedule to visit us twice. At the time of your visits we fully appreciated your strong request to continue our operations to Saipan and also to accept the petition signed by so many of your citizens. Please be assured that your intentions were appreciated and fully taken into consideration, however it is with deep regret that we suspended scheduled services as planned with the last flight on the 26th of October. Our operations to Saipan would not have been possible without your continued support in all areas including Commercial, Promotional and Safety.

Even though we have ceased operation of our scheduled flights, in order to meet the demands of our Agents and Passengers we plan to operate charter flights to Saipan and also fully utilize the activities of all of the JAL group to continue to make contributions towards the development of tourism to CNMI, in this regard I would like to ask you for your ongoing support and cooperation.

Yours sincerely,

Toshiyuki Shinmachi
Chief Executive Officer
Japan Airlines Corporation

J. Presidential Proclamation 8335, January 6, 2009 – Commonwealth of the Northern Mariana Islands: Reserving Certain Submerged Lands in the Commonwealth of the Northern Mariana Islands.

Presidential Proclamation -- Commonwealth of the Northern Mariana Islands

RESERVING CERTAIN SUBMERGED LANDS IN THE COMMONWEALTH OF THE NORTHERN MARIANA ISLANDS

BY THE PRESIDENT OF THE UNITED STATES OF AMERICA

A PROCLAMATION

The submerged lands surrounding the islands of Farallon de Pajaros (Uracas), Maug, and Asuncion in the Commonwealth of the Northern Mariana Islands are among the most biologically diverse in the Western Pacific, with relatively pristine coral reef ecosystems that have been proclaimed objects of scientific interest and reserved for their protection as the Islands Unit of the Marianas Trench Marine National Monument (marine national monument) by Proclamation 8335 of January 6, 2009. Certain submerged lands adjacent to the land leased by the United States of America on the islands of Tinian and Farallon de Medinilla under the Lease Agreement Made Pursuant to the Covenant to Establish a Commonwealth of the Northern Mariana Islands in Political Union with the United States of America, dated January 6, 1983, as amended (Lease) are essential for ensuring that United States forces forward deployed to the Western Pacific are adequately trained and ready to respond immediately and effectively to orders from the National Command Authority, and for ensuring the safety of citizens of the Commonwealth of the Northern Mariana Islands.

Certain of these submerged lands will be conveyed by the United States to the Government of the Commonwealth of the Northern Mariana Islands on January 16, 2014, pursuant to section 1(a) of Public Law 93-435, as amended by section 1 of Public Law 113-34 (the "Act"), unless the President designates otherwise pursuant to section 1(b)(vii) of the Act.

NOW, THEREFORE, I, BARACK OBAMA, President of the United States of America, by virtue of authority vested in me by section 1(b)(vii) of the Act, do hereby proclaim that the lands hereinafter described are excepted from transfer to the Government of the Commonwealth of the Northern Mariana Islands under section 1(a) of the Act:

the submerged lands adjacent to the islands of Farallon de Pajaros (Uracas), Maug, and Asuncion permanently covered by tidal waters up to the mean low water line and extending three geographical miles seaward from the mean high tide line; and

the submerged lands adjacent to the islands of Tinian and Farallon de Medinilla permanently or periodically covered by tidal waters up to the line of mean high tide and extending seaward to a line three geographical miles distant from those areas of the coastline that are adjacent to the leased lands described in the Lease.2

Nothing in this proclamation is intended to affect the authority of the Secretary of the Interior (Secretary) under section 1(b) of the Act to subsequently convey the submerged lands adjacent to the islands of Farallon de Pajaros (Uracas), Maug, and Asuncion when the Secretary, the Secretary of Commerce, and the Government of the Commonwealth of the Northern Mariana Islands have entered into an agreement for coordination of management that ensures the protection of the marine national monument within the excepted area described above. Furthermore, nothing in this proclamation is intended to affect the authority of the Secretary under section 1(b) of the Act to subsequently convey the submerged lands adjacent to the land leased by the United States on the islands of Tinian or Farallon de Medinilla when the Secretary of the Navy and the Government of the Commonwealth of the Northern Mariana Islands have entered into an agreement that ensures protection of military training within the excepted area.

IN WITNESS WHEREOF, I have hereunto set my hand this fifteenth day of January, in the year of our Lord two thousand fourteen, and of the Independence of the United States of America the two hundred and thirty-eighth.

BARACK OBAMA

K. Executive Order 12572 of November 3, 1986 – Relations with the Northern Mariana Islands.

Federal Register / Vol. 51. No. 216 / Friday, November 7, 1986 / Presidential Documents 40401

Presidential Documents

Executive Order 12572 of November 3, 1986

Relations With the Northern Mariana Islands

By the authority vested in me as President by the Constitution and laws of the United States of America, it is hereby ordered that, consistent with the Joint Resolution to approve the "Covenant To Establish a Commonwealth of the Northern Mariana Islands in Political Union with the United States of America," approved March 24, 1976 (Public Law 94–241; 90 Stat. 263), the relations of the United States with the Government of the Northern Mariana Islands shall, in all matters not the program responsibility of another Federal department or agency, be under the general administrative supervision of the Secretary of the Interior.

Ronald Reagan

THE WHITE HOUSE,
November 3, 1986.

[FR Doc. 86-25466
Filed 11-6-86; 11:18 am]
Billing code 3195-01-M

L. Letter from Former Lt. Gov. Francisco C. Ada.

FRANCISCO C. ADA
P. O. Box 500381
Saipan, MP   96950

April 14, 2005

The Honorable Juan N. Babauta
Governor
Commonwealth of the Northern Mariana Islands
Office of the Governor
P. O. Box 10007
Saipan, MP   96950

Dear Governor Babauta:

Mrs. Ada and the children join me in extending to you our heartfelt appreciation and "Si Yuus Maase" for a very memorable celebration held on March 31, 2005 on the occasion of the naming of the Saipan International Airport in my name. Members of your staff put many hours in preparing for the celebration. All of those were, of course, due in large part to your leadership and attentiveness. Your remarks on my behalf during the ceremony were profoundly touching, and we shall forever cherish and remember them.

It is most comforting and reassuring to know that you as our leader cherish and recognize the deeds of others however big or small; however important or insignificant they may be. The airport is in good hands under your stewardship and will continue to contribute to the development of our Commonwealth.

Sincerely,

Francisco C. Ada

M. Letter from A. Kerry Strong.

```
ARCHIVES BRANCH
MARINE CORPS RESEARCH CENTER
MARINE CORPS UNIVERSITY (C 40RCA)
2040 BROADWAY STREET
QUANTICO, VA  22134-5107
(703) 640-4685/4538
(FAX) 703-640-4306
(DSN) 278-4685/4538
```

20 July 1994

Juan N. Babauta
Resident Representative
Commonwealth of the Northern Mariana Islands
Office of the Resident Representative to the United States
2121 R Street, NW
Washington, D.C. 20008

Dear Representative Babauta:

We are in receipt of the publication, IN REMEMBRANCE AND HONOR OF THE BRAVE US SERVICEMEN WHO MADE THE ULTIMATE SACRIFICE IN THE MARIANAS CAMPAIGN DURING WWII. Thank you so much for sending us a copy of the first issue. It will be placed with our WWII collection and indeed will be a very valuable addition to this collection.

If in future, we can be of any further assistance to you, please do not hesitate to contact me. Again, thank you for the publication.

Sincerely,

A. Kerry Strong (Ms)
Archives Director

N. Letter from R. E. Parker, Jr.

February 4, 2000

Dear Representative Babauta,

Thank you for your welcoming remarks and introduction at the recognition ceremony that took place on January 31, 2000. You made this long deserved recognition possible which allowed the United States Marine Corps to award active duty discharges and World War II Campaign and Victory Medals to the Chamorro and Carolinian Marine Corps Scouts and the family members of deceased Scouts.

It was a privilege to serve as the United States Marine Corps' representative and to pay homage to the Chamorro and Carolinian Marine Corps Scout veterans for their gallant and heroic service. I applaud your evident dedication to your constituency.

I am also deeply appreciative for your efforts in making my visit absolutely PERFECT! I shall remember this day for the rest of my years.

R. E. PARKER, JR.
Brigadier General, U. S. Marine Corps
Commanding General, Marine Corps Base Hawaii

The Honorable Juan N. Babauta
Resident Representative to the United States
2121 R Street N.W.
Washington, DC 20008

O. Inaugural Address of Gov. Juan N. Babauta

Thank you, Lt. Governor Benavente. That has a nice ring to it... Lt. Governor, the people chose well when they chose you. You have their trust. You have mine. Now the people want to know: Are we ready to go to work?

My Dear People of the Northern Mariana Islands: Diego and I are ready to work – with each other, with each one of you – to keep building this Commonwealth that makes us so proud.

Remember how we grew up – most of us poor, farmers, fishermen, without schooling, without opportunity, without freedom. Look around us today. See how our lives have changed.

Yes, we are proud because we know what we have achieved: Today is better than yesterday. Tomorrow will be better still. And now is the moment for action.

We respect our past. But we also respect the will of the people; and you have chosen a new generation – to lead. The strength of your voice in this election leaves no doubt of your intention.

You want new ideas, new ways of doing things, and renewed respect for honesty and fairness in government. The people have spoken.

And we have listened. For two years, going house-to-house, door-to-door, island-to-island. To the father in As Lito whose job is uncertain... To the family in Koblerville unsure of the safety of their home... To the businessman in Garapan whose store stands half-empty... To the mother in Tinian, who wants her children to grow up strong in body and mind... To the manamko of Luta's Songsong Village who recall their island's beauty and want it always to remain... To students in Boise and Portland and San Diego who want to return home – to good jobs that match their education... Diego and I listened to all we met.

We understand times are tough, in part because of 9-11, recession in Japan and the U.S., matters beyond our control. But there is much we can do right here to take control. We have the energy, the talent, the resources: and we will use them.

We cannot be afraid. We cannot be hesitant nor tied to the old school. We have to take action. And Diego and I will make performance matter.

You know our plan: First, we pledge excellence in education. We stake our economic future on becoming the best educated people in the island Pacific. We believe each of us – young, old, in between – must always be learning – and having learned, put our wealth of knowledge in service to our community.

Students out there, are you ready? Are you ready to be innovative problem solvers, independent thinkers who act with integrity? We expect great things from you – and we will make sure you have what you need to learn.

A guest who, unfortunately, could not be here today, Mr. Dwight Ovitt, and his family gave me what I needed to learn: a home away from home in Enosburg Falls, Vermont, where I went to high school. My mother let her young son go halfway around the world – and she found the money to make that happen – because she knew: even in the midst of financial uncertainty education is the foundation for each person and for a strong, successful society. I am forever grateful for her gift to me.

We pledge Economic prosperity. We will offer new investors – and those already in business here – stability in the law, fairness and efficiency when dealing with the government, and an educated workforce. We will put the tens of millions of dollars in CIP funds we already have to work, building the infrastructure new investors need; and, yes, they will come. This will be a government that believes in the free hand of commerce, but understands all hands – public and private sector alike – must sometimes join together to provide for the common good.

We pledge to Care for our environment. We will do more than simply protect our islands and waters from further pollution and injury; we will work to bring back their beauty and health.

As our honored guest, President Remengesau of Palau, eloquently says: Protect the best. Improve the rest. Mr. President, forgive me for "borrowing" from a guest… but your words deserve repeating. Me sulang.

All of us in the island Pacific – Palau, Guam, the FSM – feel deeply connected to our lands and waters – and to each other.

We know our economic health, the health of our bodies, minds, and cultures, are forever joined to the well-being of our environment. So we will work within our communities – protecting the best, improving the rest; and we will work with the other island communities in our region, linking our efforts and learning from each other. Until our Pacific shines as an example to the world.

We pledge a Performance government. There will be no secrets in this administration. We will give you, the people, the same information we have. Call it: Transparency.

We will set goals publicly and report regularly to you the results. Call it: Accountability.

We reject the view that government is run to profit the few in power. Government exists to serve the needs of all. Call that: Integrity.

To every person who wants to work with this government we will ask: ko listo hao? are you ready to perform? are you ready to give the people more than they expect? are you ready to do more than you thought you could to build our commonwealth? The only acceptable answer is: Yes.

Finally, we pledge a healthy and a safe society. Illness in individuals weakens us all. Illness within our communities leads to violence and conflict.

We will focus on prevention: Our medical practitioners and health educators, working at the village level, will spread the knowledge needed, first, to stay well, and, then, when illness strikes, to get well. Our public safety officers will be trained – and expected to maintain – a higher level of professionalism. They will know the villages they serve, because they are themselves community members. We want our police to be a force for peace. Healthy and safe. Fit in body, free of fear – that is how we all must feel to work effectively for our personal welfare and for the common wealth.

This is our plan: a plan that is practical, realistic, doable. Thank you for embracing it. The plan is not a miracle cure, but a thousand simple correctives all aimed at the same goal: building our Commonwealth. One person can summarize it quickly. But it will take more than one person – more than one day – to bring this plan to life. We must put our faith in all of us working together over time. And we will discover, as a community, there are few limits to what we can do.

So Diego and I look to you all: We look to the Legislature and its leaders – President Paul Manglona, Speaker Heinz Hofschneider. There will be hard decisions ahead, but we know the Legislature is ready. We look to our youth who hold the future in their eyes, to the old who hold the wisdom of our past in their hearts. Never let us forget who we are and what we want to be. We look to those who seek profit in business; your efforts certainly sustain us all. We look to our national government. And let me say how pleased I am President Bush sent his personal representative, Mr. Abel Guerra, from the White House. Please, recognize that the Marianas takes pride in its self-sufficiency, but – as the Covenant framers foresaw – we need your partnership to make our standard of living equal the rest of our nation.

We call upon everyone to bring ideas to the table. We will listen and act upon the best. We call upon you to be resourceful. We will help the innovators in our society. We say to all: this is not the time to put out your hand; this is the time to give a hand.

We are not the first Americans faced with challenging times. Seventy years ago, Franklin Delano Roosevelt taking office looked over a nation devastated by depression, unemployment, bankruptcies and bank failures and reminded America that …happiness lies not in the mere possession of money…

I remember my father saying the same words to me, growing up poor in Tanapag: "Tacha balina salapé," he said. "Money doesn't matter." What does matter is working together. Again, to quote Roosevelt: we all go up, or we all go down, as one people.

We islanders hold the same truth in our hearts: Manmafanaugue' hit gine gi tano' ta na yangin ha famaoleg hau i bisinu'mu, siempre hun na maolek'na hao ki guiya. Este na klasen sensia ta nesesita guine gi mamaila'la na tiempo. Ta fan a'ayuda, ta fan a'famaolek, yan ta fan a'kumprende.

Growing up in these islands, that's what I learned. When the typhoon comes we work together to repair the damage. Working together makes us strong.

When we put our nets out, cast the chinchulu, we make sure everyone has their share – este i patin tiau. Sharing makes us whole. Even when the harvest is thin, everyone gets a share, so everyone has the strength to work for a richer harvest in the coming season.

I see a richer harvest ahead. Our nets will fill again. They will. We will look back with pride on these days, knowing we held together as a community, worked together – with the help of God – to create a new wealth in common for all for our Northern Mariana Islands.

Lt. Governor… Please… Are we ready? Yes! We are. God bless the Northern Marianas. God bless America. God bless us all.

References

Newspaper Articles

"Administration, Senate reviewing 'stateless' bill," *The Marianas Variety*, April 22, 2004.

"A Goal of a lifetime for ex-governor," *The Marianas Variety*, January 20, 2009.

"Islands Rehire Lobbyist to Fight Labor Bill," *The Washington Post*, September 3, 2000.

"Soviets Yield to U.S. on Pacific Islands' Status," *The New York Times*, December 24, 1990, p.5.

Magazine Articles

"Setting Priorities for Economic Development in the CNMI," *American Pacific Business Magazine*, July/August 2001.

Peter-Palican, Emi "Lisifanlaa." "Remauritius Clan," July 2005. The Remauritius Clan Reunion took place at the Garapan Central Park on Saipan on April 30, 2005.

Books and Articles

Alkire, William (1984). "The Carolinians of Saipan and the Commonwealth of the Northern Mariana Islands," *Pacific Affairs*, Vancouver, Canada: University of British Columbia.

Brower, Kenneth (1983). *A Song for Satawal*, New York: Harper & Row.

Laughlin, Stanley K., Jr. (1995). *The Law of the United States Territories and Affiliated Jurisdictions*, Rochester, N.Y.: Lawyers Cooperative Publishing.

Leary, Paul M. (1980). *The Northern Marianas Covenant and American Territorial Relations*, Berkeley, CA: Government Studies, University of California, Berkeley.

Leibowitz, Arnold H. (Fall 1975). "The Applicability of Federal Law to Guam," *Virginia Journal of International Law*, Vol. 16, No. 1.

Leibowitz, Arnold H. (1989). *Defining Status: A Comprehensive Analysis of United States Territorial Relations*. Dordrecht, Boston, London: Martinus Nijhoff Publishers; distributed by Kluwer Academic Publishers, Hingham, Mass.

Retzler, L. (1996). "The Northern Mariana Islands: Where America's Day Begins." Baltimore: Johns Hopkins University, Institute for Policy Studies.

Willens, Howard P. and Siemer, Deanne C. (2002). *An Honorable Accord: The Covenant between the Northern Mariana Islands and the United States*, Honolulu: University of Hawai'i Press and University of Hawai'i Center for Pacific Islands Studies.

Government Documents

CNMI Office of the Governor (March 12, 1981). *Executive Order No. 25.*

CNMI Office of the Governor (February 2003). *CNMI Integrated Fiscal Plan.*

CNMI Office of the Governor (April 1997). "Minimum Wage Analysis for the Commonwealth of the Northern Mariana Islands."

CNMI Office of the Resident Representative to the United States (December 2000). *Now For Then: Marianas Marine Scouts.* Washington, D.C.: Office of the Resident Representative.

Congressional Research Service (May 13, 1992). "Political Development of U.S. Insular Areas," Report for Congress. Washington, D.C.: Library of Congress.

Department of Education, Commonwealth of the Northern Mariana Islands (1984). *Annual Report.* Saipan, NMI: Board of Education/Regents.

Economic Impact of Federal Laws on the Commonwealth of the Northern Mariana Islands. Prepared for the CNMI Government October 2008. Washington, D.C.: U.S. Department of the Interior, Office of Insular Affairs.

Marianas Political Status Commission (1975). *Section-By-Section Analysis of the Covenant to Establish a Commonwealth of the Northern Mariana Islands in Political Union with the United States of America.* Saipan, NMI.

Miller, Rep. George and House Resources committee staff (March 26, 1998). "Beneath the American Flag: Labor and Human Rights Abuses in the CNMI."

National conference (February 8-11, 1993). *A Time of Change: Relations Between the United States and American Samoa, Guam, the Northern Mariana Islands, Puerto Rico and the United States Virgin Islands.* Washington, D.C.

NMI Commission on Federal Laws (August 1985). "Welcoming America's Newest Commonwealth." Second Interim Report to the U.S. Congress.

Northern Marianas Judiciary Historical Society (2011). *The Northern Mariana Islands: A Historical Overview.* Saipan, Commonwealth of the Northern Mariana Islands.

"Report of the La Fiesta Exploratory Team to NMC Interim President Antonio Guerrero." July 24, 2004.

"The Financial Report for the Northern Mariana Islands Commission on Federal Laws to the Congress of the United States," *CNMI Reports*, Vol. 1, 1991.

U.S. Commission on Immigration Reform (undated). *Immigration and the CNMI.*

U.S. Department of Agriculture Graduate School (October 24, 2012). *Commonwealth of the Northern Mariana Islands General Financial Position.* Washington, D.C.: U.S. Department of the Interior, Office of Insular Affairs.

Testimony and Remarks at Hearings

Babauta, Juan N. (March 31, 1998). CNMI Resident Representative to the United States remarks at hearing on S.1100 and S.1275 before U.S. Senate Committee on Energy and Natural Resources, 105th Congress. Washington, D.C.

Benavente, Diego T. (March 31, 1998). Eleventh Northern Mariana Islands House Speaker remarks at hearing on S. 1100 and S. 1275 before U.S. Senate Committee on Energy and Natural Resources, 105th Congress. Washington, D.C.

Camacho, Carlos S. (November 19, 1980). CNMI Governor remarks at 1536 Health Planning Agencies Conference. Saipan, NMI.

Clinton, William J. (May 30, 1997). U.S. President letter to CNMI Gov. Froilan C. Tenorio.

Deleon Guerrero, Lorenzo I. (December 21, 1990). CNMI Governor letter to United Nations Security Council.

Faleomavaega, Eni F. H. (December 26, 1990). American Samoa non-voting delegate to U.S. House of Representatives letter to Secretary of State James A. Baker III.

Manglona, Paul A. (March 31, 1998). Eleventh Northern Mariana Islands Senate President remarks at hearing on S. 1100 and S. 1275 before U.S. Senate Committee on Energy and Natural Resources, 105th Congress. Washington, D.C.

Montoya, Richard T. (May 17, 1986). U.S. Interior department Assistant Secretary for Territorial and International Affairs letter to CNMI Governor Pedro P. Tenorio.

Mullins, Janet G. (February 11, 1991). Letter to U.S. House of Representatives delegate from American Samoa.

Tenorio, Pedro A. (October 25, 2005). CNMI Resident Representative to the United States testimony before U.S. Senate Committee on Energy and Natural Resources. Washington, D.C.

Tenorio, Pedro P. (March 31, 1998). CNMI Governor remarks at hearing on S.1100 and S.1275 before U.S. Senate Committee on Energy and Natural Resources, 105th Congress. Washington, D.C.

CNMI Public Laws

P.L. 3-49. To establish within the Office of the Governor the Commonwealth Health Planning and Development Agency and the Commonwealth Health Planning Coordinating Council. February 24, 1983.

P.L. 14-8. To amend 3 CMC, Sections 4303 and 4312, to allow "Stateless Persons" to live and work in CNMI, May 27, 2004.

P.L. 16-51. To establish a public corporation for healthcare and related public health services known as the Commonwealth Healthcare Corporation, January 15, 2009.

U.S. Public Laws

Consolidated and Further Continuing Appropriations Act, 2015. P.L. 113-235. December 16, 2014. Section 10 amended Title VII of P.L. 110-229 to extend CW-1 CNMI-only non-resident worker program until December 31, 2019, and to remove Secretary of Labor's authority to extend the program.

National Health Planning and Resources Development Act of 1974. P. L. 93-641. A law signed by Pres. Gerald Ford, establishing planning mechanisms, including certificate of need programs. The programs required hospitals to obtain approval for capital expenditures of more than $100,000. The capital expenditure for the Commonwealth Health Center was nearly $30 million.

Natural Resources Act of 2008. P.L. 110-22. Title VII, Subtitle (A) Immigration, Security, and Labor. Consolidated May 8, 2008. Title VII Subtitle (A) amended the Covenant. The Covenant is a federal law that was approved by U.S. Congress in House Joint Resolution 549, which was signed March 24, 1976, by Pres. Gerald Ford as U.S. Public Law 94-241. Except for the mutual consent sections of the Covenant, listed in Section 105, the

Congress has authority to unilaterally amend Covenant, including immigration provisions in Section 503.

P.L. 94-241. A Joint Resolution to Approve the Covenant to Establish the Commonwealth of the Northern Mariana Islands in Political Union with the United States of America. March 24, 1976.

Court Cases

Sabangan et al v. Powell. U.S. Court of Appeals for the Ninth Circuit; Opinion of Circuit Judge John T. Noonan, Case No. 03-16426, District Court No. CV-02-00039. July 1, 2004.

Wabol v. Villacrusis, 958 F.2d 1450 (9th Circuit 1992), and 898 F.2d 1381 (9th Circuit 1990). The U.S. Court of Appeals for the Ninth Circuit held that Congress acted within its scope of authority under the Territorial Clause of the Constitution to exclude equal protection clause of section 1 of the 14th Amendment from operation in regards to owning and leasing land in the Commonwealth, and under that authority, Congress had enacted into law the CNMI Covenant, including Sections 501 and 805. Section 805 deals with the right to own and lease land in the Commonwealth.